THE GREAT CONFUSION IN INDIAN AFFAIRS

T0327213

THE GREAT CONFUSION IN INDIAN AFFAIRS

Native Americans & Whites in the Progressive Era

TOM HOLM

University of Texas Press
Austin

Requests for permission to reproduce material from this work should be sent to Permissions, University of Texas Press, Box 7819, Austin, TX 78713-7819.

∞ The paper used in this book meets the minimum requirements of ANSI/NISO z39.48-1992 (R1997) (Permanence of Paper).

Library of Congress Cataloging-in-Publication Data

Holm, Tom, 1946–
    The great confusion in Indian affairs : Native Americans and whites in the progressive era / Tom Holm.— 1st ed.
        p.   cm.
    Includes bibliographical references and index.
    ISBN 978-0-292-70962-1
    1. Indians of North America—Cultural assimilation. 2. Indians of North America—Government relations. 3. Indians of North America—Politics and government. 4. Indians in popular culture. 5. Assimilation (Sociology)—United States—History. 6. United States—Social policy. 7. United States—Race relations. 8. United States—Politics and government. I. Title.

E98.C89H65 2005
305.897'073'09041—dc22

                                                            2005003871

For my grandchildren, Ezikiel, Joaquin, and Sadie Grace

CONTENTS

PREFACE

THIS STUDY HAS SPENT A LONG TIME in scholastic limbo. Its first materialization was as my doctoral dissertation, done in 1978 under the able direction of Professors Arrell M. Gibson, H. Wayne Morgan, Jonathan W. Spurgeon, and Norman Crockett at the University of Oklahoma. From it I gleaned a few articles and a stack of lecture notes. At the time I thought that the articles would be sufficient evidence of scholarship that would, in turn, support my teaching career. Consequently, I did not put a great deal of effort into getting my dissertation published as a book. Besides, I had embarked upon a long-term study of Native American veterans of the Vietnam War—a project that was very close to my heart because I am a Native veteran of that conflict—which required a series of subsidiary studies in military history, political cultures, social psychology, and ethnological methods.

What prompted me to take up the dusty manuscript again was the fact that over the years I have gained several new perspectives and have expanded my knowledge as a result of stepping outside of my academic training. Although my doctorate was in history, I have not served in a department of history since 1979. I have been affiliated with an American Indian studies program that has encouraged inter- and multidisciplinary approaches to studying Native topics that transcend the traditional disciplines of history, anthropology, and sociology. Additionally, I spent fourteen years in a political science department, during which time I gained a good deal of know-how and appreciation for critical thought from the likes of Joyotpaul Chaudhuri, Jim Clarke, Cliff Lytle, and Vine Deloria, Jr. I also came under the influence of the late Robert K. "Bob" Thomas, who was as sharp a theoretical and applied cultural anthropologist as I have ever met.

From the multidisciplinary standpoint I picked up in American Indian studies and the political discourses in political science, I have reached the conclusion that most of the literature on Indian-white relations in the early twentieth century was inadequate, including my own humble dissertation. The main reason for the inadequacy was that every history of the topic or era, save for three or four, presents Native Americans as bit players in a Euro-American drama, with the "Euros" ultimately subduing and marginalizing Native Americans to the point of historical disappearance. In short, most modern scholars have succeeded in making Indians "vanish" where the policy makers of old could not. Second, none of the historical studies of the period contain truly edifying theoretical constructs that help explain the time and the topic in a larger context. Even the most recent books and articles seem to be rehashes of previous well-done studies. In short, nothing really groundbreaking on Indian-white relations in the early twentieth century has appeared since Hazel Hertzberg's *Search for an American Indian Identity* in 1971 and Frederick E. Hoxie's *A Final Promise: The Campaign to Assimilate the Indians* was published in 1984.

I resolved to put this period of policy making in the context of what was going on among Indians at the time and how the period fit into the overall pattern of Indian-white relations in the United States. I found three theoretical references that came together to explain a number of very important features in the relationship between Natives and whites. A student, the late Alice Brigham, an Ojibwa originally from Walpole Island in Canada, handed me the first. It was a report entitled "The Government of Aboriginal Peoples" done in 1983 for the Canadian government's Sub-Committee on Indian Self-Government of the House of Commons Standing Committee on Indian Affairs and Northern Development by the "Policy Development Group." The report had been commissioned during the repatriation hearings that led to the hammering out of a new Canadian constitution. "The Government of Aboriginal Peoples" distilled the relationships between the colonizer and the colonized into stages that follow a particular order but do not necessarily fall into a specific time sequence. The stages listed were (in order): displacement, restriction, assimilation, structural accommodation, and, finally, self-determination. The final phase is decolonization and is not explained as thoroughly as the previous four.

In every one of his classes Robert K. Thomas would make the point that colonization is the "deprivation of experience." He meant that in the colonial relationship the colonized are never allowed to experience change on their own terms. Colonization is the ultimate form of trespass, which represses the ability to act without reference to colonial terminology, paradigms, and symbols. The final stage of self-determination supposedly removes the colonizer from the mix and allows the indigenous population full, rather than limited, sovereignty. Arguably this final stage has never really been attained in any colonial relationship, except perhaps in India and some African nations, and certainly not in the relationship between the United States and Native American nations. Since the United States is here to stay, about the best that Native American nations could attain is the status of protectorates. Vine Deloria, Jr., and Robert DeMallie have argued in their fine and exhaustive two-volume work, *Documents of American Indian Diplomacy*, that under various treaties most Native nations have indeed accepted that particular status already. For the purposes of this look at the relationship at the beginning of the twentieth century, the last stage is not utilized in its theoretical framework. Additionally, the time period of this study exactly fits the transition in the U.S.–Native American relationship between the third (assimilation) and the fourth (structural accommodation) stages.

What is important to note about the first four phases in the colonial relationship is that each is punctuated by conflict and confusion, thus bringing about a search for another kind of orderly political arrangement. In looking back over my dissertation, I found that the period I studied was a phase in the relationship between whites and Indians. It was not, however, one of the stages outlined in the "Government of Aboriginal Peoples" report. Rather, it was a time of ideological conflict and institutional confusion that punctuated assimilation and created a philosophical void in policy making that John Collier's ideas would fill in the 1930s.

That this period corresponds with the phase in U.S. history that scholars have labeled the "Progressive Era" is not all that surprising. The years between 1900 and 1920 were fraught with social, cultural, political, and economic conflict and change. It was an era of modernization, overseas expansion, mass communication, and industrialization. It was a period of trust busting and muckraking as well as bigotry and conservative complacency. Americans became involved in environmental conservation and numerous moral crusades. Americans were also occupied with nostalgia for a preindustrial society. Many thought that urbanization and the industrial boom had dulled the frontier spirit and corrupted the American character. Ultimately the Progressive Era might have also been a period in which Americans were engaged in, according to Robert H. Wiebe, a "search for order."

The evidence for a period of confusion, conflict, ambiguity, and, finally, an attempt to discover a sound philosophical foundation for a new policy toward Native Americans led me to the conclusion that Wiebe's observation and the title of his fine book were absolutely correct. The well-documented movement to assimilate Indians into mainstream American society came under fire during the first twenty years of the twentieth century. This happenstance is not unusual in democratic societies when new generations clash with their more conservative elders. To a nineteenth-century American, Indian assimilation was indeed the most liberal and enlightened policy yet devised. What better way for American society to ease the Native's march to oblivion than to have them vanish into it?

The trouble with this "vanishing policy" was that a new American generation began to see it as unrealistic, destructive rather the constructive, and, in a way, totalitarian. For one thing, there was a new social consciousness in the United States that more or less countered the wildly individualistic *laissez-faire* liberalism of the previous half century. Second, the products of the vanishing policy, those Natives who had been through the Indian schools or who had obtained educations in the Euro-American world, were not exactly disappearing. Nor were they marginalized. They remained completely loyal to their own people, worked for Indian causes, produced works of art and literature that were both distinctly "Indian" and had wide appeal among the white people, and attempted to organize in the hope of gaining influence over the direction of American Indian policy. They and numerous non-Indian scholars, connoisseurs, educators, and social commentators were active in preserving elements of Native cultures. The vanishing policy had failed because it had not transformed the Indian identity into an American one; therefore, assimilation had not brought an effective or efficient end to the "Indian Problem." And if there was indeed an American consensus in the period, it was a generally held loathing of inefficiency. The "search for order" in the case of American Indian policy was the acknowledgment that assimilation had failed and that a different theoretical and practical foundation for Indian policy had to be discovered. The philosophy underpinning the vanishing policy did not die a quick death. It lingered simply because few people could conceive of an alternative, even though it conflicted with the ideas underscoring conservation, preservation, cultural sovereignty, the integration of Native knowledge and artistic achievement into American culture, and the idea that the need for social order might dent the American passion for individual rights and privileges. It was an age of confusion in Indian affairs that opened the door to new ideas. Wiebe's words "search for order" truly captured not only what was going on during the Progressive Era generally but also the fundamental nature of Indian-white relations in the same period.

The Policy Development Group that penned the "Government of Aboriginal Peoples" report essentially brought the discipline of political science into play regarding what had indeed happened in Indian-white relations in the first years of the twentieth century. The study is a comparative approach to the political relationships between the colonizer and the colonized, and as such gives us a very different way of viewing the totality of federal Indian policy. It was a fine attempt to develop a useful model of colonial relations. Robert Wiebe's skill as a historian at recognizing trends and reasoning inductively puts the study of this period in Indian-white relations into a larger historical context. His perspective on the era and its significance remains one of the best contributions to the vast literature on early twentieth-century America. Put together, these studies gave me the idea that this period in Indian policy was transitional. Wiebe and the Policy Development Group placed Indian-white relations in the correct political and historical contexts.

At least one observer in the period, Fayette Avery McKenzie, wrote in 1910 about the "great confusion in Indian policies." But what sparked McKenzie's perceptive observation? Most historians tend to view Indian-white relations in periods. Francis Paul Prucha's *Great Father: The United States Government and the American Indians* (1984), as well as many of his other superb histories, essentially places federal Indian policy into the eras of the trade and intercourse acts, removal, reservations, Grant's peace policy, assimilation, Indian reorganization, termination and relocation, and finally self-determination. This chronology is no doubt correct, and most other historians follow it without question. The early twentieth-century relationship between Natives and whites has been seen simply as a continuation of the previous century's vanishing policy. Change, from this perspective, comes abruptly with the passage of the Indian Reorganization Act of 1934, which, in turn, seems to have sprung forth from the fertile mind of John Collier like Athena from the head of Zeus. But change is rarely that marked or speedy or the result of a single person's philosophical or theoretical insight or force of will. Human beings, as Edmund Burke pointed out long ago in his *Reflections on the Revolution in France*, lean toward conservatism and the maintenance of order. The vanishing policy broke down before John Collier discovered Indians. The underlying ideas of assimilation collapsed because Natives simply refused to vanish as peoples or as individuals into the American mainstream. The resiliency of peoplehood militated against assimilation and caused whites to rethink the policy. The "peoplehood matrix" was the third conceptual framework that helps explain what happened to the vanishing policy.

In his 1980 book, *The Yaquis: A Cultural History*, the late Edward H. Spicer attempted to boil down the characteristics of peoples that had endured the colonial experience and maintained their unique group identities. These enduring peoples, to use Spicer's terminology, kept their languages, knew their territories, and possessed religious practices uniquely their own. A year later, Pierre Castile and Gilbert Kushner published *Persistent Peoples: Cultural Enclaves in Perspective* to honor Spicer and to explore the notion of peoplehood further. Like Spicer, Castile and Kushner realized that the resiliency of enclaved groups is connected with maintaining language, understanding place, and keeping particular religious ceremonies alive.

In the late 1980s Bob Thomas began to look at the idea of peoplehood and decided that the Spicer-Castile-Kushner model needed the addition of a fourth element that Thomas began to call "Sacred History." A group's sacred history (oral traditions, stories of origin, creation, and tricksters, etc.) linked the other aspects of peoplehood together. The sacred history told about a group's territory and how the group got there, was a "how-to" in regard to religion, defined the group's kinship structure, and was the resource for sociopolitical organization. Thomas also drew from Vine Deloria's cumulative work on Native knowledge to demonstrate that these aspects were interconnected and inseparable. Deloria has written a number of tracts arguing that Native knowledge is essentially the understanding that all things observed in a particular place are linked in a complex yet orderly system of harmonious balance. Language gives meaning to the sacred history and, as Keith Basso has demonstrated in his very fine *Wisdom Sits in Places*, to the landscape. Place in turn gives meaning to the people's ceremonial life. Ceremonies are always linked to the flora, fauna, seasons, and cosmos in or from the perspective of a particular environment. Peoplehood is a matrix, a complex, organic, and integrated system of knowledge, symbols, relationships, and behaviors. Moreover, it is based on information generated within American Indian studies.

Peoplehood was ultimately the reason underlying Native cultural resiliency. Indians managed, despite every effort on the part of the federal government, to maintain their identities as sovereign sociopolitical entities. The Indians who had been thought assimilated because they spoke English, wore Euro-American clothing, attended mainstream Christian churches, and practiced many of the white man's customs remained Indians in terms of politics, spirituality, and, because Western culture placed such great importance on it, racial identity. Native writers, artists, and professionals remained true to their tribal identities, their senses of peoplehood. Their work reflected this fact. They wrote about their lives; created works of genuine beauty and uniqueness; labored for Indian political causes; and promoted Native philosophies, arts, and a Native understanding of the environment. Indians did not vanish in any sense of the term.

Euro-Americans began to accept the fact that Indians were not going to go away or disappear into the new American industrial-urban culture. Whites did not want Indians to vanish either. They collected Indian artifacts, bought "Indian" designs, visited reservations, became patrons of Native artists, and wrote hundreds of books on "Indian lore." Many actually wanted to be Indians, as Philip Deloria has pointed out in his 1998 book, *Playing Indian*. Criticism aimed at the vanishing policy came from every possible source and angle. Non-Native scholars, conservationists, popular writers, and artists, as well as Native peoples themselves, undermined the philosophical foundation of the

Indian assimilation movement until ultimately most federal policy makers conceded that complete Indian assimilation was no longer feasible in the short term. Without an overarching philosophical goal for Indian relations, the federal government fell into the pattern of stopgap, opportunistic management in compliance with already established administrative regulations and policies (or interpretations thereof). The idea of completely assimilating the Native population into mainstream America did not die; it was enfeebled to the point of being bedridden.

By the 1920s, a number of people were developing another theory of Indian policy, this one based on accommodating the continuation of Native communities and promoting a Native identity in art, literature, and the development of policy. The Indian Reorganization Act of 1934, despite its well-known flaws, supported the notion that Native governments should have a hand in deciding tribal membership, determining how tribal resources should be utilized, and disbursing tribal funds. The creation of the Indian Arts and Crafts Board in 1935 to save Native arts and, specifically, to promote the economic welfare of the tribes was the result of an effort to undo the deleterious effects of bans on Native ceremonies, forced acculturation, and Christian zealotry. These policy changes were successful attempts to restructure the federal bureaucracy that handled Indian affairs into a permanent and powerful agency for maintaining Native tribal identities. Certain features of Indian life were to be accepted as part of American life rather than construed as opposed to it.

The philosophy that led to the structural accommodation phase in U.S.-Indian relations is still in place despite periodic efforts to do it in. It is more or less an idea that Natives can maintain their individual tribal identities and, at the same time, be "good Americans." It is a formula for American-style ethnicity. The problem is that Indians are not really just another American ethnic group. Although American citizens, Natives actually make up a number of autonomous and distinct peoples with very particular political relations with the United States. In the 1930s the federal relationship with the Native peoples was restructured to accommodate the fact that they had not only survived but also made numerous contributions to the culture of the American nation-state. Whites actually adopted certain features of the Native American cultural heritage as their own.

Because this phase in the American colonial relationship with Native peoples essentially allowed the re-formation of Native nation-states under the domination of the larger American state, it precluded the complete assimilation of Indians. Indigenous peoples, what Canadians have called "First Nations," have distinct political identities and are not really ethnics or, for that matter, "hyphenated" Americans. Otherwise, there could be Qualla Cherokee-Americans or Mississippi Choctaw-Americans. In the attempt to gain political efficacy over the territories that now make up the United States, the federal government entered into a trust relationship with a large number of these indigenous nations. In exchange for land and political stability, Native nations retained certain sovereign rights and entered into protectorate status. Thus Native Americans, provided that they are members or citizens of those Native nations that have this particular relationship with the federal or even the various state governments, possess certain rights that other Americans do not and cannot hold. This relationship has nothing to do with race, even though most Americans tend to place it in that context. Simply put, the United States inherited its colonial relationship with the Indian tribes from the United Kingdom and has gone through three phases of that colonial relationship, with periods of conflict and confusion marking the transitions between them.

In the chapters that follow, I will attempt to place the Indian-white relationship in the early years of the twentieth century into political, cultural, and historical contexts. The first chapter is more or less an introduction to and a summary of what has been called the "vanishing" policy, placing it in the colonial relationship model as outlined in the "Government of Aboriginal Peoples" report. The succeeding chapters explore the resiliency of peoplehood and how the vanishing policy failed to amalgamate, acculturate, or even marginalize fully the Native American population. The result of Native resiliency was the breakdown of the theoretical underpinnings of the vanishing policy and an opening for the introduction of the structural accommodation stage of American colonial relations with Native nation-states. The final chapter is essentially an epilogue. It attempts to place John Collier's reforms of the 1930s into the general context of domestic colonialism and speculates on where federal Indian policy now stands. Altogether this study essentially tests the colonial relationship model, the peoplehood matrix, and the Wiebe thesis. They are all viable conceptual tools, and in the case of Indian-white relations in the period roughly encompassing the Progressive Era, they have great explanatory power.

I hasten to state that any factual inaccuracies or flawed interpretations in this book are directly attributable to me. The real worth of this study is directly linked to the knowledge, analytical skills, and hard work of others, and I wish to thank them profusely for their help. Although I mentioned them in the opening paragraph, I nevertheless want to acknowledge the members of my doctoral committee at the University of Oklahoma those many years ago. Professors Crockett, Spurgeon, Morgan, and especially the late Arrell M. "Luke" Gibson did so much to get me through graduate school that I cannot thank them enough.

Help, commentary, and encouragement for this particular version of the manuscript came from a number of very different sources. At different points in time, two nationally known and highly respected scholars, Francis Paul Prucha, SJ, and Henry E. Fritz, scrutinized the study and provided highly useful critiques. The manuscript also benefited from the skill, discerning minds, and acute insights of two men with close ties to the Creek Nation. The first is my old friend and fellow graduate student Don Fixico. Don has helped me in innumerable ways: providing comments on my work, encouraging me to be a careful researcher, and being a friend for thirty years. The second is Joyotpaul Chaudhuri. Joy's late wife, Jean, was a traditional Creek woman who fought to maintain the sacred ways of her people. Joy's knowledge of Native peoples, his insights as a renowned political scientist, and his writing skills helped this get this manuscript in shape as a book. *Mado* to both Don and Joy.

I was lucky to have spent several years in the presence of Native thinkers like Vine Deloria, Jr., and the late Robert K. Thomas. Bob was especially encouraging and saw the need for expanding on the ideas I have mentioned in this preface. Vine knew that our fledgling Native American studies program at the University of Arizona had to produce scholars of high repute in order for the program to continue. In order to attract and teach talented students, professors had to produce. Vine encouraged me to publish, and publish some more, in order to strengthen our teaching. Once again, he was right.

I hasten to add a note of appreciation to Joseph "Jay" Stauss, who served as director of American Indian Studies at the University of Arizona for eleven years. Jay recognized that scholarship was the foundation on which nationally respected universities and their programs are built. Jay, like Vine before him, realized that research and publication are the lifeblood of an academic program. Consequently, Jay encouraged research and attempted to shield professors from administrative chores so that we could continue to build the program's publication list. His equal as a department chair has yet to be found.

I want to extend my heartfelt appreciation to those friends with whom I can freely discuss theoretical constructs, paradigms, and various other intellectual pursuits. I have a number of people whom I can bounce ideas off of and who will bounce them back. Like many of my friends in academia—Vine Deloria, the late Bob Thomas, and Jim Clarke—Richard Allen is another of my Marine Corps brothers. Bob Thomas once said that in the old days Cherokee men made war, hunted, and thought "great thoughts." I have found that my people really do love the give and take of intellectual discussion. Richard is certainly one of those Cherokees, and I am deeply grateful for his capable mind and willingness to discuss just about anything. Jerry C. Bread is another. I've known him for over thirty years and can engage him in a useful and interesting discussion at any given time. *Wado* to these Cherokee intellectuals.

I have several other intellectual compatriots who have added a great deal to the completion of this book. I would like to thank J. Diane Pearson, the first PhD in American Indian studies, and Elise Marubbio for their comments and support. My graduate students have always been a source of encouragement and new ideas. Johnnie Jacobs, Mariah Gover, Spintz Harrison, Pamela Bennett, and Lee Jackson have all inspired new ways to look at things and different approaches to the same subject matter. Traci Morris, who is an American Indian art historian, provided some welcome insights and sources. I want to be sure to include my sons and daughters-in-law, Garett, Mike, Andrea, and Sandra, as some of my most important intellectual supporters. My wife, Ina, has always been there as well to provide support and an intellectual sounding board.

I mentioned the late Alice Brigham earlier as the source for the "Government of Aboriginal Peoples" report. Her death was a blow from which few of us who knew her will recover. I must also mention that my former graduate student, Michael Two Horses, who was as keen an academic mind as I have ever known, passed away in 2003. Mike dug up some important materials for inclusion in this book. Thanks, Alice and Mike; you will be remembered fondly.

Finally, I would like to thank Theresa J. May at the University of Texas Press. If ever there was a senior editor who provided more encouragement, constructive criticism, and help in putting one's ideas on paper I have never heard of one. I deeply appreciate her e-mails and general uplifting attitude. I must also thank Lynne Chapman at the Press for her diligence and encouragement. A word of gratitude also goes out to Kip Keller, who is as fine a copy editor as I've encountered.

TOM HOLM
TUCSON, ARIZONA

CHAPTER I

THE VANISHING POLICY

BEFORE DIPPING A TOE into the murky waters of the late nineteenth-century movement to assimilate Native Americans into mainstream American society, it is necessary to explain Indian-white relations in a larger context. First, it must be recognized that the many and various "tribes" in North and South America were autonomous peoples. That is to say, each Native group had a unique language, a defined territory, a distinct and sacred history, and a ceremonial cycle that renewed and explained the group's relationship with the spirits of the land.[1] Peoplehood is the basis of sovereignty, nationalism, culture, and social organization.[2] European colonists, on the other hand, were mere fragments of peoples who came with their languages, religions, and sacred histories but who did not have a particular intimacy with the territory they sought to claim for themselves. Their esteem for the land rested more on a mechanical "cash exchange" basis; the land was worth exactly what it could produce, or what could be extracted from it, or what it could be bartered for. The European sacred lands were still across the seas.

The relationships between indigenous peoples and colonizers usually proceed through a serious of phases. First and foremost, the establishment of colonies disrupts Native societies and displaces people. More often than not, conflict follows, with a concomitant reassessment of the colonial policy of outright conquest. At that point, both colonizers and indigenous peoples begin to agree upon a policy of resetting territorial boundaries in order to maintain a degree of order. Treaty making is a very good example of this stage in Indian-white relations.

But perhaps because the acquisition of land is, by definition, the colonizer's main preoccupation, boundaries are continually violated, leading to more, rather than less, disorder and violence. The next stage in colonialism is the attempt on the part of the colonizer to integrate an indigenous group into the colonial socioeconomic structure. Assimilation could mean turning the indigenous population into a labor force or perhaps a marginalized group of "others" who speak the colonizers' language and have internalized the colonizers' versions of their history as being correct. As Albert Memmi has indicated, the internalization of colonialism by indigenous groups may well be the final outcome and goal of colonization.[3]

As soon as it became an independent nation, the United States launched a policy of expanding its territorial limits and colonizing areas ceded by Great Britain in the 1783 Treaty of Paris ending the Revolutionary War. Expansion, however, was a costly enterprise. The United States was relatively poor and had a small, meagerly paid army that was required to maintain order on the frontier. It failed miserably. Warfare between Indians and whites was constant and led to two disastrous American military defeats at the hands of a Native American confederacy in what is now Indiana. Consequently, the new nation took up the British policy of making treaties with Native tribes to regulate trade and purchasing, rather than simply attempting to conquer Indian lands. In short, the United States moved quickly through the first phase of colonialism and into the second in order to define boundaries and quell the violence. American treaty making, at least with Indians, was an expedient measure, intended to make colonization orderly and as inexpensive, in terms of military spending, as possible.

Besides land cessions, treaties, and trade, the Americans also implemented assimilation plans, the third step in colonization from the grab bag of policies that had been formulated under British rule. In 1790 George Washington and Secretary of War Henry Knox urged Congress to pass the first Trade and Intercourse Act to regulate trade with the tribes, formalize the treaty-making process, establish the federal government as the sole agent for the purchase of Indian lands, and promote "civilization" among the Indian people. Along with ceding tribal lands to the United States, tribal societies were to undergo cultural and social change; in short, Indians were to become like whites and be assimilated into the American body politic as farmers, laborers in the fur-and-hide trade and, in some cases, as artisans. In a series of Trade and Intercourse Acts, the federal government set aside funds not only to purchase Indian land, but also to buy farm implements, spinning wheels, and domestic animals as incentives to induce Indians to lead a "civilized" life. Indian men were urged "to give up the hunt," till the fields, and care for livestock; Native women were advised to give up their agricultural pursuits, stay in the home, and spin wool.[4]

Getting American Indians to accept the idea of private property was basic to the concept of assimilation. In 1808, President Thomas Jefferson urged a contingent of southern Indian leaders to advise their people to secure individual family farms out of tribal lands and work the plots in the manner of their white neighbors. Jefferson no doubt believed that if his advice were followed, the tribal members would become Indian versions of the Jeffersonian yeoman farmer, individualized and acculturated, Christian and loyal to the United States. Jefferson's advice amounted to an early attempt to promote the allotment of tribal lands in severalty. As time went on, larger numbers of whites concerned with Indian policy would begin to equate the allotment of tribal lands in severalty with the civilization or assimilation process.[5]

Humanitarian, assimilationist rhetoric cloaked even the most blatant transgressions against American Indian societies and landholdings. In exchange for vast cessions of tribal lands, Indians were sent missionaries, domestic animals, and the services of blacksmiths to make farming tools. Even the forced removal of the eastern tribes to lands west of the Mississippi was carried out to insure their "ultimate security and improvement."[6] The establishment of the Indian Territory and the reservation system, although an overt attempt to restrict Indian movement and to compress tribal territories so that Indians would be forced to take up farming, was instituted according to the American ideology of the period to prepare Native Americans for their entrance into American society.[7] Whites fully believed throughout the nineteenth century that American civilization would spread from coast to coast and that Native cultures—or, depending on the perspective, Native people—were doomed to extinction through the "natural" processes of human progress. "Civilization or death" for American Indians was the white view of the "Indian Problem"; there was no other alternative.[8]

The post–Civil War movement for Indian assimilation, which

reached its zenith with the liquidation of the Indian Territory under the Curtis Act of 1898, was based essentially on the same views that prompted the territory's establishment. In an earlier period, certain whites looked upon the reservations and the autonomous tribal states in the Indian Territory, to which thousands of Native Americans were removed in the 1830s and 1840s, as vast tracts of land wherein Indians would reside unmolested and could "advance" toward civilization and the acceptance of Christianity. This "advancement" was more or less considered an evolutionary process, slow and purposeful. But the outbreaks of warfare between whites and Indians in the 1860s pointed out that Indian-white relations had reached the nadir of a four-hundred-year decline. Indians did not go unmolested to pursue "civilized life." The November 29, 1864, massacre of the Cheyenne and Arapaho village at Sand Creek, Colorado Territory, after the Indians had signed a peace treaty and agreed to live on a reservation, finally stirred a government still occupied with the Civil War into a degree of action.[9]

On January 9, 1865, Senator James R. Doolittle of Wisconsin introduced a joint resolution calling for a special committee to be formed to investigate the condition of Indian affairs. Approved in March, the committee set at its arduous and lengthy task. A survey was taken from various sources, for not only did the Doolittle Commission conduct interviews and take testimony, but it sent out questionnaires to Indian agents, missionaries, army officers, and sundry other persons involved in implementing Indian policy. The results of the survey were shocking to some, predictable to others. According to the commission's report, alcoholism was rampant on the reservations and health problems enormous. Not surprisingly, the American Indian population was reported to be in a rapid decline.[10]

The responses to the Doolittle questionnaire typically emphasized the moral side of the Indian question. Those surveyed recommended that Indians should continue in agricultural training, receive Christian educations, and be protected from immoral and avaricious white influences.[11] When Ulysses S. Grant became president in 1869, he established a "Peace Policy" with the tribes by appointing missionaries as Indian agents, negotiating treaties that contained provisions for the establishment of schools on the reservations, and essentially instituted most of the recommendations of the Doolittle Commission.

The Grant administration's Indian policy was a stopgap attempt to quell the stirrings of the more radical wing of the Republican Party. In addition to appointing missionaries to fill agency positions, Grant set up the Board of Indian Commissioners, an unpaid group of zealously Christian, business-minded, Republican reformers. The president also picked a "civilized" Indian to serve as the new commissioner of Indian Affairs, Ely S. Parker. Parker was an old friend of Grant's, a Seneca from New York and former member of the general staff of the Army of the Potomac. It was said that Parker's beautiful and precise penmanship prompted Grant to have the Seneca officer write out the instrument of surrender at Appomattox Courthouse.[12]

The years of Grant's peace policy were hardly peaceful. The widespread corruption among members of the president's cabinet directly affected Native Americans. Rations, which were distributed to prevent Indians from leaving the reservations to hunt and, provisionally, to quell famine until they learned the tricks of civilized farming, were of poor quality and exceptionally high priced. It was later discovered that the secretary of the interior was accepting kickbacks from the ration contractors.[13] Although Parker was found not to have been involved in the scandals, he was nevertheless forced from office in 1871.

In addition to the graft, and in part because of it, whites and American Indians became engaged in a series of bloody armed clashes ranging from Texas to Montana to California.[14] Two sanguinary military engagements during the Grant administration shocked Americans even more than the Sand Creek massacre, for they proved that the president's policy of maintaining peace with the tribes while gradually acculturating individual Native Americans to Western values and life was crumbling. In 1873 the Modocs of northern California, although small in number, held off an entire U.S. military force and killed its commanding general, E. R. S. Canby. Canby's death appalled the American public, and the nation eventually revenged itself on the Modocs, but many whites began to question the causes of the war and its meaning within the context of the goals of Grant's Indian policy. The Modocs had been a sparse, peace-loving people who had essentially fitted themselves into northern California's labor force—most worked as ranch hands or in other agricultural pursuits—and had been largely overlooked as even potentially violent.[15] Their sudden outbreak vexed many Americans and created a stir in reform circles.[16] During the final year of the Grant administration, George Armstrong Custer led most of the Seventh Cavalry to its demise at the Little Bighorn. Coming as it did during the celebration of the nation's centennial, Custer's death ride stoked the fire of reform to even greater heights.[17]

Even after Grant left office, Indian outbreaks continued without letup. In 1877 the Nez Percé under the leadership of Chief Joseph and Ollicut broke out of their Oregon reservation in a desperate attempt to escape to Canada. Shortly thereafter the Bannocks followed suit, and less than a year later Dull Knife and Little Wolf led a number of Cheyenne out of their assigned reservation in Indian Territory to their homeland in the north. These attempts to flee reservation life were met with white resistance to be sure, but they also left many whites to question the reasons behind the outbreaks and to ponder the appalling living conditions at the agencies (reservations), which bred the trouble in the first place.[18]

But perhaps no other outbreak provoked as great a public demand for Indian reform as the "Ponca Affair" of 1879. Standing Bear, a Ponca leader, in an attempt to return the body of his dead son to the Ponca homeland, jumped the reservation in Indian Territory and fled to Nebraska. He was arrested there and brought into Omaha to await transportation back to Oklahoma. While the tribal leader was under lock and key, several reform-minded Omaha citizens, including the assistant editor of the *Omaha Herald*, Thomas Henry Tibbles, took up Standing Bear's cause with great fervor. Tibbles and the other concerned citizens prompted a few of the city's more prominent attorneys to file a writ of *habeas corpus* in an effort to set the chief free. The decision that United States District Court Judge Elmer S. Dundy rendered set a precedent in American Indian law. The judge granted the writ, ruling that Standing Bear was a "person" under the law and was therefore guaranteed constitutional protection. Before Dundy's decision, American Indians had not been given clear status under the U.S. Constitution. At best, Indians were members of "domestic dependent nations" or viewed by the courts as "wards" of the government.[19]

The aftereffects of the case were even more far-reaching. Standing Bear, Tibbles, and a member of the Omaha tribe, Suzette LaFlesche, toured the eastern United States, speaking out against the government's reservation policies. In the east, they met very receptive audiences and stimulated widespread white reflection on the "Indian Problem." Within weeks of the speaking tour, citizens' groups sprang up in such cities as Boston and Philadelphia to work for Indian policy reform.[20]

Criticism came swift and cut deep. Senator Henry Laurens Dawes of Massachusetts, who was to become the chief spokesman for Indian reform in Congress, openly criticized Secretary of the Interior Carl Schurz, a member of his own party and himself a reformer of great repute, for the secretary's lack of resolve in pushing an antireservation agenda. In 1879 in Philadelphia, Mary L. Bonney gathered a group of women together to collect signatures in a campaign to end the reservation system. The following year she collected more than 13,000 signatures on a petition urging Congress to move ahead with legislation concerning Indian affairs. By 1883 Bonney's organization assumed the title of the Women's National Indian Association.[21] The association immediately began to produce newsletters and other materials highly critical of the reservation policy. In 1881, Helen Hunt Jackson published her scathing attack on government Indian policy.[22] The book, entitled *A Century of Dishonor*, created even greater interest in American Indian problems, confirmed the legitimacy of the reformers' cause, and came shortly to be known as the *Uncle Tom's Cabin* of Indian reform.[23]

Between 1879 and 1883 the number of people and groups involved in the Indian reform movement burgeoned. The founding of several women's Indian reform organizations led the way, and soon some prominent American males were hopping on the bandwagon. The Indian Rights Association, which became perhaps the most influential of these reform organizations to deal with Indian legal problems, was founded, again in Philadelphia, in 1882. Finally, to coordinate these numerous and various groups and to provide a sounding board for them, the Lake Mohonk Conference of Friends of the Indian began annual meetings in 1883.[24]

The Lake Mohonk Conference was the brainchild and hope of Albert K. Smiley, a member of the Board of Indian Commissioners. He and his brother Alfred owned a hotel situated on Lake Mohonk in New York. Because he had found that the different groups had many of the same goals yet their efforts were uncoordinated, Smiley proposed annual fall meetings to be held at his resort. The meetings were relaxed and, at first, not well attended. But shortly thereafter attendance swelled, and the conference began to exert growing political power. Smiley, as a member of the Board of Indian Commissioners, began to have printed, at government expense, the proceedings of the Lake Mohonk Conference in the Board's annual reports.[25]

From the outset the conferees were completely taken with the idea of assimilating the Indian population into the American body politic. They believed wholeheartedly that Indians should immediately become thoroughly Americanized Christians in a cultural sense and fully indoctrinated in the competitive and individualized model that was, to them, the American way of life. By learning English, as well as to read and write, Native Americans would be better able to compete with their white neighbors. Moreover, the conferees firmly believed that Native ceremonies, healing practices, sacred histories, and "superstitions" were hindrances to Indian advancement. Most importantly, the conferees were in full agreement that the reservations should be broken up into individually held allotments in order to provide Indians with homesteads to serve as their economic base. Allotment would bring with it an end to tribalism and become the method of "Indian Emancipation."[26]

The allotment of Indian lands in severalty was neither a new idea nor completely the product of post–Civil War reform thought. The Indian reformers simply reached into colonialism's grab bag (or garbage can, as some commentators have suggested) and plucked out a formula that would ostensibly force an indigenous group to abandon its own sense of peoplehood and shift its loyalty to the colonial system, which was, in the final analysis, the protector of property rights, both colonial and indigenous. Thomas Jefferson suggested this policy regarding American Indians as early as 1808. The Chickasaw, Choctaw, and Creek were offered the option of taking allotments during the removal of the southern Indians to what became Indian Territory during the 1830s.[27] All of the Oklahoma territorial bills introduced during the 1870s contained provisions that would allot tribal lands in severalty and allow the surplus to be opened to non-Indian settlement.[28]

During the 1870s there had been numerous attempts to allot Indian lands. Most of these measures were quickly seen exactly for what they were: overt attempts to open Indian lands. The opening of Indian lands was very much a part of the intricate pattern of the take-off period of American industrial growth. To the Indian reformers, attempts to allot lands in particular areas or among certain tribes simply smacked of land speculation. Only a general allotment act, encompassing all Indian people and working for their benefit, would suffice. Without much apparent thought, the Indian reform movement played into the hands of the railroads, land companies, farmers, and ranchers as well as the timber, coal, petroleum, and steel industries.

The year 1879 produced several attempts to press through Congress a general allotment law. In January two such bills were introduced in the House and Senate. Although the Committee on Indian Affairs issued a favorable report on the House measure, it never progressed to a vote. The Senate bill was also eventually tabled.[29] Later, on April 21, Alfred M. Scales introduced another allotment measure in the House.[30] The Scales bill was referred to the Committee on Indian Affairs and ultimately met the same fate as the previously introduced allotment bills.

The next year the allotment onslaught became even more intense. On January 12, 1880, Alvin Saunders of Nebraska introduced an allotment bill into the Senate. This measure was an exact copy of the Scales bill submitted the year before.[31] During the same month, the House Committee on Indian Affairs issued a favorable report on a somewhat revised version of the Scales legislation. Neither bill, however, reached a vote.[32] On 19 May, Richard Coke of Texas placed before the Senate still another general allotment bill.[33] It was read and referred to the Committee on Indian Affairs, and after a favorable report the bill reached the Senate floor. It was debated in January and February 1881.[34]

The Coke bill was ill fated and brought forth some unexpected opposition. Although the Five Civilized Tribes of the Indian Territory were exempted from the provisions of the bill, their attitudes toward it became a central theme during the debates. One of the first questions raised concerning the Coke measure arose because of the very fact that these tribes were specifically omitted from its provisions. As an answer, Coke reminded his colleagues that one of the stipulations in the bill required tribal consent to allotment and that the "civilized tribes were known to the committee [Indian Affairs] not to desire it." The fact that section seven of the bill excluded not only the Five Tribes but the whole of the Indian Territory particularly irritated the Indian reformers, who were closely watching the ebb and flow of the allotment controversy. George Vest of Missouri requested that the bill be amended in order for tribes other than the Cherokee, Creek, Choctaw, Chicka-saw, and Seminole of the Indian Territory to accept allotment. Not surprisingly, Coke had intended the bill to pass as written, and led the voting that rejected Vest's proposed amendment.[35]

Henry M. Teller of Colorado led the opposition to the Coke bill on the Senate floor. Teller was apparently in close contact with the governments of the Five Civilized Tribes. As stipulated in several treaties made with the federal government, these tribes sent annual delegations to Washington to keep a close check on Indian policy. Essentially, these delegations became a formidable American Indian lobbying group that kept up the fight against railroad encroachment on Indian lands, bills to organize the Indian Territory, and measures that would have allotted particular Indian reservations. Teller asked to read their formal protest to the Coke bill into the record. When questioned about what possible relevance the memorial of the Five Tribes could have, since they were exempted from the bill, Teller explained that if the "civilized" Indians were against the measure, the "uncivilized" Indians would naturally contest it as well. His position was convincing enough, and the memorial was read into the debate.[36]

Teller's tactics worked well. Under pressure the Coke bill was greatly revised and amended. During the spring of 1882 the Senate finally passed the measure and sent it to the House. Despite a favorable report, the Coke allotment bill never reached the House floor.[37]

In the face of these setbacks to their measures, the Indian reformers stepped up the agitation in favor of allotment and targeted the Five Civilized Tribes as their chief adversaries. In 1883, the Indian Rights Association published S. C. Armstrong's pamphlet on the need to rid the federal government of the reservation system. The monograph was, in effect, a scathing attack on the governments and social structures of the Five Civilized Tribes. Armstrong urged unconditional allotment legislation, which, he claimed, would end the inequities in wealth among the tribes of the Southwest and the Indian Territory.[38] To counteract Armstrong and the Indian Rights Association's charges, the governments of the Five Tribes extended an invitation to the Senate Committee on Indian Affairs to visit the Indian Territory.[39]

In 1885, the Senate committee, with Henry Laurens Dawes as its chairman, finally did come to the Indian Territory. Dawes, firmly in the Indian reform camp since 1879, was hardly the open-minded congressional leader the Five Tribes had hoped to see. When he returned from the Indian Territory, Dawes went before the Lake Mohonk Conference and opened an attack on the tribal practice of holding lands in common. He specifically chose the Five Tribes as his target, saying, in effect, that although this system of land tenure had prevented abject poverty, it was nevertheless unprogressive and, in fact, backward. The senator then concluded that holding lands in common prevented "selfishness" and therefore stood as a roadblock to self-improvement. Dawes returned to the Senate and quickly set out to push a general allotment act through Congress.[40]

Dawes quickly introduced his own general allotment bill on December 8, 1885. The Senate, however, was unable to pass the measure until February of the following year. In the House, the bill was set aside until the autumn of 1886. Finally debated and amended, it was not passed out of the House until December 15 of that year.[41]

On February 8, 1887, President Grover Cleveland signed the Dawes General Allotment Act into law. The act provided for American Indian landholdings to be surveyed and then parceled out to individual tribal members. An allottee would receive full rights of U.S. citizenship along with a parcel of land. The new law also placed a trust period on allotments, guaranteeing that the land would be inalienable for a period of twenty-five years.[42]

For a number of reasons, the majority of those Americans with an interest in Indian policy considered the Dawes Act a triumph in every way. To corporate interests, in particular the railroads, it provided a means to deal with American Indians individually and without an exceptional amount of interference from the government. Surplus land—that which was left over after allotment—would become part of the U.S. public domain and would be easily obtained by purchase or lease. The law was also hailed as a triumph of nineteenth-century liberalism because it stressed individualism and the notion that the ownership of private property conferred on the owner a true sense of freedom. According to the reformers of American Indian policy, the individual ownership of property would force American Indians to abandon their cultural heritages, enter mainstream American society, and shift their allegiances to the federal government as the ultimate protector of the right to private property. To others of a more pessimistic bent, the Dawes Act was a generous offering to a doomed people.

Some tribes were specifically exempted from the provisions of the Dawes Act. The Five Civilized Tribes and the Osage of Indian Territory were, surprisingly, left alone.[43] These tribes, or their representatives, had after all become the bugbears of the allotment movement. As early as 1877, Alfred Riggs, a missionary to the Santee Dakota, urged that the Santee lands in Nebraska and South Dakota be allotted. Riggs specifically proposed that allotment be done piecemeal in order, he said, "to avoid raising that hornet's nest in the Indian Territory."[44] Leaving them out of the Dawes Act was not the fault of the reformers; there was nothing more hoped for than the liquidation of the Indian Territory. They were stymied in their attempts to include the Five Tribes and the Osage in the Dawes Act because all these tribes held a fee-simple title to their lands. These titles, however, did not deter the reformers or the corporate interests from the conviction that allotment in severalty was the panacea for all Indian ills. In fact, the reformers and the whites who coveted land in the Indian Territory kept up the pressure on Congress and fought hard to include the territory under the provisions of the General Allotment Act.

In less than six years Congress succumbed to the pressure from reformers, non-Indian intruders living in the Indian Territory illegally, and the railroad lobbyists. Under the provisions of the 1893 Indian Appropriation Act, Congress established a commission to seek agreements with the Five Tribes that would extinguish their fee-simple titles and allot their lands in severalty. The new commission, named for its chairman, none other than Henry Laurens Dawes, set out almost immediately on its mission to the Indian Territory.[45]

For nearly five years the Dawes Commission and the leaders from the Five Tribes struggled with the allotment question. At first the tribal leaders flatly refused to discuss the subject, leaving the commission with little to report during its first year of operation. During this period the Five Tribes actually picked up some support for their contention that forcing them to allot their land was directly in violation of the U.S. Constitution. Their treaties had guaranteed their titles, and any transgression of treaty rights essentially violated Article VI of the Constitution. Ever mindful of these potential legal problems, the Indian Rights Association sent Charles F. Meserve, president of Shaw College in Raleigh, North Carolina, to investigate the conditions in the Indian Territory. Meserve's report, entitled *The Dawes Commission and the Five*

Civilized Tribes of Indian Territory, was nothing more than a condemnation of the governments of the Five Tribes and a highly laudatory appraisal of the Dawes Commission's work. Meserve openly accused the tribal leaders of committing high crimes against their people, of becoming spokesmen for business monopolies, and of condoning corruption in government. Meserve's ridiculously biased and prejudicial pamphlet nevertheless demonstrated that the reformers were more than willing to violate the Constitution to accomplish their goals.[46]

Congress was equally ready to violate the supremacy clause as well, and time began to run short for the Indian Territory. In 1895 the federal government established two new United States district courts in the Indian Territory to undermine and dissolve the established tribal judicial systems and to erode the power of the tribal governments.[47] The next year Congress authorized the Dawes Commission to prepare tribal rolls for the implementation of allotment.[48] Finally, on June 28, 1898, President William McKinley signed the Curtis Act into law. The Curtis Act directed the Dawes Commission to proceed with allotment and ordered the tribal governments dissolved after the business of allotment had been concluded.[49] The Choctaw, Chickasaw, and Seminole had already reached an agreement with the Dawes Commission on allotment prior to the signing of the new statute. The Creek and Cherokee held out until after the act became law, but all recognized the futility of further argument.

To the reformers, the Curtis Act was a giant step toward the ultimate resolution of the "Indian Problem." Indeed, the destruction of a separate territory for American Indians could be considered the capstone of the entire movement for Indian reform. To the reformers, the Curtis Act brought justice to a corrupt and backward part of the United States. Allotment was, according to one writer,

> a marvelous expansion for the ignorant full-blood, who has hitherto controlled only his little sweet potato patch in the woods, and it is a pretty severe contraction for the shrewd mixed-blood, whose audacious fences have been enclosing thousands of acres of the tribal lands. Equality was not even a theory in the bygone days, when the tribe held all things in common.[50]

If the Curtis Act was the capstone of the Indian reform movement, it rested solidly on other reform policies and programs. Already Indian children were being sent off the reservations to be educated; missionaries were well situated at most Indian agencies; and a commission had been formed in order to give American Indians new, Anglicized names. In sum, the reformers believed that the complete Americanization and Christianization of the Indians was in sight. In early 1902, Charles Moreau Harger, in an article for *Outlook* magazine, pronounced the Indian reform movement successful and complete. Everything was in place that would give Native Americans the chance to be "uplifted" from savagery to civilization. It was now time, proclaimed Harger, for the individual Indian to prove himself, and if he could not, "the world owes him nothing."[51] The "Indian Problem" would be a lesson in history because the Indian would vanish.

The reformers held great faith in measures such as the Dawes and Curtis Acts. The policies of assimilation—or "shrinkage," as many of them called it, in the belief that the Indian population would melt into the dominant society and cease to be visible—were well within the parameters of American social thought during the period. The key word was competition. Through the Indian schools, allotment in severalty, and the abandonment of tribal cultures, American Indians would be placed on a level playing field with whites. Once there, Indians would have to ascribe to the same rules of "civilized society" and cut themselves free from tribal bonds as well as from their dependence on the United States government. Those who became independent and who fitted well into American culture "will be a contingent worth saving."[52]

The Indian reformers, however, were not necessarily egalitarian in outlook, nor did they wish to restructure American society. They believed that "progress" was a natural process and that the United States was moving steadily toward the zenith of civilized culture. Culture was not a relative term. Richard Henry Pratt, one of the most prominent Indian reformers and head of the Indian boarding school at Carlisle, Pennsylvania, stated flatly that Indian cultures should not be "even dignified with the term."[53] Attitudes such as Pratt's were not ordinary ethnocentrism. Rather, they reflected a very American understanding of history. Americans had made a revolution, established the world's first constitutional democracy, fought a bloody civil war, and finally abolished slavery. Industrialization was rapidly growing, and with it, great wealth. Inventions such as the telegraph, the telephone, and the electric light gave Americans the sense that their country was, at minimum, an enlightened, a scientific, and in that sense a thoroughly modern nation. Their ancestors had gone through a primitive stage in history, but the current generation had progressed to new heights in technology and refined culture. Christianity was not just another religion, but the only true belief of free, modern men. Indian cultures were simply the remnants of a bygone age and were doomed to extinction.

The policy of assimilating Indians attracted numerous advocates, among them, according to the delegates of the Cherokee Nation in Washington, "thousands of the best men and women in the United States."[54] The Cherokee were not necessarily referring only to those persons of intense morality or kindness, although "the best men and women" certainly believed they possessed these virtues. Rather, the delegates singled out those persons who were then considered among America's intellectual elite, the liberal reformers of the Gilded Age.

"Reformer" was something of a misnomer for these activists. They believed in economic orthodoxy, limited government in the Jeffersonian mold, and *laissez-faire* capitalism. They were individualistic to the core, leaned toward the evangelical side of Protestant theology, and held an all-consuming optimism concerning the future of mankind. Men such as Carl Schurz, Edwin L. Godkin, Lyman Abbott, Henry Laurens Dawes, Henry M. Teller, Samuel Bowles, Henry Ward Beecher, Henry Adams, and others provided much of liberal reform's theoretical and rhetorical base. Although many of them differed in opinion on some matters in the life of the nation, they were basically uniform in their attitudes concerning America's progress, its moral fiber, and its confirmation of personal liberty. They interested themselves in all of the predominant questions of the period, including reconstruction of the South, civil service reform, the gold standard, and Indian affairs.[55]

Their attitudes toward competition and individualism were confirmed in the classical economics of Smith, Malthus, Ricardo, and Say and in the most advanced scientific thought of the day. Darwin's theory of evolution by natural selection and the ever-growing interest and research in the social sciences tended to reaffirm their already held beliefs about linear history, natural law, and man's progress. William Graham Sumner put an academic stamp on social Darwinism during his long career at Yale University.[56] When the "father of American anthropology," Lewis Henry Morgan, expounded his theory, based on his studies of American Indians, that mankind's cultural evolution went through stages of savagery, barbarism, and, finally, civilization, his words were readily accepted, for they exactly fitted white America's preconceived ideas about the "natural" superiority of Western civilization.[57]

The new scientific understanding of the world, of course, directly confronted Christian dogma. But the liberal reformers of the Gilded Age seemed to have been able to embrace both creeds. Christian compassion and charity could temper "nature red in tooth and claw." Within the confines of these notions, most of the reformers sought to "uplift" Indians from what they commonly referred to as "savagery" to "civilization." And the word "civilization" was never questioned. It meant white American society. To a liberal reformer, forcing Indians to progress according to the scientific version of "natural law" was an act of Christian compassion. Even Samuel Bowles, editor of the Springfield, Massachusetts, *Republican*, who believed that American Indians were doomed anyway, advocated an Indian policy that would smooth the path of extinction and at the same time treat Indians as humanely as possible.[58] E. L. Godkin, editor of the influential periodical *The Nation*, looked upon American Indian policy as an open field for humanitarian, liberal reform.[59]

Most of the humanitarian, Christian rhetoric centered on the destruction of Native cultures and religions. "Savage habits" were to be done away with, for they prevented entrance into modern society. The notion of "peoplehood" was basic to the assimilationist mentality. Native American tribes drew their distinct identities from an interlocking matrix of a distinct language, a particular relationship with a particular place, the understanding of a specific history that was considered sacred, and a ceremonial cycle or religion that fixed the group's place in the world, utilized its language in a liturgical sense, and drew upon the group's understanding of sacred history to maintain its relationship with the spirit world. The reformers must have understood the basics of peoplehood because they focused their attacks specifically on the four elements of the peoplehood matrix. Private property would defeat the notion of Native territoriality and even spatial identity; Christianity would do to death the ceremonies that tied a tribe to the land, the cosmos, and the spirit world; science would rout tribal sacred histories; and, finally, an English education would destroy Indian liturgical and colloquial languages.

Allotment was intended to break the "tribal bond" and end the practice of holding lands in common. In 1883, Commissioner of Indian Affairs Hiram Price issued an order to establish Indian Courts of Offences on the reservations to "put a stop to the demoralizing influence of heathenish rites," which were, he wrote, "repugnant to common decency."[60] Former associate justice of the Supreme Court, William Strong, an advocate of Indian assimilation, stated that if Indians were to be incorporated into American society, it was the duty of the government agents and Indian educators not to allow Indians to "maintain their own language and habits."[61] The reformers were steadfast in the belief that nothing from tribal societies could possibly be of value to American society. Although the phrase "kill the Indian and save the man" could not be attributed to any one person, it fully expressed the sentiment of the "vanishing" policy.

If there was one person who made the vanishing policy into a career and personal crusade, however, it was Richard Henry Pratt. He was easily the most ardent spokesman for Indian assimilation and the leading philosophical exponent of Indian education in the latter half of the nineteenth century. Pratt was a career army officer who had been called to the colors during the Civil War. During the conflict he rose from private to captain. Army life, or perhaps combat, must have suited him because he remained in the army and served in the grueling and bloody campaigns against the tribes on the southern plains during the late 1860s and early 1870s. In 1875, however, he traded in his Indian fighter hat for that of an Indian educator. In that year Pratt was assigned to Fort Marion, Florida, to serve as warden over the American Indian prisoners of war who had been incarcerated for fighting in wars against whites.[62]

Pratt's tenure at Fort Marion brought out a reformist urge. He worked with the prisoners in trying to teach them English and urged them to take up the trappings of American society. He felt sure that society would accept any and all Indian people once they had given up their cultural heritage. To this end he devoted his life's work, eventually establishing an Indian branch at Hampton Institute and founding the Carlisle Indian School in Pennsylvania. He firmly believed that an Indian youth should be removed from the reservation influence, for "left in the surroundings of savagery, he grows to possess a savage language, superstition, and life." The goals of Pratt, and therefore of Carlisle, were to remove American Indians from their families and heritage and make them able to enter the public schools. Once out of Carlisle, the Indian youth, he stated, "should be forwarded into these other schools, there to temper, test and stimulate his brain and muscle into the capacity he needs for his struggle for life, in competition with us."[63]

The "outing system" was another Pratt innovation and perhaps the method of Indian education of which he was most proud. Pratt insisted that "savagery was only a habit" and that Indian people should "get into the swim of citizenship."[64] In order to get his students "into the swim," Pratt placed Indian children with white families during the summer months and even during the school year so that they could learn the white way of life firsthand and "become saturated with the spirit of it, and thus become equal to it."[65] Reformers praised the system and often referred to it as the hope of the Indian people. Elaine Goodale Eastman, a former director of the schools at the Pine Ridge Reservation in South Dakota used the following words to express her view of Pratt's method:

> The word "outing" is used in a new sense by Major Pratt, of the Carlisle Indian School. "Out" of the tribal bond; out of Indian narrowness and clannishness; out into the broad life of the Nation. The Carlisle outing is by no means a summer holiday; it has become a fundamental part of the Carlisle training a definite method—perhaps the method—of Americanizing Indians.[66]

Too often Pratt's military experience has been overlooked in explaining his and Carlisle's goals for Native American children. Carlisle was, and is, a military post. The children who were sent to the institution were uniformed, drilled, and marched to classes. Additionally, they were subjected to frequent military-type inspections and punishments such as whippings, mess duty, and cleaning, painting, and shining trivial pieces of equipment, furniture, and the exteriors and interiors of buildings. Over the years I have heard a number of Native American veterans of U.S. military service who had attended Indian boarding schools categorically state that after boarding school, recruit training in the army, marine corps, navy, and air force was easy.

In any case, Carlisle Indian School can be compared very easily with Prussian regimental "improving" schools of the eighteenth and nineteenth centuries.

The Prussian "improving" regiment was a feature of the militarization of many Western nations. In the nineteenth century, Europe was dotted with regimental garrisons in or close to a provincial town. In Prussia, the regiments recruited or conscripted local peasants for military service and relied on the local aristocracy for leadership. According to military historian John Keegan:

> At their best . . . such regiments became "schools of the nation," which encouraged temperance, physical fitness and proficiency in the three Rs. . . . [The] commander set up regimental schools to educate the young officers, to teach the soldiers to read and write and to train their wives in spinning and lace-making.[67]

The regimental schools also taught discipline and, most importantly, loyalty to regiment and nation. "There are," according to Keegan, "pathetic descriptions of Prussian veterans, too old and infirm to take the field, hobbling after their regiments as they departed on campaign."[68]

Although military spending was minimal and the military itself was remarkably small in the United States during the nineteenth century—with the exception of the Civil War years—in many ways America was just as militarized as any Western European nation, Prussia included. Americans had a long tradition, inherited from Great Britain, of frontier militias that fought on American soil. As the Civil War loomed on the horizon, local militias were formed in many American villages and towns. In California, vigilante groups took the form of militias and were utilized to exterminate Indians. The famous Texas Rangers were formed for the same reason. Responding to the fear of slave uprisings and abolitionist invasions, militias sprang up all over the South. The Civil War introduced more Americans to military life, and many of them, despite the horrors they encountered, formed strong bonds with their fellow soldiers and gained status and honor as veterans of a great crusade. Reunions of Civil War veterans became commonplace during the latter half of the nineteenth century, and hardly a man could be elected to public office without going on the stump and mentioning his service record and his specific regiment.

Without doubt Pratt viewed his Indian students in the same way that Prussian regimental colonels saw their peasant conscripts: brutish, backward, and uncultured. He very likely developed a kind of warriorhood camaraderie with those he fought on the southern plains and for whom he acted as jailer and teacher. At Carlisle he would take the children of these warriors and teach them military discipline, reading, writing, arithmetic, and, above all, loyalty to the nation and to Carlisle.

Many Indian educators also placed great value on industrial training. They were convinced that "the Indians have not been brought up to believe in the dignity of labor."[69] To teach those Indians who were too old to be packed off to boarding schools such as Carlisle the "habits of labor," the federal government initiated programs that sent field matrons to the agencies to teach homemaking, obtained the aid of farmers to teach agriculture, provided industrial training at local schools, and spent money establishing "factories" where Native American women were put to work making lace (also reminiscent of the Prussian regimental schools).[70] The Lake Mohonk Conference consistently advocated the policy of home manufacturing and on several occasions promised to help find markets for Indian-produced goods.[71]

Like every other aspect of the vanishing policy, the campaign to educate American Indians amounted to an assault on Native American customs and beliefs, and the reformers did not overlook a single aspect of Indian life in their vigorous attempt to stamp it out. Any and all American Indian ceremonies were frowned upon and in most cases forbidden. Native Americans were given Anglicized names, and Indian children were taken—in some cases, kidnapped—and shipped off to the boarding schools.[72] At one point in the early 1890s, the U.S. Army was allowed to form a few all-Indian companies of infantry and cavalry over the already established Indian Scouting Service, in the hope that, according to Secretary of War Redfield Proctor,

> the habits of obedience, cleanliness, and punctuality, as well as of steady labor in the performance of both military and industrial work inculcated by service in the Army, would have a good effect on those who might enlist, and also furnish an object lesson of some value and exert a healthy influence upon other of their tribes.[73]

Indian agents were to encourage enlistment in the army as well as discourage tribal ceremonies and even dress. The reformers even rebuked showmen such as Buffalo Bill for allowing the "public exhibition of Indians in their savage costumes."[74] Clearly, the vanishing policy had suffused the institutions and philosophies of the entire nation.

The assault on Native American cultures could be looked upon not only as a clash of cultures, but also as an intellectual duel. Although American Indian peoples differed from tribe to tribe in matters of dress, language, dwellings, ceremonials, and material culture, many philosophies and spiritual beliefs cut across tribal lines. For the most part, Native American worldviews were based on the premise that human beings were a part of, instead of being over and above, the forces of nature.[75] In Native American beliefs, there was an order to the universe, linking all things together. In Western beliefs, civilization stemmed from the human effort to control the environment so as to take best advantage of natural resources, whether human, animal, vegetable, or mineral. Western cultures essentially viewed this effort as being completely within the framework of "natural law." Native American cultures viewed these resources as gifts for which "natural law" demanded reciprocity and spiritual care in the form of ceremonies, offerings, and prayers. This idea stems from the understanding that all things—corporeal and spiritual—are bound together, and that should this linkage be broken or the universal balance tipped one way or the other, catastrophe would surely ensue.

The idea of territoriality was fundamental to the incongruity between the Western and the Native American understanding of the world. In most Western traditions, land is seen as a valuable asset, to be utilized for the benefit, indeed for the survival, of whoever possesses it. This notion is particularly true of the colonial mentality, and in the Americas it was instituted in the development of a particularly mechanistic relationship with the land. If worked, the land would produce wealth and status for the colonizer. If the colonizer had spiritual ties to any piece of land, it would be to his ancestral homeland or, because of his religious beliefs, to the Holy Land in the Middle East. For American Indians, holy lands and homelands were combined, and could not be owned by an individual person. Land was for subsistence and not for profit.

Holding land in common on a subsistence level was not impractical or in any way "backward." In 1887 the agent to the Five Civilized

Tribes, R. L. Owen, reported that there were no paupers within his jurisdiction and that each American Indian had a home.[76] Even Henry L. Dawes was forced to admit that the system in Indian Territory precluded poverty. Holding lands in common was simply anathema to Americans where land use and individualism were concerned. And American individualism directly countered the tribal outlook, which based life experiences on shared relationships. From a tribal view, the notion of American individualism was contradictory because it stressed a basic conformity, whereas an inherent part of Native American tribalism was the recognition of cultural plurality linked to the lands in which various peoples lived.

The Indian reformers of the latter half of the nineteenth century, however, believed firmly that Native American cultures and beliefs were dying or, in effect, dead, according to the "natural law" of progress and civilization. They looked confidently toward the twentieth century, feeling that their Christian compassion and philanthropy would cure all American Indian ills and thus relieve the United States of the burden of the "Indian Problem." Indians would vanish as separate, distinct peoples and would blend into the nation as Americans. The United States would truly become one nation, and all Americans would share a sense of peoplehood. But even as the new century dawned, it became readily apparent that Native American philosophies, spirituality, and cultures would not vanish. Indeed, they would survive and eventually bring about a reformation of American Indian policy.

CHAPTER II

PERSISTENT PEOPLES

Native American Social and Cultural Continuity

DESPITE THEIR OVERWHELMING CONFIDENCE, the Christian reformers who provided the ideological basis for the vanishing policy undoubtedly expected the greatest resistance to assimilation to come from the more traditional members of tribal societies. Chiefs like Sitting Bull and Red Cloud of the Lakota, or Lone Wolf of the Kiowa, who had been brought up in their own cultures and with their own particular sense of peoplehood, were not going to overthrow their ancient heritages overnight. Logically, tribal allegiance would be stronger in older Native Americans because they had known independence firsthand in the days before reservations and allotments. As one United States agent wrote in reference to the Lakota:

> The old "fogies" or "chiefs," who look to their supremacy and control over the people, fearful of losing it, discourage and advise the people to continue in the old rut. It is a contest between the old stagers and the young and progressive.[1]

Unfortunately for the reformers, Native American resistance to the vanishing policy was much more than a contest between the old and the young. Not only did Native Americans resist the vanishing policy, but also, and perhaps more importantly, their cultures proved remarkably resilient. The resiliency of peoplehood does not necessarily lie in the fact that it possesses the four aspects of place, sacred history, ceremonial cycle, and language, but in the intricacy with which these aspects are connected. Simply put, without all four elements in place there would be no order in the world. To a particular people, the loss of even one of these elements spelled the loss of the other three and, consequently, their eventual extinction. Native Americans fully realized that whites were working toward that end, however, and they fought against it with tenacity, subtlety, and a remarkable amount of understanding of just how and why the whites did the things they did.

By 1900, certainly, most Native Americans understood that what the whites wanted more than anything else was Indian land. This idea was very likely axiomatic among most tribes. What that self-evident notion meant to Native people was that the whites were committed to extinguishing not simply the aboriginal title to the land but also each tribal identity. In his 1981 book entitled *Political Organization of Native North Americans*, Ernest L. Schusky succinctly captured the relationship between place, religion, history, and being a people in his introduction:

> The Sioux or Lakota . . . often spoke of the disappearance of their people. When I answered that census figures showed their population increasing, they countered that parts of their reservations were continually being lost. They concluded there could be no more Indians when there was no more Indian land. Several older men told me that the original Sacred Pipe [the focus of the Lakota religion] given the Lakota in the Beginning was getting smaller. The Pipe shrank with the loss of land. When the land and Pipe disappeared, the Lakota would be gone. Discussions of land, and especially its loss, were cast in emotional tones. I have heard similar tones among Iroquois, in the Southwest, and in Alaska when land was an issue. For many Native Americans, an Indian identity is intertwined with rights to land.[2]

What can be said in 1981 about this linkage between particular peoples and particular territories can equally be said of Native Americans at the turn of the twentieth century. For Native Americans in that period of time, it was not simply a matter of choice. Giving up the land meant the death of the tribal relationship with the spirit world, the disappearance of entire belief and value systems, and the loss of all tribal knowledge. The notion of universal order would be extinguished along with the death of language and its connection with landscape.

Native Americans at the end of the nineteenth century were also cognizant of the fact that whites were not above using force to attain a political or economic goal. During the whole of the nineteenth century, nearly every tribe within the territorial limits of the United States had either been at war with the Americans or had been subjected to removal from their homelands, often at gunpoint. When allotment came, very many "irreconcilables"—those who refused to take allotments—were arrested, jailed, and forced to take the land apportioned to them under the provisions of the Dawes or the Curtis Acts. Only in Indian Territory was forced allotment carried out in this particular manner and in such great numbers, particularly among members of the so-called Five Civilized Tribes.[3] Although it was hailed as a "marvelous expansion for the ignorant full-blood," allotment in severalty provoked more resistance to government policies from the conservative or "full-blood" members of the Five Civilized Tribes than from any other group. They were the first to be jailed for refusing to take allotments and the first to be engaged in armed clashes with white authorities over the dissolution of their governments.

Perhaps as early as 1895, tribal conservatives from the Cherokee, Creek, Choctaw, and Chickasaw nations formed the Four Mothers' Society. Although it might be viewed as a political organization founded in large part to oppose the allotment of lands, it was truly a religious movement.[4] The members of this organization were adamantly opposed to allotment and were willing either to face incarceration for refusing to take allotments or even to take up arms to defend their homes. At one point during the negotiations between the Dawes Commission and the representatives of the Five Civilized Tribes, it was suggested that those who followed the traditional ways of life might immigrate to Mexico to avoid accepting allotment. To the members of the Four Mothers' Society, the vanishing policy promised a repetition of the traumatic period in the 1830s during which these peoples were removed from their ancient homelands in the southeastern United States to the Indian Territory. After removal the tribes underwent a period of turbulent adjustment to their new lands and fortunes. The Creek removed from the fertile "black earth" areas of Alabama and Georgia had to adjust to the thick sod of the prairie. Their national seal, which depicted a shock of wheat and a heavy steel plow, both symbolized the Creek adaptation to the new land and served as an ironic reminder of the betrayal of removal. After their removal, the Cherokee fought a deadly civil war in which most of the leaders who had signed the removal treaty were brutally executed for bowing to federal policy. The Choctaw and Chickasaw had also gone through similar experiences as a result of removal, and the Seminole fought a guerilla war in the swamps of Florida against United States troops to avoid being sent to the Indian Territory. The traumatic memories of the removal period had not dimmed sixty years after the fact. "Because of the unwritten history kept alive among the Indians of the distresses of the forced removal," wrote Indian agent Robert Owen, "the fullblood is almost unanimously hostile to any act which he imagines would disturb the present peace and security."[5]

The Four Mothers' Society made it known to the tribal politicians and to the federal government that they were unwilling to accept allotment and absorption into white society. Largely because of this conservative Native American opposition, the negotiators from the Five Tribes were able to present strong arguments to the Dawes Commission's charges of "mixed-blood" comparative wealth, corruption, and fraud that were "calculated to place our people and country in such unfavorable light before the Government as the facts in the case will not warrant."[6] Cherokee delegates proposed a plan that would keep full-blood settlements intact. The idea made it possible for those Cherokees who desired it to take adjacent allotments and hold them in trust. These settlements would then hold communal title and would be issued a federal patent. The tribal conservatives would then be able to form a corporation based in part on existing kinship and tribal relationships. Unfortunately for the tribal Cherokees, the plan "for preserving in effect the continuity of the Tribal Relations of the full-blood Indian" was callously rejected.[7] The elimination of these tribal and communal relationships was, after all, the primary objective of the vanishing policy.

After the passage of the Curtis Act in 1898, the federal government began the process of enrolling tribal members, surveying tribal lands, and distributing patents to individual Indians. Because the tribes held their lands in fee, each tribal government was forced to issue patents for separate allotments. That tribal officials issued these deeds, whether willingly or under duress, prompted the idea among the conservative Native American communities, and especially among the members of the Four Mothers' Society, that their own governments were acting in collusion with federal officials and thus were in violation of standing tribal constitutions and treaties.

In the Creek Nation, resistance to allotment centered on a group known popularly as the "Snakes." This epithet was taken from one of the leaders of the Four Mothers' Society, the Creek ceremonial chief Chitto Harjo, whose name was loosely translated into English as "Crazy Snake." The Snakes met at Chitto Harjo's ceremonial grounds at Old Hickory near Henryetta, Creek Nation, and were considered to be the legitimate Creek government by most of the Creek-speaking population. In 1900, traditional Creeks gathered at Old Hickory to reinstate a government based on the Creek constitution of 1867 and the treaty relationship established between the Creek and the federal government. At this meeting, traditional Creeks argued that the Creek government in Okmulgee, headed by Principal Chief Pleasant Porter, had violated the Creek constitution by bypassing the need to ratify any agreement with the federal government by the Creek national legislature. They reasoned that since the principal chief was acting in collusion with the federal government to usurp the constitution and violate standing treaties with the United States, Pleasant Porter's government was not the legitimate Creek system of public authority. Essentially, they formed another Creek government and picked Chitto Harjo as the principal chief. They also formed a police force, known as the Lighthorse—which was the term used for the traditional Creek law enforcement agency—to enforce the constitution of 1867. Almost immediately, the Lighthorse set out to curb the acceptance of allotments, and publicly whipped several Creek citizens for receiving deeds for land from what they considered to be the illegitimate Creek government under Pleasant Porter.[8]

Between 1901 and 1909 Chitto Harjo remained in the forefront of resistance to the dismemberment of the Indian Territory and its incorporation into the state of Oklahoma. Several times Chitto Harjo traveled to Washington to speak on behalf of the traditional ways of life and in opposition to the vanishing policy. At one point he hired a group of lawyers to represent the Snakes in the nation's capital. The expense involved in retaining attorneys and professional lobbyists, however, was wasted. According to *Harper's Weekly*, a national magazine that became sympathetic to the Creek traditionalists, Chitto

Harjo had been defrauded. "The lawyers cozened him; they cheered him; they took his money."[9]

In 1909 a large group of discontented African Americans assembled near the Old Hickory grounds. Oklahoma had gained statehood in 1907 and had immediately adopted Jim Crow statutes in imitation of the border states of Arkansas and Texas. The black people who gathered near Old Hickory had been driven there by segregationist policies. Whites in the vicinity, already hostile toward the Creek conservatives and now infused with fear at the possibility of a Creek-black alliance, became actively aggressive toward the encampment at Old Hickory and sought to break up the campsite under any pretext. Chitto Harjo had planned a meeting of the Creek conservatives in March, which added to the high state of white apprehension. Soon there were reports of marauding African Americans and Native Americans stealing everything from weapons to food from white farms.

During the March meeting of the Creek traditionalists, it was reported that someone from Old Hickory had stolen a piece of meat from a white farmer's smokehouse. This report touched off a series of violent incidents aimed primarily at the Creek conservatives. Upon receiving the farmer's complaint, a white deputy from Henryetta was dispatched to Old Hickory to arrest the thief. A group of armed African Americans turned the officer back. The deputy then organized a posse of whites, returned to Old Hickory, and at first light attacked the campgrounds. During the melee, one black man was killed, one white posse member was wounded, and forty-two African Americans were captured and eventually jailed.

After the battle, whites began to arm themselves and take revenge on both the blacks and Native Americans who had anything to do with the encampment at Old Hickory. The whites immediately sought to bring in Chitto Harjo as the ringleader of the "smoked meat rebellion." Another white posse was formed at Checotah, the seat of McIntosh County, to arrest the Creek leader. On March 26, a white posse arrived at Chitto Harjo's home. Although no one really knows who started the gun battle (each side accused the other of firing first), a heavy fight occurred. Two white deputies were killed instantly and several were wounded. The Creeks also suffered a few casualties, but most managed to escape the initial fusillade. Chitto Harjo, along with a few followers, escaped to the old Choctaw Nation and was aided by several Choctaw members of the Four Mothers' Society.

The battle at Chitto Harjo's home prompted Oklahoma governor Charles N. Haskell to order the militia to pursue the Creek conservatives and restore order in McIntosh and Okmulgee counties. When militia commander Colonel Roy Hoffman arrived in the area, he quickly discovered that the whites were actually prolonging the crisis. Hoffman disbanded several posses and instituted martial law over the entire area. He also launched a manhunt for Chitto Harjo, and although his search was extensive, the whites never saw the Creek leader again. After fleeing his home during the gunfight, Chitto Harjo took up residence in McCurtain County, Oklahoma, with a Choctaw conservative leader named Daniel Bob. Chitto Harjo died in April 1911 at Bob's home.[10]

The Creek "war" was not the only instance of armed violence between whites and Native Americans in the thirty years following the appalling massacre of the Lakotas at Wounded Knee in 1890, which supposedly ended the "Indian wars." In 1898 the Chippewa of Leech Lake, Minnesota, clashed with whites over a number of issues, not the least of which was the continued white demand for more land.[11] Two years following Chitto Harjo's death, several Navajos took up arms against the whites, and in 1915 violence erupted between the Ute and whites in Colorado and Utah. Matthew K. Sniffen, the secretary of the Indian Rights Association, reported that the Ute war had been largely instigated by whites and that the Ute, who had been attacked for no apparent reason, were not "spoiling for a fight, or even prepared for it."[12]

These outbreaks of violence, especially that of the "Crazy Snake Rebellion," as the violence in Oklahoma had been labeled in the press, were difficult for many whites to understand. Although many of them might have agreed that Chitto Harjo and the Creek had been provoked—just as had the Chippewa, Navajo, and Ute—whites could only wonder why anyone would continue to defy the obvious power of the U.S. military and the state militias. It seemed that any act of tribal resistance after 1890, especially of a political nature, was, in the minds of most white Americans, a completely futile and impotent gesture. Americans believed that the expansion of Western civilization was inevitable and, most importantly, beneficial to everyone who accepted it. In that belief they failed to assess the very real strengths and the persistence of peoplehood.

The conservative Native American rejection of the vanishing policy did not emerge from a mindless effort to cling to the past. At the heart of the resistance were the beliefs that religion was organically connected with the land and that societies were living entities that could not be changed without creating a degree of chaos. Native American religions were alive; God, the Creator, the Great Mystery, the spirits were still part of the landscape and heavens and were still interacting with human beings. Native Americans could live in the expectation of extraordinary, even supernatural occurrences. The resistance to the vanishing policy was a spiritual as well as political movement. Chitto Harjo was the chief of a ceremonial center at Old Hickory. In fact most of the leaders of the Four Mothers' Society were religious and ceremonial leaders in their respective tribes. Many of these religious leaders did, in fact, agree with the whites that armed conflict with the whites was futile. Consequently, many of them sought to bend but not break in preserving their spiritual connection with the land. Native American social and religious adaptations ultimately became the primary expressions of resistance to the vanishing policy in the first twenty-five years of the twentieth century.

Redbird Smith, Chitto Harjo's contemporary and a fellow leader of the Four Mothers' Society, focused his energies on restoring the Cherokee religious order, and even though he was adamantly opposed to allotment, he sedulously avoided any form of armed confrontation with the whites. Removal had been extremely traumatic for the Cherokee, but it had nevertheless affected the tribe less traumatically than it had the Creek. Whereas the Creek had been removed to a completely different environment from their fertile homeland in the east, the Cherokee had been moved to the southwestern foothills of the Ozarks, a landscape not totally unlike their southern Appalachian lands in North Carolina, Tennessee, and Georgia. After removal, the Cherokee continued to live in small settlements of related families in the secluded hollows of the Indian Territory hill country, much as their residence patterns had been in the east. Gone, however, were the "fires" or the ceremonial centers that had been the focus of Cherokee religious life. An ancient religious group, the Keetoowah Society, existed, but it became more of a political group of Cherokee conservatives who had opposed removal.

Removal had struck a serious blow to Cherokee religion. Not only that, but many Cherokees had filtered forms of Christianity, especially practices from the Baptist Church, though their own matrix of peoplehood. The removal had extinguished the old ceremonial life, but it had not completely done away with Cherokee medicine, philosophies, customs, and worldviews. During the early part of the nineteenth century, Sequoyah invented a method of writing the Cherokee language. With the introduction of the Cherokee syllabary, the Cherokee became literate almost overnight. Many whites applauded the invention of the syllabary and saw it as a mark of sophistication that would lead to a more widespread acceptance of American values and institutions. From books and newspapers printed in Cherokee, missionaries believed, tribal members would more readily understand the benefits of agricultural production and Christian salvation. Although they had little doubt that the Cherokee syllabary would serve those purposes, the whites were wholly aware of the fact that it also was used to preserve Cherokee culture. Cherokee medicine men, for example, could record rituals, the proper use of medicinal plants, and sacred formulas to assure their survival. In addition, the syllabary served to preserve language, one of the four aspects of being—and surviving as—a people.

The vanishing policy threatened even these Cherokee adaptations. Allotment would mean the destruction of the local settlements as well as the ancient practice of holding lands in common. The removal had meant the loss of homelands, the decline of ceremonial life, and the weakening of the notion of balance and order in everyday life. With allotment the Cherokee conservatives literally "faced social death."

Redbird Smith was born in Arkansas in 1851. His father was Pig Smith, a blacksmith and noted Cherokee medicine man and ceremonial leader. The elder Smith was also a prominent man in the Keetoowah Society councils. It was at one of the Keetoowah meetings that Pig Smith received a vision indicating that his descendents were to lead the society and revitalize Cherokee life.

Redbird Smith became involved in Cherokee politics early and did indeed become a leader in Keetoowah ceremonies. As the allotment movement grew in influence and the pressure to force the Cherokee to submit to federal policy rose in intensity, Smith began to concentrate more and more on the religious, rather than the political, side of Cherokee life. In the 1890s the Keetoowahs obtained the sacred wampum belts from the son of a former principal chief. Smith, along with several tribal elders, looked to the belts as the path toward restoring "God's Seven Clan Law." In his research on the belts themselves, Smith consulted Creek and Shawnee elders and learned that religion was the base for rebuilding the social and cultural bonds that could lead to Cherokee unity. With this aid from other Native American conservatives, the Keetoowah leader was able to revitalize several ceremonial dances, and by 1903 Smith had rekindled twenty-three traditional fires. These ceremonial centers, known as stomp grounds, served primarily to concentrate population. They were generally located on land used by one of the principal ceremonial leaders and in an area that could accommodate those Cherokee, and members of other tribes as well, living in several small settlements within a larger geographic region. The revived ceremonies gave the conservative Cherokee a greater sense of community and a religious sanction for their resistance to allotment.[13]

The Keetoowah challenge to the vanishing policy served other purposes. Smith believed that the Cherokee had a specific mission. If they held fast to their idea of community and sense of peoplehood, they could offer to non-Indians a model on which the foundation of a greater national unity could be built. Despite having been harassed and arrested by white authorities for refusing to take allotments, Smith still had hopes for white society. When the United States entered World War I in 1917, he called upon the Cherokee of draft age to go into the army in order to prove that they thought in wider terms and believed in a common human goal of peace, harmony, and generosity. To Smith, white society was ill, and the Cherokee offered a model, based on Keetoowah ways and the Seven Clan Law, which could be used for "the betterment of mankind."[14] The Cherokee offered knowledge that would aid the socially isolated and, by Keetoowah standards, culturally deprived non-Indians.

According to Smith, his people were "endowed with intelligence," "industrious," "loyal," and "spiritual." "But," he stated, "we are overlooking the particular Cherokee mission on earth, for no man is endowed with these qualifications without a designed purpose." "Work and right training," in the mind of the Keetoowah chief, were the ways in which the Cherokee would maintain universal equilibrium and order. Persistence in these beliefs, he thought, would eventually reach the whites, who would, in turn, see the benefit of living in harmony with the spirit world. Native American spirituality would, in short, save a depraved, greedy, and predatory white world. "A kindly man," Smith once said, "cannot help his neighbor unless he have [*sic*] a surplus and he cannot have a surplus unless he works." Smith reminded the Cherokee that the prevention of catastrophe for both Native Americans and whites depended on the strength of the Keetoowah effort to preserve Native American knowledge and the communal code of generosity. Thus Cherokee ways lived on even as the Cherokee Nation government was being undermined by the vanishing policy.[15]

Like the Creek "Snakes," the Keetoowahs were constantly accused of rebellion. Although jailed on occasion, the "Nighthawks," as they were called, avoided conflict, withdrew into the hills of eastern Oklahoma, and continued to live in small, outlying settlements centered on the stomp grounds. They kept the traditional men's service groups (*gadugi*) alive and continued to take part in religious ceremonies. At one point, Smith's followers took part in a communal dairy farm operation, but it was not a long-lasting venture. Most of the "irreconcilables" eventually took their allotments and became adjusted to them, despite the incongruity between holding them and the traditional way of holding lands in common. After Smith's death in 1918, his sons became the leaders of Cherokee ceremonial life. Pig Smith's vision that his descendents would rekindle and keep the sacred fire burning was fulfilled.[16]

The preservation of Native American knowledge, spiritual understanding, ceremonialism, and peoplehood was not, of course, left only to conservative Creeks and Cherokees. Numerous other Native American peoples sought to maintain their relationships with the spirit world through adaptation, syncretism, secrecy, and even deception. The vanishing policy had no apparent respect for the notion of freedom of religion as whites expressed it in the First Amendment to the Constitution, and oftentimes the suppression of Native American religious practices took precedence over other policies. Bans on ceremonies were initiated on many reservations during the late nineteenth century. Interestingly enough, these bans were never enacted by

statute, but were the result of administrative fiat. In 1883, the Indian
Office gave local reservation agents the authority to establish the Indian courts of offenses. Essentially, "Indian offenses" were defined as just
about anything offensive to the sensibilities and prejudices of the Indian agents and especially to Secretary of the Interior Henry M. Teller
and his subordinate, Commissioner of Indian Affairs Hiram Price,
who drew up the directive. According to Price, the courts were set up
to "put a stop to the demoralizing influence of heathenish rites" that
were, "repugnant to common decency."[17]

Apparently the most "repugnant" Native American ceremony was
the Sun Dance, for it was easily the most suppressed: in Teller's eyes it
inspired a warlike spirit among young Native American men.[18] As
usual, the policy makers had misinterpreted the function of the ceremony and had capriciously viewed it as an immoral and seditious act.
They also failed to gauge its strength among—and spiritual relevance
to—the people who practiced it. For most of the peoples of the Great
Plains—the Lakota, Cheyenne, Kiowa, Crow, Blackfeet, Arapaho, and
others—the annual performance of the Sun Dance reaffirmed each
tribe's place in the world, provided for a restrengthening of intratribal
relationships, and, like most other Native American ceremonies, fulfilled tribal obligations to the Creator's universal scheme. The yearly
assembly for the ceremony served religious, social, and political functions. As such it was spiritual, and essential to the harmony of each
tribe.[19]

In its basic form, the ceremony took eight days to complete and
involved a sacrifice to symbolize the humility of mankind before the
Great Mysteries of the world. During the ritual, those who had committed themselves to its performance either to fulfill a vow or to com-
ply with a divine vision received lessons regarding the substance and
reasons underlying the ceremony. They fasted, then danced to the
point of exhaustion over a period of four days. Among many tribes, but
certainly not all, the Sun Dance pledges sacrificed even more.
Cheyenne, Lakota, Blackfeet, and Arapaho men would pierce their
skin with skewers attached by strings of rawhide to the center pole of
the Sun Dance lodge or to a sacred buffalo skull. The attempt was
made then to pull against the strings in order rip the skewers through
the flesh. This part of the ceremonial was never done to demonstrate
imperviousness to pain but to sacrifice the flesh as the most important

and sacred offering a human being can make. The pledges were highly regarded for their willingness to undergo self-sacrifice for the continued health and prosperity of the tribe as a whole.[20]

The notion that the Sun Dance incited or intensified a martial spirit among the tribes of the plains was the result of the wars that had recently been fought with these peoples and had no real foundation in an understanding of the ceremony itself. The ceremony varied from tribe to tribe, and even the names for the ceremony differed from one group to another. In translation from the Ute language, it was the "Thirsting Dance"; the Cheyenne called it "Medicine Lodge"; the Assiniboine gave it the name "Making a Home," and so on. The blood sacrifice was important for some; in other tribes it was unheard of. As an annual ceremony of renewal it had little or nothing to do with warfare.[21]

Still, bans on its performance were put into place as early as 1883. In spite of white objections and government suppression, the ceremony persisted and did so because of the considerable accommodation to white ideas that Native Americans made to protect it. On the Cheyenne reservation at Tongue River, Montana, the tribe modified its version of the Sun Dance prior to the strict ban placed on its performance in 1897. Noting that in ancient form the ritual had not included the infliction of wounds on the bodies of the pledges, the Cheyenne freely omitted, at least within sight of the federal agent, that part of the ceremony.[22]

After the 1897 ban at Tongue River, Cheyenne leaders made request after request to their agent, pleading that the ritual be allowed to take place again. The agent refused permission despite one Cheyenne elder's convincing and constitutionally sound argument that the Cheyenne people, like other religious groups in the United States, should be permitted the right to worship freely. The ban on the Sun Dance at Tongue River was eventually lifted in 1907, in part because of the reasoning underlying the Cheyenne elder's compelling argument, but not before the Cheyenne there had made several attempts to make the ceremony more palatable to the white Christians.[23]

During the ten-year ban on the Sun Dance at Tongue River, the Cheyenne asked for and received permission from their agent to hold a "Willow Dance." This ceremony was actually a greatly modified Sun Dance. It contained no element of self-sacrifice during the cycle of dances and was held, according to Cheyenne Sun Dance priests and elders, as a religious service for the benefit of all mankind, which, in a larger sense, it was. By removing the ceremony from a familiar tribal context, the Cheyenne religious leaders sought to preserve their rights in matters of the spirit and to demonstrate to the whites that they were paying due respect to a universal creator and not some local deity. Another modification, minor but indicative of the insight the Cheyenne had of the importance to the white man of American nationalism, was to announce that the Willow Dance would thenceforward take place on the July Fourth holiday. This accommodation was not a major change in the timing of the Sun Dance ceremony. Before the Cheyenne were confined to the reservations, no precise date was ever fixed for the offering of the Sun Dance, but it was always held during the summer months. This small concession of establishing a permanent date was particularly perceptive simply because no patriotic government official would, in good conscience, prohibit Indians from celebrating Independence Day.[24]

Between 1907 and 1911 the ban on the Sun Dance at the Tongue River agency was lifted. Free to hold the ceremony again, the Cheyenne still omitted those aspects of the cycle of dances that the white people found repugnant. These concessions were futile, for the ban was reinstituted in 1911. The Cheyenne, despite the ban, continued the dance and argued for their constitutional rights in defiance of the federal agent's conviction that the ceremony was detrimental to Cheyenne progress. Eventually the Cheyenne cut the ceremony in length to two days because of their agent's insistence that they were wasting time better spent raising crops. The Cheyenne increased their emphasis on the dance's social elements and, while holding it in front of the whites, de-emphasized its religious connotations. When their agent decided to hold firm in the enforcement of the ban, even on the Willow Dance, the Cheyenne pledged themselves in the hills, out of sight and earshot of reservation officials. The tactic of secrecy, after all, had worked in preserving the Medicine Arrows and Sacred Buffalo Hat ceremonies. Whites had not, at that time, been allowed to view those very sacred objects of the Cheyenne religion. So the Sun Dance eventually was protected and preserved by deception and secrecy.[25]

The southern branch of the Cheyenne people who lived in the Indian Territory (Oklahoma) also modified their Sun Dance in an effort to maintain its practice. When bans were instituted, they, like their northern relatives, asked for permission to hold Willow Dances. On occasion, many Cheyenne traveled to other reservations to attend the rituals of their less constrained Native American neighbors. It seems that from the erroneous idea that the Sun Dance was somehow connected to warfare, bans were more strictly enforced among the tribes with which the United States had most recently fought. In any case, when the bans were lifted, or at least less rigidly enforced, on the southern Cheyenne reservation, the Cheyenne freely left out the element of self-sacrifice from the Sun Dance cycle. In addition, their Sun Dance priests and elders, with the cooperation of their agent, began to place more emphasis on the ceremony's social functions. Parades were held, whites were admitted to the campgrounds, and even storekeepers and provisions dealers were invited to the ceremony in an effort to give the Sun Dance a more festival-like appearance. Local white farmers and government officials, clinging to the imagery they had built around Native Americans, considered tribal cultures stagnant, backward, and doomed to extinction. Any change in religious ritual among Native Americans made it seem as if Indians were indeed bowing to the inevitable. The Sun Dance, for the whites in western Oklahoma at the turn of the last century, became more of a holiday than a "heathenish rite."[26]

Despite the festivities surrounding the Cheyenne Sun Dance ceremony in western Oklahoma, which ethnologist James Mooney of the Bureau of American Ethnology likened to a "camp meeting or county fair," the Cheyenne secretly kept the ceremony within a religious context. Some pledges continued to wound their flesh and receive instruction, and the ceremony retained its sacrificial meaning. In 1903 an incident occurred during the Cheyenne Sun Dance held near Eagle City, Oklahoma Territory, that most emphatically reminded the Sun Dance priests and tribal elders of the white man's vehement opposition to the notion of sacrifice. After completing the ceremony, which extended for five days instead of the usual eight, in deference to the white man's concern with time, a Cheyenne had skewers inserted into his back for the purpose of dragging pieces of buffalo skull in a complete circuit of the Sun Dance campsite. John H. Seger, who was the Cheyenne-Arapaho superintendent, witnessed the deed and reported it to higher officials and to the newspapers. The incident was quickly exploited in the press, and snowballed into a major controversy between white Christian reformers, white ethnologists, and the Cheyenne. Eventually the Cheyenne elders were warned that the Sun Dance would be banned in its entirety if self-sacrifice were not stopped completely. Thereafter and until all bans were lifted in the 1930s, the Cheyenne Sun Dance on the Oklahoma agency was allowed, but with strict injunctions issued from the tribal councils absolutely forbidding the practice of self-sacrifice during the ceremony.[27]

The Cheyenne, both in the north and the south, were not the only people to maintain the Sun Dance ceremony during the period of official persecution against its practice. As late as 1903, the Blackfeet, Shoshone, and Ute were still taking part in the ceremony and, according to James Mooney, "in every case with the sanction and permission of the Agent in charge." Strangely enough, the Ute ceremony was a relatively recent introduction rather than an age-old tradition. The Ute began practicing the renewal ceremony in the 1880s and 1890s as part of an effort to revive Ute spirituality and place it in a general Native American context. Christian missionaries had been at work among the Ute, and Christian symbolism was immediately incorporated in the Ute Sun Dance in order to pacify the whites and stave off their interference. The Ute Sun Dance lodge was built, for example, using twelve upright poles in a circle surrounding the essential center pole. The poles were said to represent Christ and the twelve apostles. In addition to this act of syncretism, the Ute performed the ceremony in three days instead of the traditional eight, for several reasons. In the first place it took less time to perform. Additionally, the three days were in conformity with the Christian Trinity.

Another tribe, the Ponca people, kept their yearly Sun Dance ceremony relatively intact, with little change or syncretism. They were on occasion, however, forced to hold the dance cycle on the property of the 101 Ranch Wild West Show. The Sun Dance by 1903 was hardly a dead or meaningless "primitive" ceremonial. Neither was it a revival of an "old-time" rite. It was, rather, a continuous yet highly significant adaptation of plains tribal cultures.[28]

Ceremonial and social dancing were exceptionally important to most Native American peoples. As confirmed in tribal sacred histories, the Creator and the spirits had given these dances to the people. All of the dances reinforced a people's ties with a particular place. They conformed to the changing seasons, to floral and faunal changes, or even to the movement of the sun, the moon, the planets, and the stars as seen from the particular perspective within a tribal homeland. Additionally, the dances utilized sacred objects and materials taken from the earth. Drums, feathers, hides from certain animals, terrapin-shell shakers, gourd rattles, particular stones, trees, and herbs, to name only a few, were considered sacred because they were all used in accordance with oral traditions and came from the tribal holy land.

The ceremonies and dances had to continue to ensure the well-being of the people; they were the focal point not only of social renewal, but also of the notion that without them catastrophic occurrences might threaten the very lives of the people. The Hopi Snake Dance, which many of the whites thoroughly abhorred because the participants carried live rattlesnakes during the ceremony, was still practiced throughout the period of the vanishing policy because it ensured a good corn crop. It also began to attract large numbers of white tourists interested in seeing its performance.[29] Cherokee, Creek, and Seminole ceremonies continued to be held.[30] The Apache Sunrise Ceremony, a puberty rite for Apache women, persisted despite the stern disapproval of missionaries on the various Apache reservations. The Apache Crown dancers, the personifications of the mountain spirits or *Gaans*, were utilized in nearly every Apache ceremony, and along with the ceremonies, people performed social dances.[31] In the same manner, the Navajo equivalent of the Apache female puberty ceremony, the *kinaalda*, continued to be practiced among family groups in isolation, far from the disapproving eyes of white missionaries and federal agents.[32] In the east, the Iroquois still utilized the "False Face" healing ceremonies, and the remnant of the Cherokee of North Carolina who had escaped the removal of the 1830s continued to hold dances and ceremonies to ensure good crops and combat disease.[33]

In the northwestern United States, many tribes continued their traditional dances with a good deal of aid from the whites. The usual accommodation in that region to the white man's revulsion at Indian dancing was to hold tribal ceremonies on the Fourth of July. At the Klamath agency in Oregon during the early years of the twentieth century, the people "celebrated" Independence Day with dances, feasting, and the ceremonial exchange of gifts. In a like manner, the Native Americans at the Tulalip and Lummi agencies in Washington danced and renewed tribal relationships during "Treaty Days" celebrations.[34]

After the 1890 Wounded Knee massacre, performances of tribal ceremonies by the Lakota were rigidly controlled. All of the federal agents located on the various Sioux reservations in South and North Dakota complained about the Lakota propensity to hold dances instead of working crops. Many Lakota, because of very strict enforcement of the ban that had been placed on the Sun Dance, took up the idea of holding social dances during the July Fourth holiday. Others, apparently sidestepping the constraints of reservation management, joined "Wild West" shows. With these traveling carnivals, Native American performers were allowed to wear tribal dress and take part in various social dances.[35]

It may be mentioned that today's intertribal social dances, known as powwows, very likely got their start in this period. In part stemming from the various "Treaty Day" dances, Independence Day dances, and warrior-society dances of the prairie and plains tribes—known in different languages as *heyruska*, *hethuska*, or *heluska* dances—and some of the dances done in the Wild West shows, the powwow became a very important expression of identity for peoples such as the Lakota, Omaha, Oto, Kiowa, Comanche, Ojibwa, and numerous others. One dance, the Sioux "grass dance" instituted and kept alive as the result of a vision received by a young man in the nineteenth century, was performed throughout the reservation period and was also incorporated into powwow dancing. Grass dances were held both on and off the reservations with the Wild West shows, and became a particular favorite and necessary component—for blessing the grounds on which the powwows took place—of northern plains intertribal gatherings. The grass dancers wore bundles and braids of sweet grass, and their dancing was done in imitation of tall grass moving in the wind; in short, they reinforced the tribal spiritual connection with the environment. These religious and social dances reinforced intertribal relationships and aided in the development of a larger "Indian" identity.

The syncretic nature of the Native American attempt to maintain a proper relationship with the spirit world and at the same time propitiate the whites led to the foundation of completely new ceremonies and religions that nevertheless managed to maintain an "Indian" identity. Among the tribes of the northwest coast, for example, there arose a new religion that not only was accommodative and acceptable to the whites, but also utilized one of the area's most important tribal ceremonies to retain status among its Native American converts. This new religion, known as the Shaker Church, began in 1882 under fairly unusual circumstances. In that year John Slocum of the Squaxin people of Puget Sound reportedly died and was resurrected after having received a message from God prompting him to begin a ministry to all Native Americans. Slocum did not want, as did the whites, to turn Indians into Christians of the Euro-American variety. Rather, he wanted Indians to remain Indians; but he also wanted to infuse numerous Christian ideals into Native systems of belief in order to curb the growing problem of alcoholism, a disease from which Slocum himself suffered.[36]

Shakerism was remarkably adaptive and widely appealing. Based on Christian-like evangelism and possessing an element of the Protestant conversion experience, the church gained a number of adherents. By 1910 there were many Shaker establishments in the northwest, organized under a system of bishoprics. Largely because of its strict doctrine of temperance, white officials allowed the religion a great degree of latitude in its practices and rituals. Although conforming outwardly to white religious functions, the Shakers maintained several important tribal customs. As one white observer noted in 1910, the Shaker church was "based on Christianity and intermixed with heathenism."[37]

Slocum's followers retained the practice of the potlatch, which was perhaps the most significant social, economic, and religious function of aboriginal northwest coast culture. Although different patterns and emphases were placed on the various facets of the traditional potlatch, in general this ceremonial display of generosity involved the validation of individual or family status with each of the culture area's tribal groups. In the hierarchical social structures of these cultures, status was extremely important for the maintenance of order and stability. Amassing wealth for the purpose of giving it away to others not of the same lineage, clan, or, among some peoples, moiety, was the principal means of preserving harmony within. Because lineage was extremely important among these groups, the status gained through the holding of a potlatch was extended to the entire clan. For this reason, family cooperation in the accumulation of goods to be given away was necessary and usually freely given. Thus, the potlatch not only preserved good relations between members of different family groups, but helped maintain sound clan relationships as well. Within the tribal economy, the potlatch continually helped redistribute wealth. Potlatches also served a diplomatic function, for other tribes invited to attend would receive largesse from a wealthy person or would at least be impressed by the riches of their hosts.

The potlatch had its spiritual side as well. During a potlatch, songs connected with a person's spirit helper were sung. The dances accompanying the songs mimicked the person's animal totem. The leader of the dance might even wear an elaborately carved mask that not only represented but also carried the power of the spirit helper. In addition, all the things given away at a potlatch came from the environment: wooden boxes, fish oil, meat, masks, carvings, and blankets woven from the wool of mountain goats. The spiritual connection between the tribe and its land was very much evident in the ceremonial redistribution of wealth. A potlatch might be given in accordance with a vision, for the safe return of a warrior, to ensure a successful whaling expedition, or upon the occasion of naming a new child.[38]

The Shakers, under the guidance of Slocum, kept up the practice of the potlatch. They did not, however, maintain it strictly out of deference to northwest cultures. The "holding of great potlatches" was primarily a missionary effort. The Shakers continued to practice the potlatch in order to produce sympathetic responses from the conservative members of their tribes, who were still loyal to their traditional religious customs, and also, in accordance with tradition, to gain status for their church and beliefs. Generosity inspired loyalty, which, in turn, translated into more adherents to the Shaker religion.[39]

During approximately the same period that Shakerism was gaining its first converts, another new and adaptive religion began to find many adherents among the Native peoples of the Great Plains and in the Southwest. Peyotism was nontraditional in the sense that it was, like Shakerism, intended to unite all Native Americans, regardless of tribal affiliation, under the banner of religious belief. The new religion spread rapidly and continued to grow strong throughout the twentieth century.

The use of peyote as a sacrament and medicine was, by the late nineteenth century, already a very old practice among several tribes in Mexico. The Cora people, for example, were reported to have a ritual involving the use of the cactus button in 1754. Among the Native Americans living within the boundaries of the United States, the use of the peyote button as a sacrament began in the 1870s. The Comanche and Kiowa, who obtained it from the Apache, turned the ritual surrounding the use of the plant as a medicine into a ceremony involving the use of the button as a sacrament. The peyote button was not the object of worship: it was used as a medicine and as a method of obtaining a spiritual connection with the Creator. Peyote use and the ceremonies that linked it to the Creator spread from Oklahoma during the period 1880–1910 to the Native peoples of Nebraska, the Dakotas, Minnesota, and Wisconsin.[40]

In spite of its pan-Indian theme, the peyote movement accommodated the tribal customs of the peoples who adopted it. The degree of Christian practice in the peyote ceremony, for example, varied from tribe to tribe and from region to region. Some adherents sang in the name of Jesus Christ, and many accepted the Christian Trinity. Others downplayed the Christian elements in their ceremonies and prayer meetings. The "peyote road" was ethically similar to Christianity in that it emphasized a "golden rule" philosophy and salvation through right living. In fact, the peyotists' own tribal codes differed little from Christian philosophies regarding personal conduct and the relationships between people. The concept of original sin, however, was absent from most Native religions and only peripheral to the peyote religion. In peyote meetings, the worshippers emphasized the ideas of brotherly love, maintenance of a strong family group, and abstinence from alcohol.[41] As the adherents constantly stressed, the peyote road was a hard road to follow, perhaps even more difficult than the "Jesus Road," and consequently was a very narrow path to take to understanding the mysteries of God.

In most cases, the worshipper ingested peyote to obtain a vision, not necessarily one related to a Christian conversion experience, but one similar to the vision quest practiced among the peoples of the Great Plains. The vision quest was used to find peace with the supernatural or to seek solutions to personal problems. Visions were also sought to determine one's destiny or to obtain spiritual power from a supernatural being. The peyote ceremonies also utilized a good deal of regional Native American material culture. The water drum, the eagle-bone whistle, the bird tail-feather fan, cedar incense, and the gourd rattle were just some of the tribal manufactures used in the ritual.[42]

The emphasis that Native Americans placed on religion—whether for preservation or syncretism—was not merely an effort to cling to the past or even to maintain the distinctions between themselves and whites. Native American life centered on the knowledge that all things were connected and that the extraordinary things that occurred in life could not simply be ignored or explained away as meaningless or unreal. Anomalies in nature were understood as realities that fitted into a universal order. The Native American respect paid to the supernatural, the ceremonies that renewed the relationship between the tribe and the spirit world, and the belief that the universe was a living, organic entity made it quite impossible for Native Americans to view societies in mechanical terms. Peoples could not simply remove an aspect of life and replace it with another as one could a cog in a machine. In this period some important ethnologists, primarily Franz Boas and his students, began to realize that culture determined behavior and, consequently, that cultures were self-perpetuating.

The maintenance of shared tribal relationships and kinship patterns was perhaps the most prevalent feature of Native American life that ran counter to the intentions of the vanishing policy. Lakota families' adaptation was an excellent example of cultural persistence in the face of contrary Indian policies adopted during the latter half of the nineteenth century. During the reservation period, the federal government sent rations to the Lakota agencies in order to feed the people until they established an agricultural economic base. Because of corruption in government contracts, most of the rations were inferior, often tainted with disease, late in delivery, and always meager to the point of causing malnutrition. Nevertheless, when the time came to ration beef, which was delivered to the reservations on the hoof, the men of a Lakota family mounted their horses, rounded up the steers, and killed them in almost the same manner as they had previously hunted buffalo. After the animals were killed, the women of the kin group took over the task of butchering. First, the steer was skinned, and then the meat was removed from the bones and placed in containers for transport back home. The women then stripped the meat and dried it, in the same way that buffalo meat was once cured for transportation. The Lakota continued to use nearly every part of the steer, from hoof to horn, for the manufacture of numerous utilitarian objects. Hides were used for drums and tipi covers; hooves and horns for glue; and sinews for sewing. Ration camps surrounding the agencies during the food distribution were not unlike the old Lakota hunting camps, and quite often members of the banned men's warrior societies kept order and settled disputes that arose from time to time. In effect, the Lakota families managed to maintain several cultural and social features and patterns associated with the life of freedom on the plains prior to the reservations.[43]

When allotment was instituted on the Lakota and Dakota reservations in North and South Dakota during the 1890s and early 1900s, it did not produce the changes in tribal kinship patterns that reformers of American Indian policy had hoped for. The intent of allotment, according to most of the whites who supported it, was to have an Indian choose a homestead for his nuclear family, work the land, and become economically and socially independent. Implied in the policy was the idea that Indian tribes would lose their power over individual members, thus allowing the institution of private property to produce a breakdown in traditional Lakota systems and allegiances. At the Pine Ridge reservation, for example, the Lakota manipulated the policy so as to produce the opposite of the intended effect. At that reservation the Lakota either selected their allotments or exchanged them so that all the lands of an extended family group adjoined each other, thus preserving the shared relationships on which the tribe's social arrangements were based.[44]

Like the Lakota, many other Native American tribes retained strong kinship ties throughout the reservation and allotment periods. "Irreconcilable" members of the Five Civilized Tribes, even after allotment had been completed, remained in small rural settlements composed of extended family members centered either on the stomp, or ceremonial, grounds or near one of the Baptist or Methodist churches. During the 1890s, the Crow of Montana were forced to accept the idea of tracing their family lineage through paternal relations in preparation for the assignment of allotments and in anticipation of having to conform to Anglo-American inheritance laws. The Crow, however, continued to use the Crow language and their own particular kinship terminology based on their traditional matrilineal clan structures. All of the Apache groups in the Southwest kept intact their extended family arrangements while moving from hunting and gathering to subsistence farming to market agriculture. The entire family aided in tilling the soil and raising cattle. Women, children, and the elderly became the reapers and sowers, and adult Apache men focused on either wage labor or becoming working cattlemen. Apache cowboys were excellent riders, gifted horse trainers, and superb ropers and herders, essentially utilizing the very same skills they had used when raiding.[45] In tribe after tribe, extended families stayed together, often with three generations and several adult siblings living in daily contact with one another. The tribal community—those shared relationships and family structures that formed the basis for human cohesion—remained intact among Native Americans; families continued to work, worship, and play together, all within the matrix of being a complete people.[46]

Concomitant with the maintenance of Native American extended families was the retention of the many patterns of something as basic as well as significant as childbirth and child rearing. When Native women gave birth, they were generally well attended by their immediate female relatives and skilled midwives. These women, who prided themselves on their skills and experience, often had prescribed ceremonial duties to perform during the process of birth and upon the delivery of a child. Native American parturition practices continued throughout the nineteenth and early twentieth centuries despite the teachings of white missionaries and agents and despite the advent in many areas of white doctors, nurses, and Indian hospitals. Early anthropologists and federal agents recorded and complained about these practices well into the twentieth century. Around 1900, the ethnologist Clark Wissler observed that a doctor friend of his serving as an Indian agency physician had " no obstetrical cases for the good reason that the culture of this tribe did not sanction the presence of a male on such occasion."[47]

One important reason for maintaining the practices surrounding childbirth was simply because they were generally practical. Giving birth in a supine position was almost unknown in Native American cultures. Native mothers either knelt, stood, or were propped upright during delivery, clutching either a post implanted in the floor of a lodge or a strap hanging from a tipi cover or, in the case of Cherokee mothers, the back of a chair in their log cabins. An upright position during parturition used the natural force of gravity to the birthing mother's benefit. According to most Native American women, giving birth from that position was less protracted and not as painful.[48]

Childbirth was highly ritualized among many tribes. The birth of a child was, to Native Americans, more than a function of biology. It was a miraculous strengthening of the kinship bond that was the key to tribal unity. Like most other ceremonies in Native life, the ritual of childbirth was a renewal and a cooperative endeavor. At the turn of the twentieth century, Cherokee mothers were required to have exactly four midwives in attendance during the birth of a child. This number, along with the number seven, was considered sacred in the Cherokee worldview; it matched the number of seasons as well as the elements of fire, earth, wind, and water. When a Tewa mother gave birth, certain duties were performed according to the Tewa kinship system. The woman was usually attended by her mother and her mother-in-law. At the time of parturition, the Tewa mother-in-law was designated as the person who cut the umbilical cord "with an arrow-shaft if the baby was a boy and with a corn-gruel stirring rod if the baby was a girl."[49] Rarely were men, except for medicine men called in to assist with difficult cases, present during childbirth. A prospective Tewa father, for example, was barred from the room where the birth was taking place, and blankets were hung from doors and windows not only to darken the room but also to keep prying eyes, including the father's, from witnessing the birth. Similarly, Arapaho, Cherokee, Cheyenne, and Ojibwa men were banned from the household during their wives' labor. In some cases, the husbands were ordered to perform certain rituals or tasks while remaining outside the home, such as intoning prayers, circumambulating the house, or even simply chopping wood. This practice was probably intended to keep the husbands busy. As one Arapaho woman stated: "My husband busied himself chopping wood or working in the field. He didn't do this to help me; he did it to keep himself from worrying."[50]

Child-rearing patterns survived with Native American family structures. Prior to the widespread establishment of government-operated schools in the late nineteenth century, Native American children, because they were brought up in extended families, were made well aware of their responsibilities and identities through constant contact with older members of their kin groups. Native American grandmothers and grandfathers, who had experienced prereservation culture firsthand, continued to relate to their children's offspring in the same manner that their ancestors had related to them. Native American children, especially those who had not been caught up in the boarding-school system, continued to enjoy strong relationships with aged relatives, who taught through storytelling and example. In many ways, the strong extended family structures gave the children a good deal more freedom than white youths had. Many Native American children were encouraged to learn through experience and observation rather than by rote, and in general there was a strong aversion to submitting a child to corporal punishment. Native Americans often expressed the fear that their children might not consider their home a refuge if they were struck or even harshly scolded. In 1915, ethnologists Alanson Skinner and John V. Satterlee observed that the Menominee of Wisconsin not only were averse to punishing a child physically, but also believed that white people had probably invented the practice in the first place. "Only white men," according to one Menominee informant, "are capable of such barbarities."[51]

Native American children, in addition to learning the ancient stories of their people, were also taught to fashion numerous utilitarian items such as baskets and pots as well as bows and arrows for hunting small game. Menominee and Ojibwa parents took their children to gather wild rice and taught them to build canoes for such work in the wetlands of the Great Lakes. Cheyenne, Arapaho, Comanche, and Kiowa girls were still taught how to do beadwork and to sew buckskin dresses. Peyote ceremonies were conducted in tipis, which continued to be fashioned in the old way. Navajo girls were taught the art of weaving, and Navajo medicine men continued to teach young men how to sing the healing songs, perform ceremonies, and make the sand paintings that went with particular ceremonies.

Notwithstanding the survival of these traditional practices, government officials remained confident that Native Americans would eventually forsake the ways of their ancestors and become integrated into the social and economic life of the nation. Even though most Native American arts and crafts were strictly utilitarian; even though childbearing and child-rearing practices were very practical; and even though ceremonies continued to enliven Native American communities, whites continued to believe that all these things were fated to disappear in the new century. In 1909 Commissioner of Indian Affairs Robert G. Valentine reported that "the dance, like the blanket and the bead toggery, will drop off the race as time goes on." Valentine was apparently so consumed with optimism that he failed to recognize that nearly thirty years of the vanishing policy and the effort to "put a stop to the demoralizing influence of heathenish rites" had not destroyed Native American cultures.[52] Native American lives had been changed, to be sure; but distinctly Native American cultures remained.

The advocates of the vanishing policy expected that tribal family structures would also give way because of changed economic conditions to Anglo-American norms. Certainly the Indian boarding schools were affecting the behavior of Native American youths. Many of the white reformers pointed to the products of institutions like the Carlisle School as examples of "New Indians," who dressed and acted like typical American citizens in almost every way. Given time and constant effort, these New Indians would lead their race into civilization and spurn the old ways of their ancestors.[53] Yet it was also undeniable that efforts to break up the tribal mass or lessen the influence of tribal ceremonies had been less than successful. Returned boarding-school students quickly adopted many of the old tribal ways or became involved in the new syncretic religions like peyotism and the Shaker Church; educated Native Americans generally found ways to work for Indian causes; traditions remained firmly implanted in most reservation communities. Although many Native Americans outwardly adopted the trappings of American civilization, in isolated places on the reservations the old ways remained potent and influential. It would take considerably more time and effort to pry Native Americans loose from their cultural moorings.

CHAPTER III

THE NEW INDIANS

"INDIAN" WAS AN INVENTED TERM. Robert F. Berkhofer, Jr., in his classic book, *The White Man's Indian*, made the case that the term "Indies" was already in use by the time Columbus made his voyage to find King Prester John and that it was given generally to those lands east of the Indus River, except for China and other known nations. The Indies, according to Berkhofer, "was the broadest designation available for all of the area he [Columbus] claimed under royal patent."[1] *Los Indios*, in Spanish, then, was the generic term invented to designate those human beings living in those lands. Following the Spanish lead, the English developed the term "Indian"; the French invented *Indien*, and the Germans *Indianer*. On the other hand, "Indies" might stem from the Latin *In Deus* or *In Dei* and could have been the Western academic term used in medieval Europe for uninhabited or vaguely known lands that were simply understood to be "in the hands of God."

In any case, Indians of course did not think of themselves as "Indians." As Berkhofer related:

> If the term *Indian* and the images and conceptual categories that go along with that collective designation for the Native Americans are White inventions, then the first question becomes one already old in 1646 when an unnamed tribesman asked Massachusetts missionary John Eliot: "Why do you call us Indians?"[2]

Indians thought of themselves as belonging to distinct groups having mutually unintelligible languages, specific territories, and special relations with the deities of a particular place. Members of tribes called themselves "the people" or "the people of" a specific territory or deity. There were early reports of Indians referring to themselves in speeches as "Red Men," thereby implying that Indians classified themselves according to racial categories or physical appearance; but this notion is dubious at best. The term "red" might have carried a large number of connotations in the various tribal languages: "red" may have been associated with a paint color, a direction, or possibly blood or fire or the sun. And it is not too unreasonable to suppose that the person who did the translating at the time simply used the term "red" without explaining what it actually meant. Moreover, it is difficult to imagine Indians thinking in racial categories, especially in the seventeenth or eighteenth centuries, because Indians were adopting and assimilating non-Indian captives in fairly large numbers without apparent concern for skin color. Not only that, but Native Americans varied widely in skin color: some were darker, some were lighter. None, of course, were or are crimson or magenta.

In the seventeenth century, however, Native Americans from different tribes began to think of themselves as sharing common interests, particularly as those interests related to the invading Europeans. "Pan-Indian" political coalitions began to emerge, as did religious movements. This is a relatively common occurrence in colonial situations. Anthropologists Neil L. Whitehead and R. Brian Ferguson have argued that "both the transformation and intensification of war, as well as the formation of tribes, result from complex interactions" in what they call the "tribal zone." This zone "begins . . . where central authority makes contact with peoples it does not rule." Traditional indigenous groups experienced the introduction of new technologies, animals, diseases, plants, and philosophies even before colonizers appeared in their midst. These changes disrupted existing systems and social relationships, thus "fostering new alliances and creating new kinds of conflicts." The creation of new alliances, even new tribes, was a reaction to Western European imperialism.[3]

To be sure, Native American nations, empires, and confederacies were in existence prior to the coming of white settlers. But the confederacies and nations were brought together, like the Iroquois and Creek Nations, because of their linguistic ties. Native American empires, such as Powhatan's of Virginia and the Aztecs of central Mexico, were hegemonic rather than colonial in nature. Subjected peoples paid tribute to these "empires" but were not forced to undergo cultural change or evacuate their lands.

Whatever the case, Pan-Indian politics and Pan-Indian coalitions began to be forged in warfare with whites. By the middle of the nineteenth century, Native Americans certainly knew that whites viewed them as a racial group. As distinct peoples, they were necessarily sovereign, but the power differentials had changed and Native Americans had collectively become the Indians of the "Indian Problem."

The policy of assimilation was intended to individualize Native Americans and extinguish the "tribal bond." This third step in colonization tends to create among indigenous peoples a marginalized or, in this case, an "Americanized" racial group. They wore "citizens'" clothing, spoke English well, became at least nominal Christians, received Western educations, lived in Western-style housing, and some married whites. But instead of becoming everyday white Americans, many Native Americans essentially became American *Indians* who, despite their clothing, speech, and religion, continued to orient themselves toward Native American communities. They worked for Indian causes and became spokespersons for Indian rights. They also knew, truly loved, and were accepted by the peoples that gave them birth. They were marginalized only on the fringes of white society, and even in that sense of marginality they were recognized as contributors to American culture. As Hazel Hertzberg, the leading historian of the Pan-Indian movement in the early twentieth century put it:

> To define their [the New Indians'] position as marginal, however, is not to imply that it was unhonored, useless, or passive. The particular kind of marginality which these men [and women] represented was exceedingly useful both to the tribes and to the wider society, and was frequently honored by both. The position of honest broker between two cultures often involves difficult inner conflicts, but it may also bring prestige, recognition, and the satisfaction of service to one's fellow man.[4]

They knew their cultures and surely felt the sting of the assimila-tionist doctrine that defined their peoples as savages who had nothing whatsoever to contribute to "modern" society. As the new century dawned, many of these American Indians took up a crusade to educate whites in the truth about their heritages, cultures, knowledge, and philosophies. They would attempt to dispel Western myths and stereo-types of Indian savagery and explain that Native American societies were as complex as any found in Europe. Native men and women such as Charles Eastman, Carlos Montezuma, Laura Cornelius Kellogg, and a number of others would also attempt to explain to whites that Native values, philosophies, and knowledge, especially regarding the idea of community and the living human relationship with the land and environment, were as practicable as or better than those of whites. To assure the survival of the tribal traditions they thought worthy of sharing with the white world, the New Indians came to believe whole-heartedly that the Indian race had "its own particular mission in the Cosmic economy."[5] They and their cultures were quite resilient, and the New Indians were emotionally much closer to their traditionalist kin than their outward appearance of marginality indicated. Marginal-ity, in fact, gave them a degree of status, which in turn lent them cred-ibility among both whites and Native Americans.

At the same time that the federal government had in place all the essentials needed to complete the task of making Indians vanish, a great many Americans revived an interest in Native American knowl-edge and practices concerning the environment. These aspects of Native American knowledge spread in the period between 1900 and the early 1920s and became part of the philosophical underpinnings of twentieth-century Pan-Indianism (they could have just as well been its impetus). Moreover, in the same period whites began to share some of these ideals concerning universal order and balance in nature. It was indeed ironic and perhaps fateful that the white man became more and more interested in conservation, environmentalism, and a collective world order at the precise point in time when he had all but destroyed Native American peoplehood and the Indian knowledge of the envi-ronment.

Europeans, from the time they first set foot on North American shores, looked upon the continent's inhabitants not only as "primitive," but also as seemingly part of the flora and fauna of the New World. The American descendents of English colonists consistently referred to Indian peoples as being "children of the forest" or "children of nature." This attitude no doubt reflected the view that American Indians not only were locked in a prepubescent stage of human development but also were totally dependent on, and subject to, the vicissitudes of nature. By the early nineteenth century, many white Americans, caught up in the romanticism of the period, adhered to the idea that American Indians were mystically in tune with the wonders of the natural world. Given this romantic view of nature, it was little wonder that Henry David Thoreau died with the words "moose" and "Indian" on his lips. Native Americans, in the minds of the whites, were forever linked with the untamed forest, fields, and streams. With this concept in mind, it was easy for whites to accept the doctrine that American Indians, along with the forests and streams, would be crushed under the advance of a "civilized" society and its offspring, industrialization.[6]

Hand in hand with the growth of industrialization and thus the spread of civilization came an interest in science. With this interest came the advent of a science of human development, anthropology. For the new discipline, the reservations offered the chance to study a primitive people before civilization completely took over and destroyed not only the "untamed" wilderness but its inhabitants as well. There was a great amount of urgency involved in collecting American Indian data, and for the most part it was gathered in a most scientific manner. By the early part of the twentieth century the urgency of the anthropologists' mission was intensified—the old chiefs were quickly dying off and the vanishing policy was presumed to be pushing aside the last remnants of American Indian lifeways. To the great relief of the scientific community, ethnologists, anthropologists, naturalists, folklorists, and western history buffs went to Indian country in ever-greater numbers to gather information. It was the beginning of what has been correctly called "salvage" anthropology.

The scientists accomplished a remarkable task in collecting and recording the customs and basic knowledge of Native people, even if the photographs, field notes, recordings, items of material culture, and reports were utilized only to further the careers of those collecting them. In large part, the scientists worked only to prove their theories of social and cultural evolution or to store their Indian souvenirs in dusty museum vaults. Native American knowledge was similarly preserved in the ethnologists' field notes and even in early sound recordings, but they were quickly locked away as collections of "dead" myths and legends.

But Native American knowledge and values survived as viable social and ecological wisdom. This wisdom was kept intact among the aged and the relatively isolated, in the kivas of the Pueblo peoples, and on the reservations where the vanishing policy was only in its first tentative stages. More importantly, Native American knowledge was being kept alive among those Natives who had been under the most pressure to cast it aside.

One of the essential aspects of Native Americans' sense of peoplehood is a particular tribe's relationship with its own landscape.[7] It is a living or organic relationship. Land was intimately linked to a tribe's ceremonial cycle, sacred history, and language. Ceremonies were usually held during times of seasonal, floral, faunal, or meteorological change or when, as seen from a particular place in the tribe's territory, celestial bodies moved into certain places in the night sky. These changes were often foretold in a tribe's sacred history, and each language had particular terms for places, both sacred and secular, that held special meaning for the group. Retaining the knowledge of these cycles, changes, and the orderliness of these phenomena was a sacred as well as pragmatic duty. For example, when animals were killed for food, it was customary among most Native American tribes to ask for forgiveness from the animals' spirits or a deity and to explain the reasons for the deaths. If a hunter failed to fulfill these obligations, the common belief was that nature would almost certainly take vengeance upon the hunter or perhaps on the tribe as a whole. The practicality of this knowledge was self-evident. The reverence involved in the ritual of killing reminded the hunter that rampant exploitation of a given resource could lead to a catastrophic decline in the numbers of game animals, followed by famine and pestilence. Several tribal elders have told me that in the old days the spirits would periodically let it be known that certain areas of tribal territory were not to be hunted in for particular lengths of time. Game animals would migrate into these "taboo" areas and replenish their numbers.

In short, Native Americans have oral traditions of deliberately and actively practicing conservation. In tribal economies based on agriculture and gathering, these ideas were extended to what was grown in the garden or collected in the wild. Again, fields might be left fallow for a period of time so that they could replenish themselves. Some tribal customs indicated that people should also express their thanks and need for forgiveness to the earth and the spirits of the land even when cutting trees, digging for clay, or preparing meals. Much of Native American ceremonialism stemmed from efforts to meet the obligation of frugality that nature and the spirit world had set upon the tribes for reaping the earth's bounty.[8]

Charles A. Eastman was one man who never forgot his own tribe's knowledge of the land and the environment. Although he had left tribal life at the age of fifteen and never questioned "the advantages of a civilized life over our earlier and primitive existence," Eastman was at his best when writing about American Indian knowledge of the land.[9] In his numerous books and essays, Eastman urged every American to "recognize the Indian's good sense and sanity in the way of simple living and the mastery of the great out of doors."[10] In his devotion to prove to whites that American Indians possessed the capabilities to learn and adapt, he gained fame among conservationists and won popular approval for Native American environmentalism.

Eastman was Santee Sioux or Dakota, born in 1858 and brought up according to Dakota customs. Although his younger days were filled with strife—the Santee War broke out in Minnesota when he was four—he understood the Santee sense of peoplehood and listened to the stories of his elders. His father, Many Lightnings, was lost during the Minnesota war of 1862 and presumed dead. Because Eastman was orphaned at a young age, according to tribal law he became the responsibility of his grandmother and uncle. Eastman, then named Ohiyesa, was instructed in the manners and knowledge of his people. There can be little doubt that he would have lived the rest of his life in Santee society had his father not unexpectedly reappeared.

In his mid-teens, Eastman was wrenched from the tribal life. At that time, Many Lightnings, who had received a pardon from Abraham Lincoln for his participation in the war against the Americans, returned to the tribe to reclaim his son. During the period between the pardon and the return to his tribe, Many Lightnings had learned Christianity, taken up homesteading, and renamed himself Jacob Eastman. The newly christened Jacob took the name from a white ancestor, as was his inclination, and had no intention of letting his son, whom he renamed Charles, remain in the tribal life. Almost immediately the younger Eastman and another son, John, were sent off to the Reverend Alfred L. Riggs's Santee Indian School. Riggs became one of the more vocal and righteous proponents of allotment, and he gave the Eastman brothers a notably rigorous Christian education. John followed in Riggs's footsteps and become a minister; Charles became a physician.[11]

The former Ohiyesa, "The Winner" in Santee, eventually went on to Knox College, then to Dartmouth on that college's American Indian scholarship, and then to Boston University Medical School. Upon graduation from medical school, Eastman accepted the position as agency doctor at the Pine Ridge Sioux reservation in South Dakota. He was thirty-three years old. During his tenure at Pine Ridge he met and married the superintendent of the agency school system, Elaine Goodale. Elaine, a white woman, was a firm believer in the vanishing policy and a follower of Richard Henry Pratt's philosophy of Indian education. She would go on to write Pratt's biography, *Pratt: The Red Man's Moses*, an uncritical and highly laudatory look at Pratt's methods and ideas concerning Indian education and the processes of the vanishing policy.[12]

When federal troops massacred Big Foot's band of refugees from the Standing Rock reservation at Wounded Knee Creek on the Pine Ridge reservation, Eastman immediately wanted to proceed to the site in order to treat the wounded. The agency superintendent, however, prevented him from doing so. Whether the superintendent feared for Eastman's life because the doctor was an Indian—as he later claimed— or was concerned that Eastman might denounce the carnage and therefore threaten the superintendent's position has never been firmly established. Probably it was the latter reason, because Eastman and Elaine launched a series of scathing protests about the Wounded Knee massacre at the federal government. Not only did the agent's apparent insensitivity gall the Eastmans, but they also evidently had long-standing grievances concerning conditions at Pine Ridge that they felt had led to the massacre in the first place. In the end, the Eastmans both resigned their positions and left South Dakota.[13]

They moved to Minneapolis, where Charles set up a private practice and began to write. While in the city he became affiliated with the Young Men's Christian Association, eventually becoming the organization's area field secretary. He later traveled extensively among the western tribes and represented some of their interests in Washington. At one point in his career, he became involved with a program for giving Anglicized names to the Sioux. By 1901 his writings were being reviewed and recognized by the literary world. In 1911 he attended the Universal Congress of Races in London as one of the American Indian delegates.[14]

By 1912 Eastman was probably the most well-known American of Native ancestry in the United States. His enormously successful books were translated into several languages. His very success made him perhaps the most highly respected of all the "progressive" Indians, and most whites considered him a "race leader."

The notion of a race leader, if viewed from within the context of the prevailing mindset of the Progressive period in American history, fitted Charles Eastman perfectly. He was striving to become part of the "melting pot" of American society. Eastman's education and writings were, in the American mind, the result of an enlightened Indian policy. More importantly, he was making a contribution to American life with his hard work and middle-class standing. He was married to a white woman, and although some Americans may have thought he had committed wrongful "miscegenation," his marriage was solid proof of his craving to become a member of the American mainstream. In nearly everything he did, he sought to legitimize himself in the eyes of white America. And although white America never forgot that he was an Indian, it was as a "new" or "progressive" Indian that he made his mark. The title fit him well, and when, in 1911, a white sociologist named Fayette Avery McKenzie proposed that he and a few other well-educated Native Americans form an organization to aid in the "transformation" of the Indian "race" into American citizens, Eastman felt duty-bound to attend.[15]

The organization, which became known as the Society of American Indians, was made up primarily of those Indian people who firmly believed in the American notion of progress and, only to a certain extent, acculturation. They had not necessarily cast aside their tribal notions of who they were as a people, but they certainly were beginning to think of themselves as an American ethnic group. Their immediate goals were many and somewhat complex, but they all thought that the society would be the preeminent organization that would take the lead in helping other Indians bridge the gap between tribal life and mainstream American society.

Toward this end, the organization's leaders sought to instill in all Native Americans an "Indian," rather than a tribal, identity and, with that, a sense of race pride. To them, race pride was the open demonstration that there were certain aspects of American Indian life that were "worthy" and should be incorporated into modern American society. According to Arthur C. Parker, one of the founders of the SAI, "all of the best things in the old Indian life . . . must be brought into and developed higher in the new civilization."[16] Society leaders stressed that Indian people possessed the virtues of generosity and loyalty and certainly had the intellectual capacity for citizenship in the United States. Moreover, American Indians were not only morally suitable for membership in the American mainstream, but also fully capable of entering on the same level as whites.

These ideas broke away from the old reformers' conclusion that there was nothing of value in the old tribal life. Eastman and the other founders of the society essentially were saying that although the tribal life was no more, it was a past that could be held up as virtuous, healthy, and knowledgeable as any other. The old and the new could be combined into something that was as promising as anything the white man had said to them. They had accepted the invented term "Indian" and quite possibly the white man's version of their own history, but they had not completely accepted the stereotypes or the mythology of colonialism. If other Indians followed their lead, they too would be able to move from "primitivism" into the economic and social life of the nation.

Eastman, although he would later become disenchanted with some of the other leaders of the Society of American Indians, was committed to proving that Indians were morally and intellectually capable of the task of accepting the responsibility of American citizenship. In all of his articles and books he stressed the equality of whites and Indians; but his writings were also instructional. American Indians consistently demonstrated courage, honor, and the "beauty of generosity."[17] In his first book, *Indian Boyhood* (1902), Eastman emphasized the idea that Indian people learned and had the capacity to learn, even while in the transition from "savagery" to "civilization." Indian cultures, however, placed emphasis on a different understanding of the world in which they lived. Indian knowledge was based on observing the workings of nature. It was the knowledge of surviving on what was at hand: Indians were self-sufficient and, most importantly, still retained their spiritual connection with the world. To Eastman, cultures may have been unequal, but Native American knowledge was very much on a par with that of the whites.

For general scientific understanding, Eastman most often gave the edge to Western European civilization. He was, after all, a product of American missionary and scientific education and was married to one of Richard Henry Pratt's most ardent supporters. But when the conservation movement began to show a widespread popular base in the United States, Eastman proudly was able to write about and demonstrate not simply the equality but the superiority of Native American knowledge and spirituality. In *Indian Boyhood*, he thought that he had proved that Indian people were capable of learning the white man's ways (his own life was demonstrative of this fact). The book also indicated that Eastman felt sure that white Americans could certainly benefit from Indian ways: for, according to Eastman, an Indian's education "makes him a master of the art of wood-craft."[18]

It was easy for Eastman to move from being a philosopher of racial intellectual capabilities to becoming a teacher of "Indian lore." In addition to the widely read and admittedly instructional *Indian Boyhood*, Eastman continued his autobiography in *From Deep Woods to Civilization*. His most popular tracts were youth books, *Red Hunters and the Animal People*, *Indian Scout Talks* and *Indian Heroes and Great Chieftains* among them.

For a more mature audience, Eastman expressed his ideas concerning the American Indian reverence for nature in *The Soul of the Indian*; he reported on conditions within Native American groups and listed Indian contributions to American society in *The Indian To-day*. Not only did Eastman's writings reveal a great deal of nostalgia for the life he lived growing up in Santee society, but they also glowed with his own pride in and enthusiasm for the growth in popularity of Native American ideals and knowledge concerning conservation. He undoubtedly thought that his popularity and acceptance in the white world would enhance American Indian self-pride and provide an avenue for white acceptance of other Native Americans. He also believed that the cause of conservation was a morally and socially sound undertaking and that it would provide a means for Native Americans to make their greatest and most long-lasting contribution to American society. Living in and knowing the "great out of doors" was to him the right and best way for mankind to exist. It was natural and balanced, and like his people, "the wisest Americans" gave over at least part of their lives to hunting, camping, hiking, and fishing, thus "receiving the vital benefits of the pure air and sunlight."[19]

As a physician very much in touch with the trends going on within his profession, Eastman wholly recommended outdoor living as the foundation of good health. He firmly believed that his ancestors owed their strong physical development to their "natural" lifestyles. Detriments to Indian health, in his mind, were measles, smallpox, tuberculosis, and alcohol—all European introductions. In fact, he once expressed the opinion that these European diseases would have totally annihilated the Native American "race . . . save its heritage of a superb physique." He became a resounding critic of the overcrowded Indian schools and their lack of outdoor training. He considered that the "close confinement and long hours of work were for these children of the forest and plains unnatural and trying at best."[20]

Eastman had tapped into another widespread movement of the period. By the early 1890s many Americans had taken up a mania for clean air, pure food and water, simplicity of life, sanitation, and athletics. Industrialization had brought pollution, slums, and some unsavory practices connected with the processing of foodstuffs. Theodore Roosevelt, who loved "fresh air," exercise, and the outdoors, became president after the assassination of William McKinley in 1900. He busily promoted the establishment of a national park system and pursued legislation that would clean up various industries, such as the meatpacking business, that directly affected the health of the nation.

The focus on a healthy, sanitary, and vigorous life affected American ideas regarding Native peoples. There was, on the one hand, the image of the "dirty Indian" mired in poverty and living in unclean conditions on the reservations. Countering that stereotype, however, was the image of the Indian as a "natural athlete." Between 1909 and 1912, Jim Thorpe led the Carlisle Indian School football team to victory over several American colleges and went on to win the decathlon and pentathlon at the 1912 Olympic games in Sweden. And he was not the only Indian athlete of note in the period. As Charles M. Harvey, writing for the magazine *American Review of Reviews*, stated, Indians "excel in many civilized sports."[21]

The popularity of the movement for fresh air and athleticism further motivated Charles A. Eastman to promote among whites other "beneficial" aspects of Native American life. He took great interest in the preservation of American Indian crafts, which of course to him were the utilitarian manifestations of a life in the great outdoors. But he also supported programs that aided in the development of the Native arts of painting, basketry, beadwork, weaving, and pottery making in order to advance them as true manifestations of the aesthetics, knowledge, and spirituality of Native American people.[22] Because of his status as a physician, writer, and "New Indian," he was able to promote the preservation of Indian art in such magazines as *Craftsman* and *Overland Monthly*. He consistently made use of the thematic idea of balance in nature and the notion that Indians were master practitioners of conservation who still maintained strong spiritual connections with the landscape. He was deeply concerned that without the aid of Native American knowledge there would be no wilderness areas in the future where whites or Indians could reap the healthful benefits of nature. For this reason Eastman gave his full support to such "back-to-nature" youth groups as the Boy Scouts. In *The Indian To-day*, Eastman bade

> the parents of America to give their fullest support to those great organizations, the Boy Scouts and the Camp Fire Girls. The young people of to-day are learning through this movement much of the wisdom of the first American [*sic*]. In the mad rush for wealth we have too long overlooked the foundations of our national welfare. The contribution of the American Indian, though considerable from any point of view, is not to be measured by material acquirement. Its greatest worth is spiritual and philosophical.[23]

Eastman was firm in his advocacy of American Indian knowledge concerning the environment and quite accurate—largely because he had lived with this knowledge during his youth—in its description. Although romantic in style, his words were based on sound ethnological research, his own data collected during his visits to the reservations, and his background as a physician. He wrote that Native American peoples were true conservationists, endowed with a spiritual reverence for the land. The earth's bounties were to be taken with a spirit of thankfulness and due humility. He constantly reminded his readers that American Indians killed animals and took from the land "only as necessity and the exigencies of life demand, and not wantonly."[24]

Most of all he kept alive the tribal conception of order and balance. After visiting the Leech Lake Ojibway in 1910, Eastman wrote that, despite all efforts to eliminate tribal value systems in relation to the earth, they were nevertheless still very much alive. The Ojibway, once his own tribe's enemies, were living in a "miniature world of freedom and plenty" maintained by the tribe's traditional beliefs and spirituality. "With them," Eastman explained, "nothing goes to waste; all meat or fish not needed for immediate use is cut into thin strips and smoked and dried; the hoofs of deer and moose are made into trinkets, the horns into spoons or tobacco boards, and the bones pounded to boil out the fat."[25] According to Eastman, man must meet the demands of nature or else lose its benefits of health, beauty, and security. He deeply believed that if the conservation movement died, the future of mankind was in grave peril.

He and his wife, Elaine, actually put these ideas into practice in 1915 when they opened an all-girls summer camp in New Hampshire and called it the "School of the Woods." The next year they made room for a boys' camp; they continued to operate these businesses until the couple separated in 1921. Eastman had given up private practice to promote and operate what he believed would become a widespread health and back-to-nature movement for young people.[26] As he stated on many occasions, Americans had much to learn from the Natives of the land.

Essentially, Eastman was attempting to create what might be called a "race ethos" that would be preserved and made a part of the larger American sense of purpose. He, like many of his contemporaries, thought of the United States as a nation in the midst of an evolution— changing with the times, confronting difficulties with an enlightened and forward-looking liberal attitude, and developing into a paragon of virtuous behavior and progressive thought. Of course he also knew that American society was segregated and remained, by and large, racist in politics, social structure, and economics. Still, he persisted in thinking that a Native American race ethos would fit into the ideology of an idealized American society. It would take a remarkable amount of hard work to undermine and refute the notion that Indians were a remnant of the American past, doomed to extinction and possessing nothing that could possibly contribute to the social, cultural, and economic well-being of the nation. Eastman was a "New Indian" in every sense of the word. He had become an American of Indian descent and had accepted "Americanism" as his ideological identity.

He was also, according to his biographer Raymond Wilson, an "acculturated rather than assimilated" Native American. His wife, Elaine, was, as a follower of Richard Henry Pratt, a staunch assimilationist. Charles attempted to harmonize Native spirituality in nature with American beliefs and perspectives, and even though Elaine heavily edited his writings, she could not "conceal her husband's syncretism."[27] Essentially, Charles Eastman filtered everything from the white world though his own sense of peoplehood, and in doing so he came up with a new identity for himself and other Native Americans who could fit in with whites but still maintain their own particular understanding of the world.

Eastman focused on the conservation movement as the method for gaining widespread acceptance of Native American philosophies. In his books and articles, he effectively erased tribal boundaries, stereotyped tribal customs, and created a broader Indian identity based on tribal concepts of balance and order in the environment. In short, he synthesized tribal practices and knowledge into a conservationist ideology. He popularized Native American ideas and created the notion that, as a race, Native Americans were "natural conservationists." He succeeded, perhaps for the first time in American history, in giving this Native American racial ethos a degree of valued status in white American society. His other contribution lay in the fact that he paved the way for other Native Americans to preserve and make popular other important products of the Native American intellect.

Hazel Hertzberg, in her excellent 1971 book, *The Search for an American Indian Identity*, places Pan-Indian movements during the early years of the twentieth century in secular and religious categories. "Reform Pan-Indianism," into which Charles Eastman might be placed, seems to have taken its cues from the general American reform movements of the Progressive Era. Although most reform Pan-Indians advocated the eventual assimilation of Indians into American society, they were determined not to have Native Americans simply disappear as distinct groups of people—or as they would have put it in that era, as distinct races. At the same time, they were not exactly sure what constituted "the Indian race." Membership in the Society of American Indians, for example, was limited to those of at least one-sixteenth "Indian blood"—as nebulous a distinction as could possibly be made— probably to include people who did not "look" Indian but nevertheless had Native ancestry.

But the New Indians were searching for a more meaningful definition of Native Americans than some hazy racial categorization. Peoplehood really belonged to the individual tribes, with their distinct languages, ceremonies, territories, and histories. For the New Indians, Indianness was more or less a state of mind combined with a tribal identity, tentative though that identification may have been in some cases. One did not necessarily have to participate in the everyday life of a tribal community, although most of the New Indians maintained ties with their own tribes. To be a New Indian, especially a reform Pan-Indian, one had to adopt an ideology of advocacy for causes, philosophies, arts, and values that could be immediately identified with Native Americans.

As Hertzberg pointed out, the New Indians took a cue from Progressive Era white Americans and attempted to organize an all-Indian interest group that became known as the Society of American Indians. Interest groups flourished during the early years of the twentieth century, and the New Indians fairly leapt at the chance to found a group that could unite Indians and influence the American social and political agenda.

They also took a cue from reformers in the period and wrote and published profusely. Thanks to technological improvements in high-speed printing presses, the print medium expanded enormously in the latter half of the previous century. Popular magazines proliferated during the early years of the twentieth century, and inexpensive books became more readily available to the general public. New Indians like Eastman found the publishing industry receptive to Native American writers, and many of them did not feel at all reticent about putting their ideas, histories, complaints, and hopes in print. One New Indian, Carlos Montezuma, even began to publish his own personal newspaper, *Wassaja*, so called after his Indian name meaning "the signal," to air his views and to promote Indian freedom.

Like Charles A. Eastman, Carlos Montezuma was a medical doctor who had, at one time, been in the employ of the United States Bureau of Indian Affairs. He was also a prolific writer and a champion of the idea that his race could indeed make great contributions to American society and become upstanding American citizens. But instead of proving Indians worthy of American citizenship—which, in his mind, did not need to be proven or established—Montezuma spent most of his adult life attacking the roadblocks that he believed stood in the path of Native Americans' freedom and their full membership in the American commonwealth. In short, Montezuma became an advocate of Native American freedom in the most sweeping and most traditionally American sense of the term. He joined a long line of Americans—Indian and otherwise—who struggled with the question of whether or not freedom meant doing as one's conscience dictated or subordinating oneself to the will of the majority and American political institutions. Ultimately he opted for the notion of personal freedom and, typically for Montezuma, went against the grain of political and social thought in the Progressive Era. He worked in an era of polemical writing and muckraking, but also in an age when government controls, civil management, and bureaucracy were on the upswing. At the same time, Montezuma was creating a new identity for American Indians as an oppressed racial group.

According to his biographer, Peter Iverson, Montezuma's life made a complete circle. He was a Yavapai who had been captured by the Pima and sold to an itinerant photographer by the name of Carlos Gentile. Gentile gave the young boy, then only seven or eight years old, his own name and picked "Montezuma" as the boy's surname to maintain some kind of tenuous connection with an "Indian" heritage. Eventually a fire ruined Gentile's finances, and after staying with a family named Baldwin in New York, Montezuma was placed in the care of W. H. Stedman, a Baptist minister in Urbana, Illinois. He enrolled in the University of Illinois and received a bachelor of science degree in 1884. After working as a druggist for a time, he was able to attend the Chicago Medical College, from which he obtained his MD in 1889. He was in his early twenties at the time.

His first private practice did not prove to be lucrative, and, nearly broke, Montezuma accepted a position with the Indian service. After spending several years on the reservations, he finally became a physician at the Carlisle Indian School, then under the superintendence of

Richard Henry Pratt. Montezuma later returned to a moderately successful medical practice in Dr. Fenton Tuck's clinic in Chicago. In 1916, partially to counterbalance the editorials of Arthur C. Parker, the Seneca ethnologist who had editorial control of the Society of American Indians journal, Montezuma began to publish *Wassaja*. He devoted the last years of his life to preserving the Fort McDowell reservation for his own people, the Yavapai, with whom he had maintained steady contact for much of his adult life. It was obvious that his Yavapai relatives meant a great deal to him, and despite his longtime antipathy toward the reservation system, he moved to Fort McDowell in 1922 and there died in January 1923 of tuberculosis.[28]

While still in medical school, Montezuma had corresponded with Richard Pratt. Like-minded and of the same dogmatic and aggressive temperament, Montezuma and Pratt, ironically perhaps, became one another's staunchest supporters. Montezuma was everything Pratt had hoped for in his Native American charges; Montezuma looked upon Pratt as an enlightened thinker and perhaps the most noble of men involved in the Indian reform movement during the late nineteenth century. Throughout his life, Montezuma wrote and spoke in the same vein and with the same passion as his mentor, but with far greater eloquence.

He was an absolute enemy of the Bureau of Indian Affairs, especially after Pratt was dismissed from his position as head of Carlisle Indian School in 1904. Montezuma had always been an ardent advocate of "Americanizing" Native Americans and saw the assimilation of Indians into American society as inevitable and beneficial for both whites and Native peoples. He believed that Native Americans had lived peaceful and happy lives before the coming of the whites and remembered his early years with his Yavapai relatives as being happy and prosperous. But historical circumstances had changed Native Americans for the worse. The reservation system had locked Indians up and had stopped what Montezuma saw as the natural human progression from the savage state to enlightened civilization. Freedom was the answer to the "Indian question."

In Montezuma's view, the reservations had frozen Indians in time and place. Unallowed to progress naturally, Native Americans had become wards of a growing bureaucracy that cared little for personal rights or, for that matter, human dignity. The reservations were prisons that demoralized and stultified the inmates, and Montezuma preached passionately against the continuation of what he considered an un-American system of injustice and a wholly immoral practice. "Neither are habits of dress, color of skin or descent," he wrote "grounds for exceptions in the matter of personal rights."[29]

To Montezuma, Carlisle Indian School was the bright light in the shadowy world of Indian affairs, and when Pratt was dismissed from its leadership, Montezuma was outraged. On June 29, 1904, Montezuma expressed the depth of his feelings to both Pratt and President Theodore Roosevelt in separate letters. To Pratt, he wrote:

> What is the matter? Can no one speak the truth? Must the Indian be an Indian forever? . . . It is not a [sic] for the Government to lay claim to the Indian any longer. This idea of expending public money to cripple the Indian race is outrageous. . . . The injustice is over whelming, it should not be tolerated or continued any longer.[30]

To Roosevelt he wrote in the voice of a stereotyped noble Indian speaking to the "Great Father" in the White House, possibly to mock the president's own stereotypes of Native Americans:

> In silence I have looked upon you as a great father at Washington to my people, but I am much surprised and dumbfounded at the position you have taken in permitting the dismissal of the foremost student of Indian affairs in the service of the Government, General R. H. Pratt. . . . His dismissal is unjust to the wards of our nation, who deserve the rare talents, wide knowledge and accurate judgment he displayed in Indian matters. It is a dark blot in your administration, a backward movement for my people. . . . There is not a wigwam throught [sic] the country that can smoke the pipe of peace with you for such an act of injustice to our veteran leader. . . . It is not too late for you to right this wrong by reinstating General Pratt, and then we shall again smoke the pipe of peace with you.[31]

Montezuma's outrage at Pratt's dismissal led him to feel a deep antipathy toward the Republican Party and to reject leadership in what may have been the first all-Indian political organization. In August 1904, Lusena Choteau, a Native American resident of San Francisco,

California, wrote to Montezuma, asking him to become the vice president of the National Indian Republican Association. Although the organization was open to Indian men only, Choteau, a woman, had been installed as president. The group had "appointed officers for this Association without first consulting them," but nevertheless contacted Montezuma, as a Native American both "highly educated and of unusual ability," to take up the task of encouraging Native American men "to take interest in politics and to claim all the rights of an American citizen." Choteau also asked Montezuma not to let it be "known that a woman is the President of this political Association."[32] Montezuma rebuffed the offer on the basis that Pratt had been dismissed by a Republican administration. On August 13, Choteau urged Montezuma to put aside his anger and let the new organization work for Pratt's reinstatement. "Your present attitude," she wrote, "is hurting him and the whole Indian CAUSE."[33] Montezuma, however, remained adamantly unwilling to work with any Republican organization so long as Pratt was banished from Carlisle. Choteau's organization apparently died a quick death after Montezuma's rejection.

Pratt's dismissal had largely been the result of the old reformer's diatribes against the Bureau of Indian Affairs and the reservation system. Pratt firmly believed that the bureau itself was a hindrance to Indian progress because it treated Native Americans as wards. It was a hindrance to freedom and a roadblock to Indian citizenship. Actually, it was Pratt who was standing in the path of a trend in government and in American cultural perceptions.

Bureaucracy was expanding from the increased demands on government to solve problems and provide more services to an ever-increasing American population. Bureaucracies were gaining more and more discretionary authority over the problems they were put in place to fix. The Bureau of Indian Affairs had taken on the responsibility of managing allotment, Indian health, the dissolution of Indian Territory, Indian education, and the reservations, as well as land claims and water rights. In short, the bureau's discretionary authority over the management of these issues and services grew as Indian affairs became more complex. Gone were the quick-fix solutions and highly generalized philosophies of Pratt's era of reform. His demands for the dissolution of the bureau threatened the livelihoods of a growing body of government officials, which by that time included more than a few Native

Americans. Management was fast becoming quantifiable, and the bureau could point to statistics that essentially proved that it was providing numerous services to Native Americans. This hard evidence of bureau functions—whether the figures for Indian patients in hospitals, acreage put under the plow, allotments taken, or buildings erected for Indian industries were accurate or even relevant—began to outweigh the more abstract ideologies espoused by Richard H. Pratt and his supporters.

On a different level, many Americans were becoming interested in preserving a few features of Native American cultures that were deemed worthy of incorporating into American life. Collecting Indian arts and crafts was on the upswing, and Native Americans such as Charles Eastman were advocating the acceptance of Native American knowledge and aesthetics in the widespread conservation movement. Pratt's—and Montezuma's—advocacy of total and speedy assimilation of Native Americans was simply becoming *passé*.

Carlisle itself underwent great change after Pratt's exit, and Montezuma was adamantly against what he viewed as the school's new direction. Moses Friedman, the new superintendent, instituted a new program that essentially encouraged students to produce "Indian Art." In 1907 the bureau erected a new building at the school to be named "The Leupp Indian Art Studio." Named in honor of Francis E. Leupp, who had succeeded William A. Jones, Montezuma's old friend, as commissioner of Indian Affairs, the building was symbolic of the new interest being paid to the production and marketing of Native American arts and crafts. Montezuma railed:

> As a building, in itself, we make no cry against this structure lately erected at Carlisle, for there are many uses to which it could profitable [*sic*] be put, but what we do object to is the use proposed to be made of it. And this for the reason, first that there is no such thing as Indian Art, in the proper sense of the word, and second, any attempt to perpetuate this non-existent thing has a tendency to undermine the foundational purpose of the school.

Montezuma further stated that Carlisle had been

> founded, and for more than twenty years, conducted strictly with one end in view—to so train and instruct its pupils that at the end

of their school work there, they could begin life in competition with those of the other races, self-supporting and self-sustaining by virtue of their ability to perform the practical every day things that men and women are called to do in the various pursuits of life.

Montezuma correctly pointed out that, moreover, "The purpose of the School is not to preserve the characteristics of Indian life, but rather an admonition to the Carlisle students to forget it."[34]

That the building was to be named for Commissioner of Indian Affairs Francis Leupp must have particularly galled Montezuma. The doctor had clashed with the bureaucrat before. Concerning Indian education, Leupp favored the idea of having Indian students read materials to which they could easily relate. In a 1905 *New York Tribune* article entitled "The Future of Our Indians," Leupp spoke of giving Indian children books that contained stories about familiar animals. The "young Indian," he said, "will read them eagerly because they have some relation to things he has seen and known."[35]

Montezuma quickly responded to Leupp's statements in a printed review. Leupp's ideas of environmental relevance in reading materials for young Native Americans prompted Montezuma to write:

> Simply because the Indian in his former environment had actual knowledge of the appearance of some of the wild animals, it seems, therefore, according to the Commissioner, that books for his early entertainment and reading must consist of stories about the wolf, the prairie dog, and Mr. and Mrs. Bear and the juvenile bears. It would seem to one not looking through a smoked glass, that if the object is to civilize the Indian, then the farther we remove him, bodily and mentally, from wolves, coyotes and the whole bear family, the more we are liable to make life attractive to him.[36]

Throughout the rest of his life Montezuma protested against the reservation system and the Bureau of Indian Affairs. He saw both as impediments to knowledge and Native American freedom. Although he was involved in founding and organizing the Society of American Indians, he became one of its most nagging critics. He consistently assailed those Natives who worked for the bureau and aimed written barbs at members of the society who advocated the preservation of Native American arts. In short, he did not believe in syncretism or in the ideology underlying cultural relevance in education. On the other hand, he felt that adaptation—perhaps in the old social Darwinian sense of the word—did not "demand a complete renunciation of the Indian heritage."[37]

He did, however, believe in absolute freedom. In April 1916 Montezuma began to publish *Wassaja* precisely to air his own ideas concerning Indian freedom. In essence, Montezuma defined and identified Native Americans as members of an oppressed and segregated racial minority. Unlike him, most Indians were neither allowed to rule themselves nor to move freely in mainstream society. The only differences between Native Americans and the dominant whites were skin color and unequal levels of economic and political power. If Native Americans were allowed the opportunity to receive educations like the whites' and if the Bureau of Indian Affairs were dissolved, then Indians could take their place in the national polity, free of administrative tyranny and what Montezuma considered imprisonment on the reservation. He was uncompromising in his stand on the Bureau of Indian Affairs, and he very likely felt as if the Republican Party had betrayed its own liberal foundations.

His fight to save the McDowell reservation for his relatives, the Yavapai, did not in the least contradict his hatred of the reservation system. After the establishment of the reservation in 1903, a movement began to remove the Yavapai to the Salt River reservation so that the whites could exploit the more fertile lands of the Fort McDowell reservation. Montezuma urged his relatives to "stay put" and to stand together to defeat the blatant attempt to rob them of their lands. At first, Montezuma thought that allotment might be the solution. The fifty-odd square miles of the reservation would be split up among the Yavapai to be owned individually in fee. The problem was that the Yavapai needed a guarantee that they would have rights to water, timber, and pasturelands, which the government was unwilling or unable to give. If the Yavapai were moved to Salt River, they would have little arable land and would be placed in a subordinate position to the Salt River Pima, who were once their traditional enemies. To Montezuma, the effort to dispossess the Yavapai was simply an overt expression of government domination and administrative control. In his mind, freedom for the Yavapai meant the retention their lands and autonomous control over their own destiny.[38]

The fight to save the Fort McDowell reservation was Montezuma's last, and perhaps his only real, victory. Most often he stood for a nineteenth-century brand of personal freedom that was fast becoming irrelevant in mainstream political thought. If progressivism could be defined with any accuracy at all, it could be seen as a willingness to establish controls over a polity so that certain citizens or groups of citizens could not impinge on the rights of others or become burdens on society as a whole. Government could become a countervailing force to offset the power of big business or any other collectives—such as labor unions—that might disrupt an orderly society. In a way, it was a "collective" mentality that abhorred the idea of smaller collectives controlling certain parts of the national polity.

Big business, for example, meant wealth, but that could be dangerous because a free market economy engendered poverty, which could, in turn, be disruptive in and of itself. On the other hand, interest groups and other "collectives" like big business and the labor unions were what really drove the political and economic processes. In fact, politicking by interest groups, including those organized along racial and ethnic lines, was common and even characteristic of the Progressive Era. In Montezuma's mind, Indians were a racial group, perhaps even an interest group, that warranted the right of political and economic participation in the American polity. Indians were not able to participate fully in American society because of a wardship status conferred upon them by an ever-growing bureaucracy that had been legitimized precisely to manage the collective "Indian Problem."

In the fight to save Fort McDowell, Montezuma urged a collective resistance. He realized that the ability to organize was perhaps inherent in tribal societies, simply because they functioned on the basis of shared relationships. Even though he espoused what was basically a philosophy of personal freedom, he knew that political power lay in associations of like-minded people.

Montezuma was one of the first Native Americans to join with Fayette McKenzie in developing plans for the conference of educated Native Americans that ultimately led to the founding of the Society of American Indians. Typically for Montezuma, he did not attend the first meeting, because he realized that many of the people in attendance had close connections with the Bureau of Indian Affairs. He did attend the second meeting of the SAI in 1912 and passionately argued against the bureau and the idea of gradually assimilating American Indians. When the conference attendees more or less rejected Montezuma's proposal to dissolve the bureau instantly, he was angered, but he stuck with the SAI. He very likely thought of himself as representing the loyal opposition, but as time wore on and the organization's ideological stances did not seem to agree with his own, Montezuma became more and more critical of society members. In *Wassaja*, he openly attacked Arthur C. Parker's editorials in the society's journal and carried on a personal feud against the Reverend Sherman Coolidge, the president of SAI, for his work with the bureau.[39] Montezuma certainly favored unity, organization, and collective effort in order to attain a political goal, but his objectives were rarely, if ever, in accord with those of his fellow "New Indians."

Had Carlos Montezuma been in attendance at the first meeting of the SAI, he would have heard Laura Cornelius, an Oneida from Wisconsin, deliver a paper that extolled the virtues of Native American communities and explained how those virtues could lead to an attainable solution to the "Indian Problem." In fact, her proposals, according to Hazel Hertzberg, "foreshadowed the New Deal era in Indian affairs." Montezuma probably would have viewed her remarks with a certain amount of disdain and written them off as an attempt to keep Native Americans in the "tribal state." On the other hand, Cornelius's presentation also emphasized Indian self-sufficiency, autonomy, and progressive reform, which no doubt the good doctor would have endorsed.[40] Where and how did this progressive Native American woman come up with her ideas? Her ideas directly countered the vanishing policy. Not only that, but they also went against freezing Native Americans in time and place on the reservations, the policy against which Montezuma had fought so long and hard.

Like several of her contemporary "New Indians"—Francis LaFlesche, Arthur C. Parker, J. N. B. Hewitt—Cornelius was interested in the study of ethnology. Unlike most of them, however, she had taken anthropology courses at several colleges and had apparently developed an interest in tribal organizational structures and the theoretical underpinnings of cultural evolution. She was also an activist who would later be called "the Joan of Arc of the Indians" and "the Battling Indian Princess."

Laura Minnie Cornelius was born in Wisconsin on the Oneida

reservation. She was the granddaughter of the famous Oneida leader Daniel Bread, or Dehowyadilou (Great Eagle), who had secured land for his people from the Menominee in Wisconsin in 1822. Bread, who spoke both Oneida and English and was a friend of both Henry Clay and Daniel Webster, was missionary-educated and a believer in the notion that the Oneida had to acculturate themselves to the white man's ways in order to survive. Cornelius followed her grandfather's lead and became one of the few Native American women to attend college. After graduating from Grafton Hall, an Episcopal boarding school primarily for non-Indians in Fond du Lac, Wisconsin, she studied at Barnard College, Cornell University, the New York School of Philanthropy—which eventually became the Columbia University School of Social Work—Stanford University, and the University of Wisconsin. Although never attaining a degree from any of universities she attended, Cornelius became a linguist of note, speaking Oneida, Mohawk, and English fluently.

She also became an enthralling lecturer on the League of the Haudenosaunee (Iroquois) and an activist regarding Iroquois land claims in New York. In fact, her pursuit of these claims and the methods by which she and her husband, Orrin Joseph Kellogg, a white attorney from Minneapolis whom she married in 1912, collected money to finance their activities led to their arrests for fraud in Oklahoma in 1913 and in Montreal in 1925. They were found not guilty both times, and went on to press the case of *Deere v. St. Lawrence River Power Company* in U.S. district court. The court did not rule in their favor, and she would carry the charges that she had defrauded many Native Americans and divided the Iroquois Nation for the rest of her life.[41]

But Cornelius's real contribution to Indian affairs and to the creation of a larger Native American identity lay in her farsighted activism in pursuing land claims and her belief that Indian problems would be remedied only through Indian means. As a student of the Iroquoian laws and ways, she was no doubt aware that traditionally women held great political and social powers. Among the Oneida, Mohawk, Onondaga, Cayuga, Seneca, and Tuscarora, women were the focus of each tribe's culture. Clan lineage was traced through mothers. The women raised the crops and therefore provided the larger share of tribal subsistence. Iroquoian women were also the tribal political powers, for they alone picked the representatives to the league's councils.

Additionally, the primary purpose of warfare among Iroquoian peoples was the abduction and adoption of others to replace lost family members. Iroquois women normally decided the fate of captives in this form of raiding, known as "mourning war," and thus held the power of sanctioning warfare.[42]

Cornelius projected Iroquoian organizational strengths on to other Native Americans and essentially framed the idea that tribal social organization based on shared relationships could serve as the basis for each tribe's economic development. Land—the reservation—was important primarily because it would serve as a base for the tribal industrial collectives that Cornelius envisioned as being the salvation of Native American life. Although it has never been hinted that Cornelius was a Marxist, she certainly was a strong advocate of communal economic systems based on the idea that those who worked the land or manufactured goods should control the means of production and share in the wealth thus generated. Of course there were a number of Americans in the period who were interested not only in the ideas of Karl Marx, but also in Jean-Jacques Rousseau's notions of social organization based on human cooperation and compassion.

Political organizations were rife in the early twentieth century, and there was a strong belief in collective activism. But there was also a progressive belief in the idea that humans were basically cooperative and, most often, compassionate. John Wesley Powell, the noted ethnologist and linguist who became the first director of the Bureau of American Ethnology, spent time toying with Lewis Henry Morgan's ideas concerning the steps in human cultural evolution. In 1877 Morgan published his masterwork entitled *Ancient Society*, outlining the thesis that human cultures evolved "in imperceptible steps" from "savagery" through "barbarism" to "civilization."[43] Basically, Morgan applied Darwinian biological theory to human culture, much as Herbert Spencer had done in applying Darwinism to human social structures. Powell, however, suggested that there might be a fourth stage of cultural development, which he termed "enlightenment." According to Frederick E. Hoxie, Powell was an organizer and an eclectic who thought that the corporations and bureaucracies of modern states would make people interdependent and raise them above competition. "He was confident," Hoxie wrote, "that the extension of modernity would produce a single world language, international peace, and the rule of benevolent associations."[44] Powell's ideas might have been anti-Marxist, but they were utopian and mildly socialist nonetheless.

When Cornelius helped found the Society of American Indians, she undoubtedly thought that she could not only enhance the position of Indian women but also undo the damages done by the vanishing policy to Native American societies. At the first meeting of the SAI, held in Columbus, Ohio, in 1911, Cornelius took a very active part and won a place on the organization's executive committee. She took a deep interest in Indian art, proposing that another group be formed to regulate its production in order to prevent the widespread introduction of its "deteriorated forms."

Second, and more importantly, she presented a paper entitled "Industrial Organization for the Indian," perhaps her most unsettling statement to the body of New Indians assembled at the conference. In her talk, she proposed that self-governing "industrial villages" be organized among Native people living on reservations. The industrial villages could produce whatever could be manufactured from the local resources. One tribe could go into dairy farming; another could manufacture shoes; still another could concentrate on Native arts and crafts for sale to tourists. The villages would be organized along the lines of joint-stock companies, but no one person would be able to obtain a controlling interest in the communities' stock, and everyone would be entitled to a share of the profits. Cornelius had in her mind a touch of Wall Street business combined with "the Mormon idea of communistic cooperation" and what she referred to as the "natural clannishness" of Native Americans. Through the industrial village plan, Cornelius believed that Indians could "teach the white man" the benefits of group cooperation and equal economic justice for all.[45]

In many ways, her plan was a critique of the ills that were inherent in corporate capitalism during the period. The development in big business of trusts, interlocking directorates, and oligopolies was in some ways like the fully enlightened modern state that John Wesley Powell envisioned. Congress and the federal bureaucracy were in the first stages of becoming the forces that would countervail corporate excesses. Big business ruthlessly exploited labor and provoked unionism and socialist sentiment, which, in turn, threatened to undermine middle-class stability, security, and relative prosperity. Cornelius did not necessarily share Powell's vision of "one world, one people" enlightenment. Indians, like other oppressed minorities and colonized peoples, were being left out of the formula. But Cornelius thought that her industrial-village plan would integrate Native Americans into the American economy yet maintain their particular sense of peoplehood. Her idea seemed to be that people would be more productive if they were free from interference from the outside world of policies and management and from the threat of losing their land to corporate interests.

She looked upon her industrial-village plan as a workable solution to Indian problems because, she said, it was totally in keeping with Native American lifestyles. Like other New Indians, she wanted Native Americans eventually to become independent from what she considered to be the administrative tyranny of the Indian Office. But, unlike many of them, Cornelius felt sure that there should be something to replace the bureau. The tribally run corporation seemed the logical choice, provided that a reservation land base was kept intact. In essence, she opposed the centerpiece of the vanishing policy, the wholesale allotment of Indian lands.

Eleven years after presenting her "industrial village" paper at the first meeting of the Society of American Indians, Cornelius published a book on the subject. Entitled *Our Democracy and the American Indian: A Comprehensive Presentation of the Indian Situation as It Is Today*, the book was an elaboration of the original presentation. The plan, now called the "Lolomi" after a Hopi word, would provide for self-government first and the establishment of industrial communities once the tribes had the power to make contracts and set up locations for the villages. It would be no problem to found these communities, argued Cornelius, because "all Indians understand village organization . . . and want it." She was certain that the idea incorporated the best of both the Indian and white worlds: tribalism with productivity, communalism with capitalism.[46]

Although she was positive that the plan would integrate American Indian manufacturing into the mainstream American economy, she was decidedly vague on what exactly could be produced for the open market. Corporate farming or ranching was an obvious choice, given that all reservations were rural by definition. She became involved in a communal dairy farm project among the Cherokee of northeastern Oklahoma for a time, but the experiment ultimately failed. Her interest in the preservation of Native arts and crafts—and the fact that there was a growing market among whites in the period for these products—gave her, at one point, the idea that the curio industry might be the salvation of some reservations. She was firmly convinced, however, that the solution to Indian problems lay in curing Native American social ills. Economic problems would be solved in the process of revitalizing tribal social structures because, according to Cornelius, "so interdependent are the business and social problems of the Red Man they cannot be separated in his life."[47] If she could cure the latter, the former would simply fall into place.

She recognized not only that tribal societies were complex, but also that tribal knowledge emphasized the interdependence and relationship of family ties with politics, the spiritual with the mundane, and the person with the earth. Indian ways, to her, were the only means of addressing the problems on the reservations, and the Indian Office and the land speculators stood in the path of the application of tribal knowledge in the modern world. She was convinced that the Lolomi plan was the "Indian way" and also the way out of poverty, social ills, and the demoralization caused by the stripping away of all the positive attributes of tribal life. The Lolomi plan emphasized the concepts of group cooperation, shared relationships, balance, and the understanding that there was a natural order in the world. If village life was restored, American Indian pride would soar to new heights, Native American dignity would be reestablished, and the solidarity of Native peoplehood would be attained.

Cornelius believed that the trouble with the vanishing policy lay in its complete disregard for Native American values and knowledge. According to her:

> Of the philanthropists outside the race, who have given themselves to the Cause, and of those of the race who have ardently longed to do something for their own, there did not happen to be one whose experience was that of the race itself. Not one has lived so close to the old days that he could honestly glory in the Red Man's inheritance.[48]

Even though Cornelius was wrong to think that most of her fellow New Indians did not have the experience of tribal life, she rightly saw that many of them had indeed internalized and come to believe in the white man's version of who they were. Although some New Indians like Eastman had indeed experienced tribal life and ultimately believed in syncretism, they more or less accepted that "progress," in the white man's terms, was inevitable. Others, like Montezuma, were convinced that tribal life was, in fact, dead and that its last vestiges seriously impeded Native Americans from taking their rightful place as equals in an ever-changing society.

Cornelius was a syncretist, but one with a different perspective on Native American customs and cultures. "I am not the new Indian," she once said, "I am the old Indian adjusted to new conditions." She valued Native American philosophies, customs and ideals over the notion that the acceptance of Western culture was inevitable and truly progressive.[49] She traveled extensively through Indian country and came to know tribal people well. She wrote plays based on Indian themes and was considered to be a "real daughter of the race."[50] Interestingly, she dedicated *Our Democracy and the American Indian* to Redbird Smith, the Cherokee "irreconcilable" who she said "preserved his people from demoralization and who was the first to accept the Lolomi."[51] In her lectures, she truly gloried in the Oneida people and in the League of the Iroquois, and despite her extensive education in the largely white schools and colleges and her Episcopalian religion, she believed that only when Indians could utilize their own knowledge, gained through centuries of experience, to solve their own problems would they stand on a par with whites.

Although some of the New Indians might not have agreed with Cornelius's open advocacy of tribal socialism, all of them shared her opinion that Native Americans needed the uplifting sense of ethnic pride and accomplishment. To encourage Indian self-respect—and because many of them thought that Native American cultures were rapidly deteriorating—the New Indians, with the possible exception of Carlos Montezuma, favored the preservation—at least in print—of tribal histories, customs, political systems, and philosophies. A number of them encouraged the scientific study of the tribes; several had already formed close ties with the discipline of anthropology; and several had entered the profession itself. The Society of American Indians had a number of Native ethnologists who served on its governing board or as executive officers. Cornelius, although she never received an academic degree, was a noted linguist and a student of Iroquois history. J. N. B.

Hewitt, a Tuscarora who worked for the Bureau of American Ethnology, became a member of the SAI's executive committee in 1912. Another member of the executive committee was Francis LaFlesche, an Omaha whose long collaboration with ethnologist Alice Cunningham Fletcher produced several major studies of Native American cultures. Later, his own work on the Osages would bring LaFlesche great recognition as a competent anthropologist in his own right.[52]

Undoubtedly the Native American anthropologist who had the greatest impact on the direction of the Society of American Indians was Seneca author and museum curator Arthur C. Parker. Already a noted folklorist, Parker was a nephew of the famous Ely S. Parker, the first Native American to hold the office of commissioner of Indian Affairs. He was a strong advocate of Native American unity and an ardent supporter of the formation of the SAI. Significantly, when the society began to publish a quarterly journal, Parker was installed as its editor.[53]

As the editor of the periodical, which was first called simply *The Quarterly Journal of the Society of American Indians* and later changed to *The American Indian Magazine* to give it broader appeal, Parker filled its pages with his own philosophies and observations. Proud of both his white, New England missionary, and Seneca heritages, Parker was convinced that America could indeed become the great melting pot that would blend the virtues of the old world with those of the new. At the same time, however, he thought not only that the noble traits of Indian life were deteriorating, but also that non-Indians viewed Native Americans in the least positive light. To counter white stereotypes, Parker spoke and wrote in glowing terms about Indian achievements and actively supported any group that advocated the learning of Native American philosophies and knowledge. Like Charles Eastman, he looked fondly upon scouting and the conservation groups of the period because they helped perpetuate Native ecological practices. Parker was also dedicated to proving that Indians were the intellectual equals of whites. His editorials were larded with examples of the ways in which tribal philosophies closely corresponded with the mores of white middle-class America.[54]

Not an academically trained anthropologist, although Franz Boas once offered to take him on as a student at Columbia University, Parker was continually intrigued by contemporary anthropological theory. Perhaps because many of his relatives had contributed to Lewis Henry

Morgan's studies of the Iroquois Confederacy, Parker was drawn to Morgan's social evolutionist interpretation of the development of culture and away from the Boas school of cultural determinism. He accepted Morgan's idea that all societies underwent substantial and continuous change and progressively moved from primitivism to higher forms of civilization in small, incremental steps. Very likely, Parker preferred Morgan's ideas because he thought of himself as a thoroughly progressive, competent human being who happened to be racially native to North America and linked to the same "natural" processes of evolution that whites had gone through. In any case, Parker thought that Native Americans should remember their histories with pride and rejoice in modern Native American achievement. To that end, he urged Indians to "avail themselves of every bit of business training they can get" so that they could adapt to and compete in an increasingly complex world of industrialized societies. According to Parker, only after becoming competitive and well adapted to American civilization should Indians be allowed to "parade in buckskin and plumes." Learn the white ways first, he admonished, then Indians could be "Indian."[55]

Parker was markedly ambiguous concerning the preservation of tribal lifeways. On the one hand, he could lament the passing of some worthwhile aspects of tribal societies as a result of the introduction of the ceremonies associated with the peyote sacrament. "More than all the labors of the missionaries, perhaps," he wrote, "it (peyote) has led to the abandonment of the old native religious customs." On the other hand, in the same issue of the *Quarterly Journal* Parker could justify the destruction of Indian art—a facet of Native American life that was rapidly gaining in popularity among whites—to force Native Americans into American society. He wrote that "many sentimental white men and women" mourned the fact that "the old Indian type is passing away and that his art and craft are being swept away." But such were the consequences of progress. "Would these same good-hearted friends be willing to say," he asked, "that they would like to go back to the days of Queen Elizabeth, or hie back to the time of Chaucer?" Did they believe, Parker continued, "that the loss of simple arts of early England" was "not paid for by modern invention?" The idea that the loss of tribal arts was justified in the quest to modernize Native Americans was, by the time Parker wrote this tract, totally unacceptable to many whites and to most of his colleagues in the SAI.[56]

Parker was trapped in a dilemma that affected many other people, both Indian and white, during the early years of the twentieth century. He was convinced that individualism and the idea of making "individuals" out of Indians were sound philosophies. But individualism as an all-consuming ideal was experiencing a good deal of modification in his era. Several noteworthy whites wrote to Parker urging him to impress upon other Native Americans that citizenship was not merely the gaining of personal liberties. President William Howard Taft, for example, reminded the members of the SAI that citizenship involved "more than benefits to the individual." There were also "obligations and burdens toward the community" that Indians "must recognize and assume." Any plan "for the development of the Indian as an individual must," according to Taft, "include efforts to impress upon him the fact that he must accept the responsibilities if he demands the benefits of citizenship."[57]

These ideas often conflicted with notions of competition and personal liberties, but Parker readily adapted. In 1916 he wrote, "we must demonstrate what the attitude of the individual is to the body of people and prove that Indians in the same proportion as the whites are 'social minded!'"[58] This collectivist attitude was evident in Parker even before the reception of Taft's letter of admonishment. The formation of the SAI itself, Parker believed, was a communal, racial effort to secure basic personal liberties for themselves and aid in the transition of all Native Americans from the old ways to the new. In 1914, he had offered his own definition of civilization and the way in which a person should act in a progressive society. According to Parker, civilization meant "order and the respect of the rights of other men." Ironically, his definition coincided with the shifting values of many white Americans and at the same time captured the essence of what many Native American tribal conservatives defined as basic tribalism. Perhaps Parker merely transferred his own Iroquois social ethos to a larger stage and coincidentally happened to pinpoint the direction that the American middle class was also moving in its reconsideration of individualism.[59]

What Parker often failed to recognize in his role as editor of the SAI's periodical was that the society itself was composed of members as diverse in opinion as any other organization basing its unity solely on race or presumed social status. Carlos Montezuma, although he might have agreed with Parker regarding cultural evolution, was a constant thorn in Parker's side in his editorials for *Wassaja*. Parker's views on Native American arts often ran counter to the predominate idea that they should be carefully preserved, encouraged, and nurtured. Having been a museum curator, perhaps he thought of Indian art as a collection of materials that had been used in the past. To him, arts and crafts certainly could serve as a source of pride and definitely had scientific value, but they had minimal functional use in "modern" culture. In this attitude, Parker was definitely at odds with most members of the SAI and with many of his colleagues in anthropology. Art was tangible evidence that Native American creativity was very much alive, and it demonstrated that spiritually and aesthetically Native Americans had a great deal to contribute to American culture. In essence, the creation of a new Indian identity demanded that a racial ethos be supported by a major contribution to the larger society. Native American art not only became something creative that the New Indians could take great pride in, but also came to symbolize Native American survival in a changing world.

SYMBOLS OF NATIVE AMERICAN RESILIENCY

The Indian Art Movement

A T THE FIRST CONCLAVE of the Society of American Indians in 1911, a Winnebago (Ho-Chunk) woman named Angel DeCora rose to deliver a talk on the need to protect Native American arts from becoming corrupted in the modern commercial market.[1] As much as anyone else at the conference, DeCora was devoted to promoting "race progress," conferring the fundamental rights of American citizenship on Native Americans, and demonstrating that Native people did indeed possess many things that could contribute to the larger society. A skilled painter in her own right, she was also a teacher and the leader of the art program that was developed after Richard Henry Pratt had been removed as superintendent of the Carlisle Indian School. It was as an arts advocate that she found herself in opposition to those at the conference who tended to think that any continuation of the old ways—including the manufacture of traditional arts and crafts—would hinder the full assimilation of Native people into the American mainstream. Fortunately, her case was strong, and she had support from the likes of Charles Eastman and Laura Cornelius. She was also responding to a growing demand among whites for the development of Native American art and following what she believed was the best course to pursue in the cause of "race progress."

DeCora, as an educated, middle-class New Indian, knew that most liberal-minded whites regarded her and her colleagues at the SAI conference as "race leaders" and role models for other Indians and that her essential purpose in American society was to symbolize "Indian progress." At the same time that the New Indians were filling this role, they were also concerned with maintaining their own tribal relationships. They worried about raising the morale of their relatives still on the poverty-stricken reservations, and they knew that their successes in American society could not alone fulfill this function. They, like their reservation relatives, were proud of their heritage, and they realized that bowing to complete assimilation would be a denial of their tribal birthright. Even Carlos Montezuma, who because of his friendship with Pratt believed in full assimilation and often stood in opposition to the "Indian art" movement, would in later life defend the upkeep of the Fort McDowell reservation on the basis that the land was indeed part of the Yavapai right to exist as a distinct people. DeCora, like Eastman and Cornelius, thought that her special mission was to inform whites about the good things in Indian life. DeCora sought to save American society by introducing it to Native American spirituality through the medium of art.

Integration, rather than assimilation, according to those who sided with DeCora in the Indian art movement, would become the real answer to the "Indian Problem." The United States, a newly developing society without long-standing traditions, was open to experimentation and expansion. True to the liberal tradition, DeCora, Cornelius, Eastman, and others believed that Americans, despite their various ethnic backgrounds, could share their different cultures and create a unique, completely new American way of life. As an expression of twentieth-century liberalism, this view was more social and secular in outlook, but it still retained the optimism and the emphasis on change that characterized the previous century's liberal ethos.

The New Indian mission was, therefore, an effort to prove to whites that there were aspects of tribal societies worthy of incorporating into the new American culture. Integration of the kind these New Indians advocated suggested an acceptance of the good in both societies and an automatic mutual respect between the races. An Indian identity would be preserved because the cultures were to be shared rather than blended together. What was originally European and what was originally Native American could be exulted in by everyone. The message was not a glorification of the melting-pot theory of American society. Rather, it was focused on pointing out that much of American culture was actually Native in origin and that there were even more unnoticed, distinctly Indian contributions to come. The New Indians also began to realize what their relatives already knew, that the various aspects of culture were interlocking and interrelated. One could not destroy Native American spirituality without sacrificing the intrinsic spiritual content of Native American art.

Many of the New Indians and their non-Indian supporters had already begun to churn out books and articles about past and potential Indian donations to the betterment and evolution of American society. Readers were informed that much of the food they consumed—corn, tomatoes, beans, squash—was American Indian in origin and that a multitude of Indian words and place names were used in everyday American English. Articles were published about Indian athletic achievements and about Native American spirituality. But as much as the popular press swayed American thought about Indians, the news-papers, magazines, and books also reflected public opinion. The reading public displayed an interest in the Indian image, and soon there appeared in print more information on Native American subjects than had ever been disseminated before.

The list of Native American contributions became extensive, but from the outset both white and Indian writers focused on Native American art as the preeminent tribal gift to American life. There were several reasons for this focus, not the least of which was the production of uniquely Native American artifacts as a present and continuous contribution, and not only for preservation in natural history museums. Indian art was tangible evidence that Native Americans were creative, peaceful, spiritual, aesthetic, and thus worthy of admiration. But most importantly, Native American artwork represented a heritage to glory in rather than be ashamed of. When this fact became universally recognized, according to nearly every writer on the subject, it could serve only to uplift the collective morale of Native Americans everywhere. Art became a symbol of survival as much as a focus of Native American integration.

For most Native American tribes, art was not just a peripheral aesthetic accomplishment of the talented few, but an integral part of the community, shared and produced by many people. Native American men, particularly among the plains tribes, even though deficient in many technical skills, nevertheless covered tipis, buffalo robes, and clothing with paintings representing their exploits in war and hunting. Often these drawings, depicting great swirling battles, gave the Lakota, Kiowa, or Blackfeet viewer a feeling of motion and inspiration. War shields painted with symbols of personal medicine power were utilitarian as well as spiritually inspired. The artist-warrior firmly believed that the symbols on the shields were far more powerful and protective than the rawhide from which the shields were made. Plains women gained status as artists through such media as beadwork, quillwork, and painted designs on buffalo robes.[2]

Art in tribal cultures, as in European societies, also served religious functions. The beautifully carved Hopi kachina dolls helped a priest explain the Hopi way and teach young people about the tribe's sacred history. The simple but elegant Kickapoo prayer sticks, the individual fetishes, and the various Sun Dance dolls were just a few examples of Native American religious art. Akin to these products were the carved masks of the Cherokee, Yaqui, and numerous other tribes. The masks of the Iroquois false face society were used in curing ceremonies. The beautifully and precisely executed Navajo sand paintings were drawn to add to the power of the various healing songs or ceremonies as well. More utilitarian were the ceramics and baskets of the different tribes. Although highly decorative and generally functional, the designs on pots and baskets were often linked with the artist's religious beliefs and represented motifs that illustrated familiar themes in the tribe's religious traditions.[3]

Without doubt the most striking example of the integration of art into tribal societies was among the tribes of the Pacific Northwest. Within the hierarchical social structures of tribes such as the Tlingit, Kwakiutl, and Haida, art validated familial and personal status. The elaborately carved totem poles were much like heraldic crests, tracing the lineage and distinguished heritage of the tribal clans. Painted and carved masks, hats, boxes, and woodwork on houses served to mark a person's position in the tribe. The potlatch, perhaps the most important ceremonial for most of these tribes, prompted a dependence on skilled craftspersons. The artisans who created items for distribution in the potlatch were absolutely essential for families conscious of position and rank.[4]

In addition to the demand for art made necessary by Native American ceremonies and everyday life, whites fostered tribal arts. From almost the first days of European contact, whites began collecting and using Indian arts and crafts. Of course the first Indian-made items of value to the Europeans were those made of precious metals. But the first European settlers also made use of Native American ceramics and basketry to store foodstuffs and water. White soldiers also collected Native American weapons and even clothing, either from battles or from the "hang around the forts" Indians, and decorated their barracks with these trophies.

During the latter half of the nineteenth century, the non-Indian urge to collect the products of Native American manufacture became scientific as well as personal and nostalgic. To most white collectors, Native American handicrafts were the arts of a vanishing people; remnants of a bygone age soon to be lost forever and, therefore, precious and valuable. By 1890 there had developed among anthropologists and dilettantes something of a "furor for Indian curiosities." This urge to collect even prompted Philip C. Garrett, a prominent reformer and member of the Lake Mohonk Conference of Friends of the Indian, to speak out at this bastion of the vanishing policy in favor of fostering the continued production of Yuma pottery as a possible method of educational and economic improvement for the tribe.[5] The interest in collecting Indian artifacts greatly affected the consensus at Lake Mohonk. Thoroughly imbued with the old adage that "idle hands are the devil's workshop," the men and women who attended the conferences had been searching to find a way to keep the government's Native American charges gainfully and busily employed. In 1894 the conference welcomed the suggestion that an Indian Industries League be founded in order to "build up self-supporting industries in Indian communities."[6]

The suggested industries at first largely centered on the idea of setting Native American women to work producing items that the reformers thought would reflect Indian progress in civilization and would at the same time be marketable in white society. They immediately set out to establish lace-making factories on various reservations. By 1897, however, Albert Smiley, a member of the Board of Commissioners for Indian Affairs and founder of the Lake Mohonk Conference, agreed to provide financial support for other industries and stipulated that aid would be given to Native American crafts such as ceramics and basket weaving. The next year the Conference provided $1,200 to establish the Lake Mohonk Lodge at Colony, Oklahoma, for "industrial work." But instead of making lace or weaving baskets, the Cheyenne and Arapaho women in Colony worked at their native art of beadwork. Fostering native crafts among Native Americans certainly belied the theory that in order to assimilate Indians into mainstream society their cultures must first be destroyed and that they must lose any and all facets of a tribal identity. In spite of their deepest beliefs to the contrary, the old reformers and numerous other whites had to admit that there was something of real value in Native American cultures.[7]

Not only that, but the very idea of developing Indian industries in Native American communities suggested that certain vanishing-policy ideologues were thinking in terms of tribal, as opposed to individual, economic uplift. This "corporate" model of American Indian development, which was first outlined by the Oneida activist Laura Cornelius, in fact contradicted the vanishing policy, the underlying assumption of which focused on the "transformation" and "Americanization" of Indians into atomized individuals and essentially doing away with tribes as social, political, and economic entities. Although they studiously avoided using the terms "tribe" and "tribal" when speaking of the development of Indian industrial cooperatives, proponents of the corporate model were clearly thinking of Native American communities as aggregate bodies. Given the age and the then-positive views of industrial growth, it would be a very short step from thinking of Indian tribes as corporations to thinking of Indian tribes as polities once again.

Therein lay the contradictions of the vanishing policy. In a market economy, manufacturers fashion the items that they have the ability to produce and for which there is a demand. Setting Indian women to work making lace was a doomed project in the first place. Although they made lace of high quality, these Native American women were placed in competition with large, well-financed lace producers. Demand for Indian-made lace was probably no higher than what white manufacturers could produce. The fact that Native American hands produced it may have increased its marketability; but whoever made it, lace was still lace—a product that could be made by anyone with the correct skills. The Cheyenne and Arapaho women, however, had the remarkable and unique ability to produce very beautiful beadwork distinctly their own, for which there was a growing demand.

To organize production and market Indian handicrafts, there had to be a corporate base. Ultimately, the Lake Mohonk Lodge in Colony served as a Cheyenne-Arapaho "industrial village" such as the ones

Laura Cornelius later advocated. In forming the Indian Industries League, the Lake Mohonk Conference essentially subverted its own cause. Indians and their tribal identities could not simply vanish; the demand for their continued existence both as individuals and as groups of people producing something for white consumption was becoming too great for them to be dismissed as being simply "backward" and doomed to extinction.

Actually the first Native American handicrafts to gain widespread popular acclaim were the blankets and ceramics of the Navajo and Pueblo peoples of the southwestern United States. Candace Wheeler of New York City, who was introduced to the Lake Mohonk Conference in 1901 as "the foremost authority in this country as to what is worth perpetuating in Indian art," stated categorically before the assembly that Navajo blanket weaving represented "the best weaving that has ever been done in the world."[8] A year later, George Warton James, outdoorsman, conservationist, and writer, was no less enthusiastic in his praise for Navajo weaving in an article published in the influential conservationist magazine, *Outing*.[9] The poet Edwin L. Sabin wrote an ode in tribute to Navajo weaving entitled "Indian Weaver" that was published in 1908 in *Craftsman*, another outdoor periodical of the era. Reprinted under the title "The Navajo Blanket," the poem also appeared in the Carlisle Indian School publication *The Red Man* two years later.[10] By 1911, George Warton James, continuing his studies of Native American life in natural settings, had compiled an entire book on Indian weaving that included a chapter on "Reliable Dealers in Navaho Blankets."[11]

Native American pottery, basketry, and beadwork similarly drew praise as works of great beauty and utility. It was during the period from 1900 to 1925 that the Pueblo potters of San Ildefonso, Acoma, and Taos were first recognized for their artistry in ceramics. The world-famous Maria Martinez of San Ildefonso began her work during this period.[12] In 1903 the widely recognized art magazine *International Studio* praised the expressionism captured in the symbols woven into Native-made baskets and reproduced several photographs of Native American basketry to support its contentions and to serve as examples of the quality of these items of Indian craftsmanship.[13]

The beadwork produced in the Lake Mohonk Lodge at Colony, started at the behest of the Lake Mohonk reformers, was admittedly meant to be sold to white collectors of Indian curios. Yet according to Mrs. F. N. Doubleday of New York, a collector of Indian art, it still "retained the old symbolism and artistic value."[14] The popularity of the beadwork industry had become so great by 1903 that the *Ladies' Home Journal* offered tips to its readers on the selection of beaded material for collections.[15] In 1919 the renowned ethnologist Clark Wissler published a general-interest book on beadwork that, according to its subtitle, would provide "A Help for Students of Design."[16] Even Native American–made birchbark canoes were applauded as "almost deserving to be put under glass as specimens of absolute symmetry of form."[17]

Without doubt some of the impetus for collecting Native American arts and crafts grew from the widespread notion that Native Americans were vanishing. Thus, objects of Native manufacture may have been thought of as artistic investments that would become more valuable as time went on and the Native American population, especially the numbers of Native artists, diminished to the point of extinction. On the other hand, as demand grew, so did production, causing collectors and "New Indians" such as Angel DeCora and Charles Eastman to worry about the effects of commercialism on the quality of Native American crafts. Essentially they feared that production shortcuts and the demands of white consumers for particular designs might lead to the "corruption" of "old" styles, symbols, and artisanship. Care and creativity, in short, might be sacrificed to increased production.

This concern spilled over into the question of whether Native American manufactures should be considered art or craft. Popular as they became and aesthetically pleasing as they were, ceramics, basketry, and blankets served practical, utilitarian functions. For that matter, so did the symmetrical Indian canoe. From the standpoint of most white collectors of "Indian curios," a craft was essentially learned and could be passed on from generation to generation without innovation or real creativity. Art, as most Americans thought of it, was the individual, creative expression of insight and intuitive talent. The question of whether or not a Native American craft could evolve into "true" art without losing its "traditional" character arose time and again during the first twenty years of—and later in—the twentieth century. The debate concerning art and crafts often undermined the artistic influence and critical recognition of some Native American artists. On the other hand, Native artists like Maria Martinez and her husband Julian seem to have resolved the question by 1919, when they created, and were duly recognized for, a new style of highly polished blackware pottery.[18] Native Americans could be both: highly skilled technical craftspersons and gifted, innovative artists.

A variety of complex reasons led to the public recognition of Native American art. The technological boom of the nineteenth and early twentieth centuries increased the mobility of more and more Americans. The railroad and, a bit later, the automobile encouraged Americans to travel as long as they had the financial means to do so. At the same time, an increasing number of Americans, nostalgic for the idealized frontier life they believed their forefathers had led and seeking the benefits of a more healthful climate, decided to explore the countryside, away from the dreary confines of the urban areas. As a result, tourism, particularly in the western United States, burgeoned. The tourists especially came to the Southwest. There they could view the last of the frontier, visit some of the newly created national parks, and gaze upon the ancient ruins of Mesa Verde, Casa Grande, and other restored archaeological sites.

To profit from this influx of relatively well-off Americans, the Achison, Topeka and Santa Fe Railroad and the Fred Harvey Company actively promoted the American pursuit of beauty, health, conservation, and history. These two corporations pioneered tourism in the western states and created the popular image of the American southwest as a place of great charm, colorful cultures, and historic and natural monuments. In the 1870s Frederick Henry Harvey reached an agreement with the Santa Fe line under which he established a series of restaurants along the route. At these rest stops, travelers could enjoy a moderately priced meal served by the "Harvey Girls"—all well-dressed, pleasant young women imported from the eastern seaboard. The Harvey Company and the Santa Fe Railroad prospered as result of this business relationship. Railroad travel in the west became less arduous and tiresome because passengers could expect a touch of sophistication at a Harvey rest stop.[19]

As travel in the west increased, the Harvey Company enlarged its operations and branched out into the hotel business. To an era accustomed to opulent and ostentatious hotels in cities and nondescript rooming houses in rural areas, the new Fred Harvey Hotels were wonders of design and utility. Not only did they invoke the rustic charm of the "old frontier," but they also exploited the Spanish, Mexican, and Native American heritage of the Old Southwest.

In addition to the partnership with the Santa Fe line, the Harvey Company sought an alliance with Don Lorenzo Hubbell, the leading dealer in Navajo blankets. A longtime trader on the Navajo reservation, Hubbell supplied the Harvey hotels with items of Native American manufacture for decoration and, of course, for sale. By the early 1900s, the Harvey Company and the Santa Fe Railroad began to employ their own Native American craftspersons and artists with the aid of the Indian Office and opened curio shops directly adjacent to the hotels and restaurants. Living conditions for Harvey-employed artisans, however, were said to be meager, but the Indian Office could and often did brag about increasing employment for Native Americans. At a Fred Harvey Inn, travelers to the Southwest could now enjoy beautiful surroundings, dine on good food, and purchase souvenirs of their trip. The chief items purchased were Native American baskets and pottery and fine specimens of Navajo weaving.[20]

Navajo blankets were in great demand for both private and public display. As early as the 1850s the Navajos had been encouraged to develop their sheep herds for the woolens industry. In the 1870s Indian agents introduced looms and spinning wheels onto Navajo reservations and urged Navajo weavers to increase the production of blankets, then made on handlooms, for trade and sale. By the 1890s the traders had introduced new dyes and some new production methods to meet the demands of the growing market in Navajo blankets. The Fred Harvey Company and the Hubbell Trading Post, however, worked to prevent Navajo rug and blanket weaving from losing artistic merit and distinctly Navajo identity. Both companies insisted that the blankets for the tourist trade be of the best quality and be kept well within the boundaries of traditional Navajo design. Because they had the capital, these companies could afford to pay the higher prices that handloomed weaving and the best wool and dyes cost. They could absorb overproduction and inferior-quality weaving for a secondary trade. The increased costs were simply passed along to the well-heeled tourist. If the Navajo weaver suffered in poverty, the quality of her weaving did not.[21]

Among the most noteworthy admirers of Navajo weaving was President Theodore Roosevelt. Several rugs from his large collection, brought back from numerous visits to the West, adorned the walls of his residences. After viewing the International Exhibition of Modern Art in 1913—the "Armory Show" that introduced Americans to the European modernists—Roosevelt declared Navajo weaving to be superior in design to Cubist painting. According to the former president, a Navajo rug "in my bath-room" was far more satisfactory and decorative than several paintings at the exhibition, according to " any proper interpretation of the Cubist theory." From "the standpoint of decorative value, of sincerity, and of artistic merit," the former president continued, "the Navajo rug is infinitely ahead of the picture" entitled "Naked Man Going Down Stairs"—the Cubist painting by Marcel Duchamp usually known as "Nude Descending a Staircase."[22]

The interest shown in Navajo weaving and in Pueblo pottery and basketry was substantial, but the most unexpected and dramatic development to come out of the rage for Native American arts and crafts was the rise in importance of Native American painting. In the closing years of the nineteenth century, Native American painters were generally unknown and unrecognized as artists. During the first three decades of the twentieth century, however, there developed at least three different stylistic schools of Indian painting. Native American art began to be taught at Carlisle Indian School, and Indian painters finally had their works displayed in museums and art shows. Moreover, Native American paintings were shown not as museum pieces, but as examples of a vibrant, creative, and attractive force in Native American life.

One of the first steps in the development of Native American painting styles came, ironically enough, from the federal prison for hostile Native leaders and their followers that was established at Fort Marion, Florida. Even more ironic, perhaps, was the fact that the warden at the prison was none other than Richard Henry Pratt, who would become the superintendent of Carlisle Indian School and who would oppose the further development of Native American art as a hindrance to Indian assimilation. In addition to teaching his old enemies in the wars on the southern plains the ways of the whites, then Captain Pratt allowed his charges to draw and paint scenes from their former lives as hunters and warriors. Pratt thought that painting would be a way of keeping his prisoners occupied and that it would also serve as a form of recreation. Painting became a minor source of income when several of the inmates' paintings were sold to some of the Fort Marion guards and to regular visitors to the prison who collected them as curiosities. Pratt thought that this give-and-take would build good relations between whites and the imprisoned chiefs and would teach the Native Americans that their labors could bear fruit in a free market. Pratt's object lesson in capitalism at least allowed his prisoners a certain amount of creative license and spiritual expression.[23]

At first the drawings from Fort Marion were much like the skin paintings traditionally done among the peoples of the southern plains. As the prisoners' periods of confinement wore on, the more talented of the artists learned new techniques and began to work with themes that evoked considerably different feelings from those expressed in their earlier paintings and drawings. Instead of recording events and exploits on buffalo hides as they and their ancestors had done when living as free and autonomous peoples, the Fort Marion prisoners of war began to experiment with self-expression with paint and ink on paper and canvas.

One of the finest examples of the limited spiritual and creative freedom that Pratt allowed the prisoners in their art came from the pen of a Kiowa inmate named Wohaw. Done in 1877, the drawing depicted a Native American man standing between two cultures—his own and that of the white man. Wohaw drew symbols of sustenance for both cultures flanking the man's figure. On the subject's right the artist drew a buffalo and on the left, a steer. In the man's extended hands he holds two sacred pipes in offering to the two animals, which envelop his figure with words. Near the figure's right foot, in miniature, is a tipi surrounded by a buffalo herd, while at his left foot lie cultivated fields and a frame farmhouse. He rests his left foot on the cultivated field, symbolically taking a step toward a different life.

Although nostalgic for the life he knew and loved, and still recognizing its intrinsic harmony with nature, Wohaw was forced to change his view of the future. The painting demonstrated with exactness Wohaw's own inner conflicts and his understanding of what whites wanted of him. At the same time, it captured the idea that he, as a hunter, could still communicate on a spiritual level with both symbolic animals. Wohaw certainly knew who he was; but he also recognized, in keeping with his own tribal knowledge, that like birth and death, the world of human beings experiences a continual cycle of often painful change. Although taking on a new way of surviving in the world, Wohaw remained Kiowa to the core.[24]

Wohaw was not the only artist of note imprisoned at Fort Marion

Among the others were Zotom, a Kiowa; Squint Eyes, who later aided ethnologists at the Smithsonian Institution; and Cohoe and Howling Wolf, both Cheyenne. Although some drawings and paintings were technically weak, they accurately expressed their creators' moods, desires, convictions, and conflicts, and in that sense they attained true value from any artistic standpoint. Ranging from the melancholy to the nostalgic to the comic, the art from Fort Marion marked a transition in Native American painting from the old forms to new expressions without any loss of tribal cultural identity.[25]

Pratt did not take his limited tolerance for Native American artistic freedom from Fort Marion to Carlisle Indian School. Under the enigmatic yet resolute army captain, Carlisle was primarily dedicated to providing manual training with practical application in the white world. Art, particularly that which had an Indian identity attached to it, hardly conformed to Pratt's vision of the future for Native Americans and certainly not to his views of Indian education. A staunch assimilationist, Pratt wanted to provide Native American youths with an education that would either help them obtain employment in white businesses or enable them to run their own farms. Pratt saw his graduates as future missionaries of the philosophical underpinnings of the vanishing policy. They would return to their reservations to prepare their fellow tribal members for entrance into mainstream American society. To Pratt, Carlisle was an introduction to white society and a place where Indians could "get into the swim" of American citizenship.[26]

When Pratt was dismissed from his position as director of Carlisle in 1904 because of his bitter antagonism toward the Indian Office, the school became slightly more liberal toward Native American art. Moses Friedman, the new head of the school, hired two Native American artists to teach "Indian" crafts to interested students. The pair, Angel DeCora and her husband William Dietz, who was also known as Lone Star, gave instruction in metalwork, weaving, and especially painting.[27] For the most part, the couple emphasized design and decorative art. In keeping with Pratt's ideas, however, DeCora wanted to maintain the practical side of Indian industrial training. She was primarily interested in reproducing, with some innovation, the designs found in beadwork, patchwork garments, and quill appliqué from traditional societies, done primarily by women. These designs were emphasized over typically male-produced representational art.[28]

Like Pratt, and in accordance with the ideas of most of her fellow New Indians, DeCora firmly believed that Native Americans should be able to make their own way in the world. As a result of her own interests and her decidedly favorable view of practical education, she directed her youthful Carlisle art students toward commercial ventures. During her presentation at the first meeting of the Society of American Indians in 1911, she reported that the director of the Pennsylvania School of Industrial Art in Philadelphia had offered his assistance in her effort to apply Carlisle designs to "modern house furnishing." DeCora further indicated that through "careful study and close application many hundred designs have been evolved." Moreover, she added that Indian art promised to "be of great value in a country which heretofore has been obliged to draw its models from the countries of the eastern hemisphere."[29]

DeCora was a fine painter in her own right. She was born in 1871 and entered a reservation school probably in 1878. She had been enrolled in the school for only a few days when she and six other children were abducted by a "strange white man," taken on a wagon ride to the nearest railroad station, placed on a train, and transported to the Hampton Institute. She studied at Hampton for three years before returning to her family. She returned to Hampton, graduated, and entered Burnham Classical School for Girls in Northampton, Massachusetts. From Burnham she enrolled in the art department at Smith College and received a custodianship of the institution's art gallery. Over the next several years, DeCora studied illustration at the Drexel Institute in Philadelphia, the Cowles Art School in Boston, and that city's Museum of Fine Arts.

She opened a studio in Boston, but gave it up and moved to New York. Despite her vast study, she felt that it was "well that I had not over studied the prescribed methods of European decoration, for then my aboriginal qualities could never have asserted themselves." In 1906, she was appointed to teach art at Carlisle in order, in her words, "to foster the native talents of the Indian students there." At Carlisle she devoted herself to nurturing what she considered to be intuitive in Native Americans. "There is no doubt," she wrote, "that the young Indian has a talent for the pictorial art, and the Indian's artistic conception is well worth recognition."[30]

Throughout her career at Carlisle she set aside her own artistic aspirations in favor of her students' and concentrated her efforts on design. She also illustrated Francis LaFlesche's *The Middle Five* and Zitkala Sa's *Old Indian Legends*. One of her most important and poignant paintings— untitled— portrayed a boy in Native dress sitting on a bench with his left arm thrown over his eyes in obvious distress over the fact of being sent to a boarding school. In the painting another young man in the dark uniform of the boarding school, complete with kepi, is reaching out to the young boy with tenderness and sympathy. The painting no doubt reflected DeCora's own anguish, fear, and grief at being sent, without the knowledge of her parents, to Hampton years before.

DeCora, along with her husband, Lone Star, who served Carlisle as an assistant football coach as well as an art teacher, gained a good deal of recognition through their students. One of their students, Moses Stranger Horse, became well known among connoisseurs and collectors of Native American painting and western Americana. A Lakota from South Dakota, Stranger Horse returned to his home after graduating from Carlisle and soon entered military service. He was one of the many Native Americans who fought in France with the American Expeditionary Force during World War I. After the war, Stranger Horse remained in Paris, along with several other American expatriates, to study art. Dissatisfied with Europe and longing to reproduce on canvas the beauty of the land he knew as a child and young man, Stranger Horse returned to the United States. Once back on his home territory, Stranger Horse produced a number of fine paintings that reflected the style of the western artist. Most of his subjects were, like himself, Native American ranch hands and cowboys who worked for the western cattle industry.[31]

In 1912, a writer from *Literary Digest* approached Stranger Horse's mentors, DeCora and Lone Star Dietz, to record their commentary on the subject of Indians in the white man's world of art. The writer was especially interested in how much western painters, such as Charles Russell and Frederick Remington, had misrepresented Indian life. Native American criticism of one of America's most cherished art genres was unheard of at the time, but the fact that DeCora and Dietz were asked to comment on art of any kind reflected a growing respect for Native American artistic insight.[32]

DeCora and Dietz were a brilliant and eccentric couple who

enjoyed a wide range of sporting activities and raised a large pack of Russian wolfhounds. Together they collaborated on producing the art-work for the covers of the Carlisle Indian School publications as well as fostering the artistic talents of their Native students. Dietz was the son of a white trader and Indian Office agent and a Lakota mother from the Pine Ridge reservation. His father, who had become quite wealthy, evidently impregnated his mother, but did not marry her, and left the reservation when Lone Star was between two and three years old. Dietz's father returned after a five-year sojourn in the eastern United States and reclaimed the boy, who was then named *Wicarhpi Isnala*. The father named him William Henry Dietz and called him Lone Star, supposedly the English rendering of the boy's Lakota name. Lone Star's father married an old sweetheart and shipped Lone Star to various schools.

After graduating from high school, Lone Star went to visit his mother and sister on the reservation but returned to college and art school. He worked as a staff artist for various newspapers, and in 1904 supervised the interior and mural decorations of the Native American exhibit at the Louisiana Purchase Exposition in St. Louis. There he met Angel DeCora. In 1908 she hired him as her assistant at Carlisle, and they were soon married.[33] He was also taken on as assistant to Carlisle football coach Pop Warner.

In 1914 football gained precedence over art in Lone Star's life, and he accepted the head coach position at Washington State Agricultural College. Angel went with him for a time, but divorced him and returned to Carlisle where she maintained a residence but had no con-nection with the school. She returned to her art, but her life was tragi-cally cut short in 1920 by influenza, perhaps a remnant of the great pandemic of 1918–1919.[34] Lone Star gained a great reputation as a foot-ball coach and was later inducted into Pennsylvania Sports Hall of Fame.

Both DeCora and Dietz emphasized the notion that Native Amer-ican art was the expression of a spiritual connection with the natural setting. According to E. L. Martin, in an article about the couple for the Carlisle publication, *The Red Man*, they were "themselves students of nature, which the real artist must ever continue to be." For the most part, non-Indian artists "have not seen the Indian soul speaking in the Indian face" because they have not lived in harmony with the natural world of the Native peoples. Native American artists, on the other hand, capture the spirit of the natural setting because, according to Martin, they "have learned to look at nature with an artist's eye." And, as Dietz stated, "of all things the Indian has been, he has first of all been an artist." [35]

Although DeCora and Dietz were never very complimentary toward most of the white artists who painted Indian subjects, they were willing to pay tribute to the famous painter of western Americana, Charles Russell.[36] The couple, in fact, thought that Russell's work represented both a realism lost to most white painters and an understanding of Native American cultures known to only a few people other than Native Americans themselves. Russell's understanding, they acknowledged, came firsthand. He lived in the West and knew several of the older tribal leaders, whom he interviewed on occasion in order to obtain details about tribal dress, weapons, and horsemanship. In addition, Russell worked with and influenced the careers of at least two rising Native American artists.

Myles Horn, an Arikara originally from Fort Berthold, North Dakota, first expressed an interest in art while attending the Wahpeton Indian School in South Dakota. In 1915, at the age of twenty-one, Horn met Russell and began a long and productive career in painting. The association between the two artists was mutually beneficial. Russell gave Horn instruction in the use of color, composition, and technical drawing. At the same time, the Arikara artist taught Russell about the ceremonies and customs of the plains tribes and put Russell in contact with several tribal elders.[37]

Russell also aided the career of Hart Merriam Schultz, a Blackfeet from Montana. Schultz, with the western artist's blessing and after a considerable amount of instruction from him, studied at the Los Angeles Institute of Art. In 1922, Schultz was asked to give an individual presentation of his work in New York. Schultz's show was well received and marked a breakthrough for Native American painting in America's cosmopolitan center. Like Russell, both Horn and Schultz painted primarily in the western Americana genre, a type of art that was rapidly becoming popular in the United States because of its distinctly nationalist overtones.[38]

Stranger Horse, Horn, and Schultz dealt with a subject matter that was, even in that period, of questionable Native American identity. Primarily they concerned themselves with reflecting Indian life as it appeared to them at the time. Native American countenances were depicted under the broad brims of western headgear, and Indian cowboys rode bucking horses in the same manner and with the same equipment as white American cowboys. What they represented was Native American life in a state of change. Consequently, their work was considered by some observers as not truly "Indian" in the sense that it failed to depict whites' preconceived images of Native American tribal life. Stereotypes still pervaded American thought, artistic or otherwise, and not to paint images associated with a presumed Native American past was viewed as being non-Indian. What may be said about the works of Stranger Horse, Horn, and Schultz is that their art reflected not only the changes that were occurring in Native American life, but also its growing dependency on white ways. In that sense, they were capturing Native American life after it had lost its freedom. Nevertheless, Stranger Horse, Horn, and Schultz were given critical recognition for their presentations of western themes and for their technical skill.

Another form of Native American painting, the Indianness of which was never called into question, emerged in Arizona and New Mexico. Anthropological interest, although somewhat lacking at first in artistic sensitivity, accounted for the resurgence of Native American painting in the American Southwest. During the late 1890s, J. Walter Fewkes, an ethnologist working with the Bureau of American Ethnology of the Smithsonian Institution, hired several Hopi men to draw accurately their ceremonial kachina figures. In most Pueblo societies, male children were initiated at an early age into one of the various kivas of the tribal religious order. Each kiva taught the initiate about the spirits sacred to the tribe through the use of intricately carved dolls. Interested in the ceremonial function of these kachina figures, Fewkes supplied the tribal artists with all the materials for the work, and by 1900 he had collected over two hundred drawings. Most of the artists took very traditional views of their work for Fewkes. It was well within Hopi tradition to fashion the figures for instructional purposes, and drawings of them would not have been considered sacrilegious.[39]

In 1903 the Smithsonian Institution published Fewkes' collection under the title "Hopi Katchinas, Drawn by Native Artists," in the Bureau of American Ethnology's annual report. As an ethnologist, Fewkes was interested primarily in the religious activities of the Hopi and in gathering other anthropological data, rather than in artistic accomplishment. The drawings, as a result, were detailed, but lacking in personal expression. Fewkes did, however, stimulate further interest in the "scientific" implications of ethnic art, especially as it was involved in religious practice.[40]

In 1902 another anthropologist, Kenneth Chapman, perhaps borrowing the idea from Fewkes, began to seek out Navajo artists in an effort to collect drawings of ceremonial sand paintings. Sand painting may have originated among the Pueblo peoples, but the Navajo medicine men and women had elaborated its practice and enhanced its beauty and meaning. Artists sprinkled dry pigments by hand to create large pictorials of tribal deities and sacred symbols. Most often the paintings were used in curing ceremonials. Because of the materials were ephemeral and because curing the illness required the images to be destroyed, the paintings were only temporary creations.[41]

Chapman was initially frustrated in his search because Navajo sand painting, unlike kachinas, did not carry instructional connotations. For several reasons, medicine men and women were considerably more reluctant to make drawings of their ceremonial art than were the Hopis. The sand paintings were to be executed only in conjunction with songs, specialized motions, and particular prayers. If formed without these special rituals, the sand paintings could lose their power for curing.

Finally, Chapman discovered an artist who, though unwilling to commit sacrilege by detailing the sand paintings, was ready at least to commit to paper some scenes of Navajo cosmology. The artist, Apie Begay, was to become the father of modern Navajo painting. Much to Begay's astonishment and pleasure, Chapman supplied a wide range of colors and materials for his drawings. After Begay submitted several drawings, Chapman became something of a patron to several other Navajo artists and, unlike Fewkes, seemed more interested in the artistic value of the drawings he commissioned.[42]

Edgar L. Hewitt was still another anthropologist who actively fostered the development of Indian painting in the Southwest. A former professor at the University of Southern California and chairman of the department of anthropology at the University of New Mexico, from 1905 to 1915 Hewitt sponsored several Native American artists who later became well known in eastern art circles. As director of the

School of American Research at the Museum of New Mexico, he financially aided the careers of Awa Tsireh, Fred Kobotie, Ma Pe Wi, and Crescencio Martinez, all Pueblo and Hopi Indians who would later have their paintings displayed at the annual exhibition of the Society of Independent Artists held in 1920 at the Waldorf-Astoria Hotel in New York. Hewitt was decidedly interested in art for art's sake and not, like Fewkes or, to a lesser extent, Chapman, concerned with ceremonial secrets.[43]

Representation of Native American painting at the Waldorf art show was the result of growing enthusiasm in the East for the pristine quality of Indian art. The year before the show, a group of concerned artists and patrons of the arts proposed that the Metropolitan Museum of Art organize "a great exhibition of Indian art." Museum officials and other perhaps less enthusiastic patrons of the museum evidently thought of Indian art as being more an ethnological or archaeological subject, and therefore a concern of the Museum of Natural History or the Heye Foundation's recently established Museum of the American Indian. The Museum of Natural History's displays and later the Heye Foundation's continuing exhibitions focused on older or at least more traditional art forms. Dissatisfaction with these museum showings prompted the effort to have Native American painting presented at the Waldorf show in order to place "more emphasis on the work of to-day."[44]

The agitation for an exhibition of Native American art was indicative of the recognition that southwestern Indian painting had already gained. Immediately before the Waldorf show, Walter Pach, a founder of the Society of Independent Artists, writing for *Dial* magazine, stated that Kobotie's and Ma Pe Wi's paintings were "primitive . . . in the true sense of the word . . . their form and content deriving from an immediate response to the scenes they depict." Very few white artists, according to Pach, had been able to achieve the level of expression that these two painters were already attaining in their medium. Pach was positively flowery in his praise for these "untaught young Indians."[45] By 1925, these painters had indeed achieved widespread critical acclaim. The *New York Times*, for example, singled out Awa Tsireh's work and stated that "his drawings are, in their own field, as precise and sophisticated as a Persian miniature."[46] Native American painting, in short, had become a "field," and the individual contributors to it were being hailed, finally, as very real artists rather than as pure craftsmen.

By the time of the Waldorf show, southwest Native American painting had already reached Europe. Elizabeth Richards, a teacher at San Ildefonso Pueblo, allowed her students a good deal more latitude in artistic expression than was usual at other Indian schools of the time. Richards, because she had observed San Ildefonso potters at work, firmly believed that her pupils had a heritage of beautiful decorative art. Consequently she urged her students to utilize their heritage and pick their own topics for art class. Richards sent the pictures she considered the best artistic compositions abroad in 1911. Her efforts produced a small but expanding clique of Europeans very much concerned with the preservation and development of Native American painting.[47]

Richards was not, however, the only teacher in Indian schools to allow her students a degree of artistic license in the classroom or to search for further instruction and recognition for her pupils' work. Susie Ryan Peters of Anadarko, Oklahoma, who began working with Kiowa students in 1916, provided the impetus to a revitalization of painting by southern plains Indians. Peters displayed a marked interest in the development of the artistic skills of several of her young Kiowa charges and used her own funds to hire teachers to give art instruction to some she considered her most able students. As a consequence, Monroe Tsatoke, Stephen Mopope, Spencer Asah, James Auchiah, and Jack Hokeah were included in these private art classes. As their talent developed, Peters sought more and better instruction for these five outstanding students. In 1927 she was able to enroll them in the University of Oklahoma's art program under the supervision of Oscar B. Jacobson. Tsatoke, Mopope, Asah, Auchiah, and Hokeah were recognized by the late 1920s as a dominant school of Native American painting and had become almost an institution in themselves, being known as the "Five Kiowas."[48]

There were some interesting, though tenuous, connections between the "Five Kiowa" school and the earlier Fort Marion artists. Most of the prisoners at Fort Marion under Pratt were members of the southern plains tribes that became relocated permanently to reservations in Oklahoma. Consequently, after their eventual release from prison several of them made their homes in the same area where Tsatoke, Mopope, Asah, Auchiah, and Hokeah grew up. Some of the youthful Kiowa painters with whom Peters was associated were descendents of or related to the Fort Marion prisoners. Wohaw, for example, was related by marriage to the Tsatoke family. Although it is doubtful that the Fort Marion artists had any direct influence on the Five Kiowas, both groups drew upon the same pictorial traditions. Like the Fort Marion prisoners, the Five Kiowas produced compositions that were nostalgic, highly stylized, and symbolic. Using flat colors, no shading, and the flowing forms taught to them by Jacobson, who was interested in art nouveau, the Five Kiowas' paintings were decorative as well as representational. Tsatoke, Mopope, Asah, Auchiah, and Hokeah basically used the same subject matter as the Fort Marion artists, including mounted warriors, traditional dancers, and scenes of buffalo hunting. They had, however, a great deal more technical training and acquired skill.[49]

The Kiowa school was very influential in the development of Native American painting in general. In 1928 Jacobson, the Five Kiowas' instructor at the University of Oklahoma, arranged for some of their paintings to be shown at the International Folk Art Exhibition in Prague, Czechoslovakia. Later, he published a portfolio of his students' work. This volume was one of the earliest books to deal specifically with the emergence of Native American painting as a particular genre. The Kiowa school was copied and modified, and southwest Native American painters, who had actually gained their reputations before the rise of the Five Kiowas, even recognized the value and influence of its decorative, free-flowing style.[50]

The respect with which whites were beginning to demonstrate for Native American art and artists in the first decades of the twentieth century was not limited to the mediums of weaving, basketry, ceramics, or painting. Much to the dismay of the advocates of the vanishing policy, who strongly supported the abandonment of tribal ceremonialism, a great deal of white interest began to focus on the "heathenish rites" of Native American dance and music. As with painting, white Americans first took notice of Indian music out of ethnological curiosity. In fact, a member of the Lake Mohonk Conference, Alice C. Fletcher, who actually took part in the breakup and parceling out of Indian lands under the General Allotment Act, spent a great part of her career as an anthropologist recording tribal songs, thereby assuring their partial survival.

As a scientist, Fletcher was a member of the Morganian cultural-evolutionist school of thought. From her viewpoint, Indians were an evolving race just emerging from the depths of primitivism to modern civilization. There was no doubt in her mind that Indian tribal cultures were doomed to extinction. In fact, she willingly abetted the movement to assimilate Native Americans and declared often enough that her work as an ethnologist had practical application to the allotment of the Omaha, Winnebago, and Nez Percé reservations in accordance with the Dawes Act. Her concern with Indian music was purely academic. It was an effort on her part to record for posterity the folkways of peoples she presumed to be doomed anyway.[51]

Fletcher was welcomed at the Lake Mohonk Conferences of Friends of the Indian precisely because she shared the views of the founder, Albert K. Smiley, and because she gave the vanishing policy scientific validation. From 1891 until her death, she was the recipient of a fellowship funded through Harvard University in memory of Mary Copley Thaw. Thus she was able to pursue a career free from academic responsibilities and relatively untouched by the growing dissension within her chosen profession during the first twenty or so years of the twentieth century. Early in her studies she became acquainted with Francis LaFlesche, an Omaha who would become an ethnologist in his own right and a prominent member of the Society of American Indians. She utilized LaFlesche first as an informant and interpreter. Later she and LaFlesche worked together as coauthors. In the 1890s, she legally adopted him as her son, and when she died, she left to him her substantial estate. Because of her early work with allotment, the old reformers at Lake Mohonk knew her well and looked to her as an authority on Native American life. S. J. Barrows, a noted leader of the Lake Mohonk assemblages, said before the meeting of the conference in 1903 that Fletcher was "the best ethnologist in the United States."[52]

Fletcher's involvement in the Indian reform movement was as deep as her interest in ethnology. To her, any kind of "Indian work," whether anthropological study or the parceling out allotments, was "humanitarian work." From her belief that Native American ceremonies were rapidly vanishing, she became part of the effort to collect Indian goods, record languages, take photographs, make life masks, and record music. Two of her best-known books on the subject of Native American music were *Indian Story and Song from North America* (1907) and

Indian Games and Dances with Native Songs (1915). She also wrote several articles for popular magazines on Native American topics, including, in 1900, "Indian Song" for the *Nation*, a widely circulated periodical of the time. After her death in 1923, she was recognized as the person who "inaugurated the work of this interesting branch of investigation, which bids fair to enrich the music of the world."[53]

Fletcher's works on Native American music did indeed influence further study and enrich—depending on the point of view—the music of the day. Following in Fletcher's footsteps came a flood of ethnological and artistic interest in Native American music. Frances Densmore, one of the first persons to specialize in ethnomusicology, began a very long career with an emphasis on Indian music during this period. In addition to pursuing ethnological interests, Arthur Farwell, a musician and composer of some note, was recording and experimenting with Indian motifs in his own compositions as early as 1903.[54]

Six years later Frederick R. Burton published a book-length study of Native American music. Burton's volume, entitled *American Primitive Music* (1909), was intended for artistic consumption instead of being aimed at an anthropological audience, and dealt with rhythms and themes that could be developed from Native American songs. The *Nation* gave Burton's book a favorable review and wholeheartedly agreed with the author's rather ethnocentric thesis that "primitives" did not "develop rhythm to a higher plane" than "civilized" people. Despite the reviewer's and Burton's ideas regarding rhythmic themes, the review stressed the idea that the musical problem was still unresolved, and it welcomed "more compositions on Indian themes" written by trained musicians in order to test Burton's hypothesis.[55]

Composers wasted little time in answering the *Nation*'s call. By 1912 Antonin Dvorak, Carlos Troyer, Harvey Worthington Loomis, Charles Cadman, and, "to an extent," Carl Busch, had all expressed interest in developing compositions based on the music of both Native Americans and Americans of African origin. According to Arthur Farwell, Native American music was sure to become the more significant of the two types. In an article for *Literary Digest* written in 1912, he stated that "it is the Indian's music that has been seized upon by the composer in America, while the development of negro melodies has been practically at a standstill."[56] Farwell was wrong, of course, because

African American music soon became the paradigm for nearly every form of popular music in the United States.

Still, between 1890 and 1920 Indian themes became very popular in all forms of American music. Antonin Dvorak was said to have listened to recordings of tribal music and to have used their "mystic and austere" motifs in his famous *New World* Symphony (1893). Charles Cadman recorded Native American tribal songs for use in his *Thunderbird Suite* (1914). Other serious composers incorporated their idea of—rather than actual—music of Indian origin into their compositions, as Carl Busch did for his *Minnehaha's Vision* (1914).[57] Charles Sanford Skilton wrote an opera, *Kalopin* (1927), based on an Indian story; a Sioux Flute Serenade (1920); and an American Indian Fantasy (1926) for organ, among other works featuring Indian melodies and motifs.[58]

Popular composers, far less scholarly than Cadman in their approach to music, very likely did not listen to actual recordings of Native American songs and music. Still, to appease a surprisingly interested public, Tin Pan Alley produced "Indian" music in quantity if not quality. Among the most popular tunes churned out during the era were "Navajo" (1903), "Cheyenne" (1906), "Dearest Pocahontas, Her Wooing" (1907), and "By the Waters of the Minnetonka" (1921). "From the Land of Sky Blue Waters," a very popular, catchy, and long-lasting melody—it was used to score television commercials for a certain brand of beer in the 1960s—was written in 1909.[59]

The popularity of "Indian music" very likely sparked an effort in 1913 on the part of the federal government to preserve genuine tribal songs. In that year, *Literary Digest* reported that the Department of the Interior had selected an official to tour the country in order to record Native American music. The appointment demonstrated the bureaucratic confusion that was soon to characterize federal Indian policy in the period. The Interior Department was committed to the preservation and retention of Indian music, while at the same time the official stance of the Indian Office, one of Interior's minor agencies, was to frown upon any practice and continuance of Native American ceremonies. Indian cultures, then, had value for an appreciative non-Indian scholarly community and had some sentimental value, which could be caricatured for a non-Indian popular-music genre, but were not to be taken seriously by their Native American originators.[60]

Along with music, Native American dance was accorded some artistic merit. In 1918 Marsden Hartley, an academic painter and member of the Greenwich Village "Bohemian" artistic-intellectual community of New York, wrote about the lamentable government attempt to destroy Native American ceremonial dancing. Hartley was unquestionably enthusiastic about the "dramatic intensity" of tribal dance, which he referred to as "the solemn high mass of the Indian soul."[61]

The "Indian craze" was on, and during the first twenty-five years of the new century, artistic, connoisseurial, and popular acceptance of Native American painting, ceramics, basketry, music, and dance became fact. To some whites, Native American art was "the only American art there is."[62] The willingness to preserve the different forms of Indian art provided a key that would eventually unlock the shackles of cultural bias, which had justified the policy of total assimilation for Native Americans. As one writer put it, "at last we are beginning to understand that the heathen's spiritual blindness does not prevent his producing great art." It was true, according to the same author, that the "sixteenth century discovered America, the seventeenth colonized it, but it has been left for the twentieth to realize the importance of its art."[63]

CHAPTER V

PRESERVING THE "INDIAN"

The Reassessment of
the Native American Image

THE TWENTIETH CENTURY'S REALIZATION of the importance of Indian art stood not only as a symbol of Native American resiliency but also as a warning sign that the theoretical underpinnings of the vanishing policy were mere assumptions rather than unvarnished truths. The non-Indian discovery and adoption of Native American art served to bring to the surface a glaring inconsistency in white attitudes toward Indians, which had been buried under the idealism of the assimilation theory. Whites could admire the image of the Indian as an artist yet detest the Indian as a savage. The truth was that Native American cultures could indeed produce something of value. Thus Native Americans were neither backward nor doomed because of some inherent deficiency in their race or in their societies. Whites began to realize that the real culprits in the demise of Native Americans were not progress, civilization, modernity, or natural law. They themselves were at fault.

The inconsistencies in white attitudes toward Native Americans had been a part of Euro-Americans' mentality since they arrived in the New World. In American literature and folklore, Indians could be portrayed as mindless and bloodthirsty savages waylaying peaceful wagon trains, toasting pioneers over open fires, dashing white babies against trees, raping beautiful white women, pillaging outlying farmhouses, and ambushing gallant soldiers, oblivious to morality or higher civilized values. Indians could also be depicted as helpmates of the frontiersman and founding father, magnanimously demonstrating to these hardy pioneers the proper way to survive in a harsh climate. Whites could both admire and detest the Indian of literature and folklore and see little inconsistency in their attitudes.

The same love-hate view of Indians carried over into very real situations. White missionaries expressed deep concern for the welfare of Native Americans, yet the very nature of their calling demanded that they adopt a contemptuous view of the manner in which Native Americans lived and worshipped. Images of Indians were both negative and positive, and policies often reflected the most familiar imagery dealing with Indian life in any particular period of time.[1]

During the late nineteenth century, the negative view of Native Americans seemed to overshadow the more positive myths. The major difference between the early nineteenth-century negative attitudes and those of the second half of the century was that "science," in the theoretical assumption that cultures "naturally" evolved toward modernity, validated the notion that Indians remained savages in need of the uplifting influences of white society. The movement to assimilate Native Americans worked toward the elimination of Native American peoplehood by creating "civilized" persons capable of conforming to the social mores of "mainstream" America. Introducing private property would create an individual, as opposed to a collective, relationship with land; replacing a Native language with English would destroy the ability to pass along sacred history, sound the death knell for tribal ceremonies, and undermine the connection between human beings and the landscape.

In the 1890s and early years of the twentieth century, however, white views of Native Americans began to conflict with one another. Even at the Lake Mohonk conferences, where assimilationist theory was the norm, the image of the romantic, noble Indian was often cited to counteract the belief that the Indian was a savage, pagan, and backward human being incapable of salvation or higher morality. In 1896, for example, Joseph Anderson received an ovation from the Lake Mohonk members for his description of Native languages as being "stately and classical" and carrying "the stamp of intellect." His suggestion to establish an institute for "Aboriginal Research" named for the conference founder, Albert Smiley, was equally well received.[2] Despite his rhetoric and the ovation he received, Anderson's remarks were not taken all that seriously, because the conference then turned its attention to a discussion about how to force Indians to cast aside the old ways, learn English, become Christians, and work the land as farmers and ranchers. The ambivalence and inconsistency of the situation were not understood until after the turn of the century, when the old Christian reformers were placed in a quandary from which they could not extract themselves.

Between 1900 and the mid-1920s, just when it seemed probable that whites would forget about Indians, a new surge of interest fixed the attention of numerous prominent whites once again on Native Americans. Stereotypes and imagery that had not been seen for three or four decades suddenly seemed to take on new life. To be sure, members of a new generation of Americans were discovering their heritage, and of course, the Indian of myth stood directly in the path of their understanding of themselves. This confrontation with the historical Indian seems to be part of the maturing process of each generation of Americans. Unless white Americans satisfactorily orient themselves toward the Indians of history and myth, they seem unable to direct their lives properly. Perhaps the realization that they were not the first humans to occupy the land or that their ancestors had in effect built up a great society through fraud, theft, and murder prompted each generation to "do right by the Indians." Whatever the underlying reasons for this collective guilt complex, it seems that each new generation of Americans has an interest in Indians and is in some deep, mystical way compelled to invent its own version of the Indian image.

The generation that came to maturity at the turn of the century began to orient itself in quite a different direction from the older exponents of the vanishing policy. The old reformers thought in opposites. Tribalism was believed to be antithetical to modern civilization, and even though it might have produced some admirable persons and ideas, it nevertheless inevitably had to bow before the superiority of Euro-American culture. In their heyday, Indians might have been threatening, but now they were doomed unless they were brought individually into the mainstream of modern life.

The new generation also perceived that Indians, both as mythical figures and as real people, were vanishing. They held this notion, however, with a singularly important difference. To them, Indians were no longer a physical threat, and they therefore conceivably could bring something of value—such as art—into white society before they passed from the earth.

The belief that Native Americans were a vanishing race became an incontrovertible fact to most Americans in the early twentieth century.[3] Disease, poverty, and alcohol had taken their toll to be sure. But many Americans came to believe that intermarriage between Indians and whites was leading to a rapid decline in the number of racially identifiable Indians. One writer commented that "Cononchet's, Pontiac's and Tecumseh's race will be as dead as the buffalo, and a hybrid will have taken its place."[4] This conception had a good deal of "scientific" validation. The well-known anthropologist Franz Boas expressed his interest as early as 1903 in the "process" of Indian-white "amalgamation." Later he would even suggest that intermarriage might eventually become the salvation of the race and the solution to the "Indian Problem."[5] In 1916, Albert Jenks, an ethnologist interested in the Minnesota Chippewa population, stated that repeated intermarriages did not affect the whites but tended only to dilute "Indian blood." His conclusion could have originated only in an atmosphere deeply steeped in racial superiority, and his thinking was a boon to people who believed that white "blood" was the ultimate salvation of the Indians.[6]

Much of the rhetoric of the old reform movement had been curiously lacking in racial overtones. Most of the old reformers followed Richard Henry Pratt's notion that if Native Americans were infused with the Protestant work ethic, they would naturally become like whites. Hard work, diligence, and the adoption of Western values would make Native Americans the social and economic equals of the American middle class. Native Americans such as Charles A. Eastman, Laura Cornelius, Angel DeCora, Lone Star Dietz, and Carlos Montezuma had become accepted in the white world and were perceived as prospering in mainstream American society. Montezuma and Eastman, graduates of top medical schools, not only were respected within their professions but also had received the praise of the nation for their literary and philanthropic contributions to American culture. Their success seemed to verify the old reformers' beliefs and assured everyone interested in Indians that the Gospel of Hard Work was a practical working solution to the "Indian Problem."

The new belief that intermarriage with whites could substitute for diligence suggested that thrift, perseverance, and other virtues of the Protestant work ethic could be transmitted by genetic ancestry—a belief that not even Charles Darwin, Herbert Spencer, Lewis Henry Morgan, and the hardiest evolutionists would have supported. The stereotypes of Indians during the early twentieth century thus became a curious mixture of racial attitudes and quasi-scientific theories that had little except white superstition to bolster them.

Some of the early twentieth-century notions about race directly countered the idea of assimilating Indians into white society. Several scholars of the period indicated that certain inherited factors kept Indians from dropping their old habits and customs. According to these researchers, Native Americans' brain capacities were lower on average than those of the whites. These inherent limitations prevented Indians as a race from progressing along the same social, economic, and religious lines as Euro-Americans. The idea that Indians were inherently inferior was an old idea, and the belief had gained a good deal of quasi-scientific support during the first half of the nineteenth century. Indeed, there had been a wealth of rather fanciful and frankly manipulated data published in that period concerning the supposed inadaptability of Indians, written primarily to justify Manifest Destiny. The old reformers basically rejected these ideas and maintained that all people were born blanks that could be molded into civilized human beings.

In the twentieth century, the notion of racial inferiority emerged once again. The geographer Ellsworth Huntington, who had been a guest at the Lake Mohonk conference, wrote as late as 1919 that the "past achievements and present condition" of the Indian "indicate that he stands between the white man and the Negro." Moreover, Huntington asserted, this level of development was undeniably the social "position that would be expected from the capacity of his brain." Indians who adapted but maintained an Indian or tribal identity would have been seen as members of an inferior or, at best, a retarded race.[7]

The obvious abilities of the New Indians countered this argument better than any other factor. On the other hand, many of the New Indians were acting strangely enough like the old Indians. They lambasted the white man for breaking treaties, maintained direct links with their tribes, and took up the pen to tell whites exactly what they were doing wrong. Eastman wrote nostalgic essays extolling the virtues and spirituality of the older tribal life. Cornelius actively fought for Native American rights, as had her ancestors. Montezuma realized his people's (and his own) connection with the land and devoted his last years to the struggle to save the Fort McDowell reservation and protect Yavapais' freedom of action. One of the most forceful speakers and writers who fiercely guarded and maintained her Native American identity when she had been regarded as one of the most "progressive" of the New Indians was Gertrude Bonnin, who wrote under her Sioux name, Zitkala Sa.

Zitkala Sa, who was engaged to Carlos Montezuma in 1901 and later married a Yankton man named Raymond Bonnin, had been enticed by the promise of red apples at the age of eight to attend a Quaker manual-arts school for Indians in Indiana. She went on to Earlham College and became an orator and violinist of note. When she was twenty-two, Richard Henry Pratt hired her to teach at Carlisle. There she began to write short articles for magazines such as *Atlantic Monthly* and *Harper's*. In 1901 she published *Old Indian Legends*, a collection of trickster stories, that won for her a certain amount of prestige as a folklorist. She left Carlisle in 1902, moved to Yankton, South Dakota, met and married Raymond, who was with the Indian Service, and went with him to the Uintah Ouray Ute Agency in Utah. While in Utah, she collaborated with William Hanson in composing "The Sun Dance Opera," which had several performances in Utah. The New York Light Opera Company performed the opera a short time after her death in 1938.[8]

Her accomplishments in the white world very likely led to an estrangement with her mother and her people in South Dakota. As a result, Zitkala Sa sought to rectify the strained relationship by revalidating her own identity as a Sioux woman through writing. Her excellent book, *Old Indian Legends*, no doubt emerged from this tension, but more importantly she began to reassess the whole notion underlying her assimilation into white society. She became increasingly disaffected with the theoretical structure of the vanishing policy and the Christian-based philosophies that debased Native Americans' knowledge and their spiritual relationship with the natural world. Perhaps her most important essay, "Why I Am a Pagan," published in *Atlantic Monthly* in 1902, best expressed her disenchantment with the white man's religion and philosophies:

I prefer to their dogma my excursions into the natural gardens where the voice of the Great Spirit is heard in the twittering of birds, the rippling of mighty waters, and the sweet breathing of flowers. If this is Paganism, then at present, at least, I am a Pagan.[9]

The very existence of intelligent, perceptive Native Americans like Zitkala Sa, Eastman, Cornelius, and other New Indians who could express their thoughts and feelings in English forced many white Americans to rethink the notion of the supposed backwardness of the Indian. In addition, a number of whites in the early part of the century began to agree with Zitkala Sa that Christianity, modernity, and the spiritual and environmental havoc they had caused in the natural world were not exactly in sync with their vision of America's future. To these Americans, primitivism and even "backwardness" were not wholly negative terms. Americans became caught up in a widespread movement to conserve natural resources that were fast becoming depleted in the rush to industrialize the United States. This conservation movement was multifaceted. It included a program for proper land usage that emphasized the notion that efficient management would lead to a more prosperous nation. This aspect of the movement, which was embraced by most Americans, was regulatory in nature and concerned with preserving the country's resources for future use.[10]

Another side of the movement saw conservation as a method of attaining some kind of equilibrium with nature in order to counterbalance the destructiveness of industrialization. Within this facet of the movement was a growing concern for preserving, rather than conserving for later consumption, the wilderness areas of America and for protecting endangered species of American fauna.[11] As a corollary, if the Indian race was soon to become "as dead as the buffalo," then like the buffalo, according to some preservationists, the race should be protected. Although this attitude dehumanized Native Americans in much the same manner as had the American military with its infamous "squaw" targets, it produced the opposite effect. Instead of dehumanizing Indians in order to hunt them, whites dehumanized Indians in order to protect them.

Still another aspect of the conservationist mentality affected Native Americans. One element of the conservation movement was as nostalgic and romantic as its opposite was practical and structured. As a result of the census of 1890, the Department of the Interior declared the frontier closed. The pioneering spirit, which many people believed important in shaping the American character, was in grave danger of dying out. Several American leaders, among them President Theodore Roosevelt, thought that with the closing of the frontier a "national malaise" had set in that had endangered American morale. To change the relaxed attitude and compensate for the lack of a frontier, Roosevelt and others demanded that the wilderness be preserved so that Americans could hunt, fish, and generally learn to survive in a harsh climate. If they could recapture the pioneering spirit, then Americans could continue to be forceful individualists—distinctly separate from the rest of the world—and could eventually assume positions of leadership worldwide.[12]

The preservationists promoted their movement by extolling the idea that a life in the "great out of doors" was both healthful and aesthetically stimulating. Quite often their enthusiasm applauded Native American life as the epitome of a natural, spiritual existence. Many whites, despite the very real health problems that plagued Native Americans during the period, devoutly agreed with Charles Eastman's proposition that the tribal people of America had a "heritage of a superb physique." Because of their life in the wilds of America, people believed, Indians had developed a strong physical presence and were, in fact, natural athletes.

Belief in the physical superiority of Indians and other natural peoples was long-standing. As early as 1492, Christopher Columbus had reported that Indians were "very well-built, with very handsome bodies and very good faces" and that they were "all generally fairly tall, good looking and well proportioned."[13] Several persons throughout American history had echoed these sentiments. In the eighteenth century, the Indian trader James Adair wrote that Indians were "strong, well proportioned in body and limbs, surprisingly active and nimble, and hardy in their own way of living."[14] In the nineteenth century, Washington Irving would write in admiration of the "fine physiques" of Indians in the natural state.[15]

These views remained basically unaltered over the centuries, and in the early twentieth century they became widely accepted tenets of belief. Even a white missionary named Thomas C. Moffet, who sought Native American converts and so the destruction of indigenous religions, could praise the physical attributes of Indians. Writing in 1914, he stated that "the Indian as a rule is physically well-proportioned, symmetrical, straight," and, moreover, "with a large chest, small and shapely hands, a well-nourished body, he is usually prepossessing."[16] This picture became a part of the popular imagery of Indians, and was confirmed in the minds of many whites by the success of several Native American athletes during the period, the most notable being Jim Thorpe. Thorpe, a Sac and Fox, led the Carlisle Indian School's football team in victories over several white colleges, including the United States Military Academy. He was voted All American twice, and won the decathlon and pentathlon at the 1912 Olympic games. The greatest athlete of his day, Thorpe was considered a natural competitor and the very image of Indian physical development.

The growing motion-picture industry began to capitalize on the image of the Indian athlete. Two productions, *Football Warrior* (1908) and *The Call of the Wild* (1909), both about Native American football heroes suffering through tragic romances with white women, were very popular among moviegoers of the day. The films, although melodramatic, reminded their audiences of the stereotypical Indian athlete and further ingrained in the minds of the whites the idea that Indians were naturally gifted competitors, owing their physical well-being to a life in the great outdoors. These films also stressed the notion that despite their great abilities of speed, strength, and endurance, Indians would always remain marginal to the white man's growing industrial culture and that it was far better for them to stay in the wilds than to risk rejection by a fickle, urban, and urbane female.[17]

Ultimately, the romantic side of the conservation movement was about a growing sense of alienation caused by the rise of industrial culture. In the same year that *Football Warrior* was released, the wilderness enthusiast and writer George Warton James published a lengthy monograph urging whites to learn the beneficial ways of the Indians. Entitled *What the White Race May Learn from the Indian*, the book argued that urban areas and contemporary American lifestyles were most detrimental to the human body and to the overall national physical and mental health. For the volume's second printing in 1917, James retitled his "new and enlarged edition," *The Indians' Secret of Health*, a title that revealed the author's main theme even more explicitly.[18]

James was a resounding critic of white America's habits and an exponent of the idea that all progress was not necessarily beneficial. James admonished the nation:

we do not know how to eat rationally; few people sleep as they should; our drinking habits could not be much worse; our clothing is stiff, formal, conventional, hideous and unhealthful.[19]

In addition, James continued, American architecture was "weakly imitative, flimsy without character or stability," and white religious practice was a "profession" rather than a life. His attacks on society touched upon the American educational system. In James's view, institutions of higher learning in the United States were turning out "anaemic and half-trained pupils who are forceful demonstrators of the truth that 'a little knowledge is a dangerous thing.'" James himself unwittingly demonstrated the truth of his remark by misquoting Alexander Pope's "Essay on Criticism": "A little learning is a dangerous thing." In short, American civilization had become the chief culprit in the decline of the American pioneering spirit and had created the "dull and vacant eye, the inert face" of the American urban dweller.[20]

To cure society of the illness caused by "over-civilization," James urged his readers to follow the Native American lead and seek the pure air of the wilderness sky, practice deep breathing, and take up running as a beneficial exercise (long before the jogging craze). Essentially he called upon "the white race to incorporate into its civilization the good things of the Indian civilization" and "forsake the injurious things of it pseudo-civilized, artificial, and over-refined life." Whites should, he wrote, "return to the simple, healthful, and natural life which the Indians largely lived."[21]

Taking to heart much of what Charles Eastman had already written about Native American life, James represented that segment of American society that was just beginning to view "civilization" in it most negative sense. Industrialization, according to James, had become a menace rather than a savior. It had brought with it laborsaving devices to be sure, yet it had also brought complexity into American lives. The devious entrepreneur had replaced the straightforward frontiersman as the bearer of American culture. According to social critics such as James, Americans should, like the pioneers of old, learn the ways of the Indians in order to survive. The so-called "backward" Indian lived simply, enjoyed the natural wonders of the land, tended to develop a healthful physique, and maintained a spiritual purity lost to all but a few whites.

The glorification of the pioneer became a national mania. Between 1890 and 1910, American urbanites flocked to attend numerous Wild West shows held in open arenas. Buffalo Bill's show and those of the 101 Ranch and Pawnee Bill flourished. These celebrations of the pioneer experience allowed their audiences to feel vicariously, and with no danger and little discomfort, the elemental forces of the natural struggle. The productions were as nationalistic as they were entertaining. Although stereotyped and exploited, the Native Americans who toured with these wilderness extravaganzas made the most of their experiences. They traveled the world, and in spite of the exploitation they endured, Native Americans were still able to retain an "Indian" identity that had heroic overtones. Before the eyes of the audience, Buffalo Bill and his Congress of Rough Riders crushed courageous and sacrificial Indian resistance and advanced the spread of American civilization and progress. At the same time, the loyal Wild West fans realized that the frontiersman and the Indian, although enemies, were kindred spirits in their love for the land and their dwindling numbers. The Indian of the Wild West show was a noble enemy: villainous, but victimized by the same spread of civilization that led to the demise of the hardy pioneer.[22]

The motion-picture theater of urban America led to the demise of the Wild West show. Still, the motion-picture industry furthered the frontier myths in the collective mind of the American public. The audience could soak in the frontier spirit without having to endure the smells and suffer the summer heat in the open-air arenas of the Wild West shows. Hundreds of movies were produced between 1900 and 1920 with "Indian" themes or with Indians as either the noble or the recalcitrant foes of white expansionism. In 1911 alone, some two hundred "Indian" movies—as opposed to straightforward "western" adventure stories set against a frontier backdrop— were released. Many of these early motion pictures presented more benign and romantic images of Indians than the Wild West shows. A number of these Indian movies extolled the virtues of a life close to nature. Movie Indians were mostly savages, but depicted more often as the noble variety: honest, loyal, brave, and dignified. Quite often movie Indians of the early silent era were accurately costumed on screen simply because production companies hired Native Americans who were former employees of the Wild West shows and could supply their own traditional dress. Only later, when location shooting became more expensive, would Hollywood adopt a standard costume for movie Indians. There was also an incessant demand from the public for authenticity. Some "Indian" films were advertised as having been filmed "under the direction of a native Indian chief," while others claimed that there was "not a pale face in the film."[23]

D. W. Griffith, perhaps the most important director of the period, was reported to have been quite concerned with authenticity in depicting Native Americans, and even filmed *A Pueblo Legend* on location, utilizing an all-Indian cast. But Griffith also tended to reflect the romanticism of the period. Some of his Indian movies included: *The Redman and the Child*, *The Mended Flute*, *The Indian Runner's Romance* (evidently illustrating the healthful as well as romantic sides of Indian life), and *An Indian's Loyalty*. The famed moviemaker's slightly favorable portrayal of Native Americans was in direct contrast to his depiction of African Americans in his epic *Birth of a Nation*. Still, whether favorable or unfavorable, Griffith's images of both groups were examples of blatant and unmerciful stereotyping—predictable, perhaps, in the early days of filmmaking, but hardly forgivable.[24]

In the early 1900s, an influx of white visitors came to the Southwest to stay in Fred Harvey hotels and commune with nature, and they expected to see the same picturesque Indians they had seen on their hometown movie screens. The tourists of the era, although not quite as hardy as the original pioneers, were equally part of the "wilderness cult" of the day, and just as interested in capturing their bit of the American heritage as were the growing numbers of Boy Scouts and Camp Fire Girls. As a consequence, they willingly paid to see Native American dances performed, and they purchased Indian-made crafts as souvenirs of the pilgrimage back to nature in order to feel that they were obtaining a small, very romantic portion of the American past.

The curio industry boomed, and collecting items of Native American manufacture became exceedingly popular. Large collections of Indian artifacts changed the appearance of many American homes. In the East, the parlor became a "den" and took on "a North American Indian cast" that was "quite as decorative as the oriental scheme, so long in favor." The new interior designs were rugged, individualistic, and "much more stimulating to one's patriotism." As "part of the Indian cult of the day," whites displayed Pueblo pots and baskets and covered their floors and walls with animal skins and Navajo rugs and blankets. "In short," according to a feature story in the *New York Tribune* that was reprinted in the Vinita, Oklahoma, *Weekly Chieftain*, "there is nothing in birch bark or beadwork that will not fit admirably to the red man's room," provided that "one only has taste in her selection and knows how to dispose of her trophies."[25]

The collecting of Indian crafts and art reinforced among whites the idea that Native American life was spiritually stimulating. The whites seemed truly interested in aesthetics, despite their nostalgia for the roughness, ruggedness, and extreme practicality of the American frontier myth. Surrounded by natural beauty and forced to be creative by their struggle for survival in the natural environment, Indians could easily become, as painter Marsden Hartley wrote in 1918, "artists of the first degree."[26] Native American art was regarded as unique, supremely spiritual, and very "American" because the "first Americans" created it. It seemed to be part of the wilderness image, both natural and unspoiled. According to George Warton James, "frankness, honesty, simplicity, directness characterized the manufactures of the Indian." Moreover, he stated that there was in Indian art "no wild straining after unique effect; no fantastic distortions to secure novelty; everything is natural and rational, and therefore artistically effective."[27]

Other observers agreed with James and Hartley. Warren K. Moorhead, writing for the *Indian Craftsman*, commented on Native American art using nearly the same terminology as they did and, rather boldly for his period, stated that because of the high degree of art found in tribal societies, the Native American potter, weaver, carver, and, especially, painter, "never stood in the path of progress."[28] The idea and image of the Indian as artist had captivated even such a well-known personage as Theodore Roosevelt. "How many Congressmen do you suppose there are who would understand that there could be such a thing as 'Indian art'?" he once wrote. "They will say, 'Another of Roosevelt's vagaries!'"[29] For some people, collecting Indian crafts may even have been an effort to pay homage to the vanishing, aesthetically inclined "natural man." The image of the peaceful Native American potter or weaver was positive, but an image just the same.

A number of whites, however, were very much interested in the retention of tribal identity through the manufacture of Indian crafts. In this instance, therefore, whites seemed genuinely concerned with ensuring the survival of the peaceful Indian potter or weaver of reality. Several museums of natural history collected thousands of items of Indian manufacture to be put on permanent display. These ethnological collections, according to the influential art magazine *Camera Work*, "ought also to be considered as museums of art."[30] The Smithsonian Institution, the New York Museum of Natural History, and the Field Museum in Chicago all began to expand their collections of both old and modern Native American materials. The excellent Denver Art Museum also devoted a large part of its space to the display of Native American art. Most of the artifacts in these museums were acquired under the auspices of scientific research, and many of them were removed from sacred burial sites. A large number of these artifacts were displayed without regard to their original makers' beliefs, customs, or practices. The museums, however, were in fact expanding their displays of Native American material cultures because of overwhelming demand by the American public.

But the collection that stood "alone in the annals of American museums," according to *Outlook* magazine, because of its exclusivity was the Museum of the American Indian founded in 1916. The museum began as a private collection. In 1903, George Gustav Heye, a native New Yorker who had received his education in Germany, formed the nucleus of what would become the most extensive collection of Indian art in the world. A founder of the banking firm of Battles, Heye and Harrison, Heye had enough capital to finance a foundation devoted solely to gathering Native American material culture. In 1904 the Heye Foundation sent expeditions into several areas in the United States and Canada to gather new artifacts. By 1910 it had sent collectors and ethnologists to Peru, Ecuador, Brazil, and the West Indies. Six years later the Heye Foundation's collection of Native American artifacts had grown so large that its founder simply did not have enough space available to store it all. In 1916, Heye reendowed the foundation with enough money to rent a building so that his collection could be opened to public view. Although the new museum housed a great deal of archaeological material, contemporary artifacts were collected and displayed with equal attention devoted to presenting their tribal origins and artistry.[31] The museum was obviously dedicated to something much more than "salvage anthropology."

When Heye opened the Museum of the American Indian, the

movement to preserve Indian art was in full swing. Ethnologists, conservationists, artists, tourists, and art collectors were all caught up in the effort to conserve both the beauty and the distinctive nature of Native American craftsmanship. As early as 1909, A. J. Fynn had urged the conference of the National Education Association to establish special courses in the production of native crafts at Indian schools. Significantly, Fynn urged this policy because "conservation is the watchword of the hour." Native American talent, it seemed, like the forest, streams, and minerals should be fostered and preserved for the enjoyment of future generations.[32]

White academic artists were not left unaffected by the growing interest in protecting the wilderness, Indian art, and American Indians in general. Many artists left the cities of the East in order to remove themselves from the corruptive elements supposedly absent in a more pristine environment. The Southwest particularly attracted several important painters. Around 1900, Oscar E. Berninghaus and Ernest L. Blumenchien, two young artists from New York, came into the Taos, New Mexico, area in search of new subjects to paint and more generally to commune with nature. Like other artists and intellectuals of the day, they devoutly believed that urban life was stagnant and stultifying. Materialistic, industrialized society could never condone or even be cognizant of the aesthetics of the natural life. But "in the land of the Indian," these two artists "found so much to admire and respect, and were so deeply moved by the sights and the life of this beautiful valley," at Taos, that they decided to stay. By 1915 there were enough artists located in the small New Mexican town to form a league appropriately named the Taos Society of Artists. By 1916 nearly one hundred nonindigenous painters either regularly visited or lived in the town.[33]

Many of the artists of Taos became very well known. Berninghaus established a studio there early in the century and quickly gained recognition for his studies of Pueblo Indian life. Following him were Irving Couse, John Hauser, and Blumenchien, who, with Berninghaus, founded the Taos Society of Artists. All of these painters were interested in utilizing Indians as subjects for their work. Indeed Couse had left Oregon because he found the Native Americans of that area somewhat reluctant to pose for him. In Taos he had no trouble finding subjects. Couse was especially well respected because he had been a student at the National Academy of Design in New York and at the École des

Beaux-Arts in Paris. His paintings were displayed in the National Arts Club in New York and the National Gallery of Art in Washington, D.C.[34]

John Hauser painted Native American subjects from all over the United States and became a well-known figure not only in the art world but also among the people with whom he worked. The Sioux of South Dakota, in fact, formally adopted him as one of their own in 1901. Despite Hauser's acceptance elsewhere, he always returned to Taos and Santa Fe, another New Mexican artist community, both of which were quickly gaining attention for their production of excellent canvases and fine sculptures. Marsden Hartley spent two years in the Southwest before moving on to Paris for further instruction.[35]

Each one of these artists became involved in protecting Native American cultures. The artistic communities, steeped in the preservation movement, strongly opposed the federal government's handling of Indian affairs. In addition, the artist communities in Taos and Santa Fe had significant connections with several American intellectual centers. The founders of the New York–based Society of Independent Artists, Walter Pach and John Sloan, had close ties to white painters in New Mexico, and as a result they became involved in the "Indian craft as art" movement. It was largely through their effort that Native American painters were included in the Waldorf show of 1920. The connections of the New Mexico artists reached into the Greenwich Village "Bohemian" community as well. Marsden Hartley was associated with Alfred Stieglitz, who published the art journal *Camera Work* and was the leader of the Photo-Secessionist movement of New York photographers. It was probably Stieglitz, more than anyone else, who elevated photography into an art form. At various times, *Camera Work*'s editorial board carried the names of Isadora Duncan and Mabel Dodge, the renowned hostess. Significantly, Dodge was later to attract John Collier, a frequent visitor to her Greenwich Village salon and the future commissioner of Indian Affairs in Franklin D. Roosevelt's administrations, to her new home that she established in 1917 in Taos. Dodge's famous salon also attracted such literary, artistic, and intellectual personalities as Isadora Duncan, D. H. Lawrence, Max Eastman, and Gertrude Stein.

The urge to preserve Native American cultures became intense, but in a curiously circular logic, it also tended to imply that Indians were indeed vanishing. The very fact that these artists of the Southwest were intent upon painting Indian subjects before their authenticity was lost served only to give credence to the myth of the "vanishing race." The artists, however, were not the only white Americans who launched campaigns to capture some aspects of Native American life while they were still more or less pristine. Edward S. Curtis, with financial aid from J. Pierpont Morgan, devoted his life to photographing "Vanishing Indian Types." Several years later, a writer and photographer named Karl Moon would follow Curtis's lead into Indian communities to photograph the last vestiges of the "old" Indian life. In addition, a New York lawyer named Joseph K. Dixon organized the "expeditions" in 1908, 1909, and 1913 sponsored by the Wanamaker family (and its department-store fortune) to photograph and record the cultures of the "first Americans" as a means of paying tribute to them before they passed from memory.[36]

The efforts to preserve Native Americans, both as museum relics and as living cultures, had an unnatural urgency. Hundreds of whites from academic and lay backgrounds rushed to interview the old chiefs before they died. Anthropologists came in droves to Indian reservations and often departed heavily laden with artifacts gleaned from old men and women who had few possessions left to them in the first place. Ethnologist S. A. Barret, practicing salvage anthropology to its extreme and gaining fame for his methods, obtained the autobiography of Geronimo in 1905 and then left the Apache leader as he had found him. A few years later Geronimo died, frozen to death on an Oklahoma country road. Native Americans, both adults and children, were photographed in the same manner as police mug shots, in both full face and profile, to define in detail the features of the vanishing Indian race.[37]

To preserve Indians properly, many whites looked to scientific investigators like Barret or to the person who made the greatest anthropological find of the period, A. L. Kroeber. In 1911, Kroeber took a famished Indian named Ishi from the hills of northern California to his place of work, the University of California at Berkeley. Ishi was considered the last "wild" Indian in the United States and thus a perfect specimen for study. He became a mascot at the university's museum and provided Kroeber with a wealth of information about the California tribes.[38]

Along with the growing preservation movement there was a concomitant rise in the popularity of academic anthropology and archaeology. These disciplines invoked a nostalgic interest in the past, prompting whites to seek the historic spirit of the pioneer, to display antiques, and to travel to famous archaeological sites. Some the new national parks were established to preserve the ruins of ancient Native American towns. Indian antiquities began to be viewed with pride and a strong feeling of protectiveness. The ruins were also being systematically looted by those who sought to profit in the sale of Native American artifacts. As a result, several bills were put before Congress to ensure that archaeological sites would be placed under federal protection. During 1904 alone, four such preservation bills were introduced into the House and Senate. Senator Shelby M. Cullom proposed a bill that specifically designated "the preservation of aboriginal monuments, ruins and other antiquities." A House bill even contained a provision making it unlawful for anyone to counterfeit prehistoric and archaeological objects.[39]

The movement stirred a great deal of excitement on the part of numerous professional and amateur scientists. Natalie Curtis Burlin, a writer and art collector, attempted to enlist the aid of Franz Boas, who normally avoided political questions, in obtaining legislation for the preservation of all Hopi villages. "I believe in progress," she confided to Boas, "but it seems to me that the Moqui (Hopi) towns are too rich in ethnological, historic, and artistic interest to be carelessly entrusted for 'improvement' to government officials." Even if those government officials were conscientious, Burlin thought that they could have "but little appreciation of the real worth of such towns to the world's history."[40]

For his part, Boas kept up a continuing correspondence with Alice C. Fletcher and the president of Columbia University, Nicholas Murray Butler, concerning the preservation of Native American antiquities. His influence through Butler was so strong that one of the proposed preservation acts was defeated because Boas objected to its stipulation that gave the Smithsonian Institution's Bureau of American Ethnology the exclusive right to issue permits for the exploitation of federally protected archaeological sites. Boas believed that this provision would preclude foreign scholars from mining the wealth of the sites themselves and would serve only to stir up antagonisms within his own profession on a worldwide scale.[41]

The preservation movement forever linked Native Americans with the academic discipline of anthropology. To most Americans, Native Americans were living antiquities who possessed such admirable qualities as the ability to live harmoniously with nature and to create primitive art. In the minds of many whites, if one wished to gain an understanding of how the natural life gave Native Americans healthy physiques and artistic propensities, one turned to anthropology, the discipline doing its utmost to salvage these aspects of tribal societies. It followed then that one should not rely upon information about Native Americans supplied by the old reformers and Christian missionaries who had been determined to destroy indigenous customs, beliefs, and even material culture. Anthropologists were revered as scientists who could bring reason and expertise to the "Indian question." Anthropologists, after all, had introduced Indian art to the larger public and had written eloquent tracts about the physical and intellectual achievements of Native Americans in the days before the coming of the whites. As a science in the new urban and urbane American culture, anthropology was fast becoming the discipline Americans looked to for answers concerning the human condition. Perhaps it was not totally incongruous to Americans that "Anthropology Days" were staged at the St. Louis Olympic Games of 1904, during which a number of peoples living under colonial rule competed and during which a Sioux Indian won the hundred-yard dash.[42]

The effects on the American public of the movement to preserve "the Indian" were complicated but readily understandable. Although whites during the period viewed Native Americans in terms of some very old stereotypes, their attitudes concerning these myths changed remarkably. Native Americans had been considered "natural men" for centuries. In the nineteenth century this attribute was looked upon as a sign of inferiority. But many whites during the early years of the twentieth century came to view this connection with the natural world favorably. Being in harmony with the environment, according to the new attitudes, gave Indians special qualities, such as intrinsic athletic capabilities and spiritual powers lost to or overlooked by Euro-American society. Even primitivism in art, long a sign of lower civilization or mentality to people of Euro-American descent, became a positive aspect of Native American cultures, to be fostered and maintained. Moreover, many whites began to look upon Native American art as a truly magnificent achievement, suggesting a superiority in Indian life unattainable to any but a few sensitive whites. The idea that Native American cultures had little or nothing to contribute to the civilization of the white man could no longer be justified. "The Indian," wrote Natalie Curtis Burlin, "is to-day finding an increasing recognition as a human being capable of bringing gifts of his own to the civilization that absorbs him."[43] Because of these notions, Native Americans, or at least the white images of Indians, became popular and even beloved. As early as 1903, musician and composer Arthur Farwell commented on the "amazing rapidity with which the Indian and his art and traditions are growing in popularity."[44]

The great interest in preserving Native Americans conflicted with—and at the same time owed part of its existence to—the idea that Indians were, in accordance with the laws of nature, about to vanish. In the nineteenth century, when Native American cultures were viewed most negatively, whites could readily accept and condone the possibility of Indian extinction. The Indian assimilation policy sought to make Native Americans vanish into mainstream society for their own "betterment."

Beginning in the twentieth century, a new generation of Americans refused to accept completely this fate for tribal traditions, customs, manners, morals, and aesthetic accomplishments. They began to support the many Native Americans who were attempting to preserve as many of the tribal cultures of North America as possible. Their actions were in direct opposition to the tenets of the vanishing policy. They chose to maintain Indians: some did so for entertainment, but others because they truly believed that Native American cultures possessed intrinsic values worthy of emulation, in spite of previous government policies and old reform ideals. Instead of formulating a new theoretical basis for the conduct of American Indian policy, however, they simply lashed out against the assimilationist mentality and especially against the "missionary" zeal that was leading toward the absolute destruction of Native American tribal cultures.

CHAPTER VI

PROGRESSIVE AMBIGUITY

The Reassessment of the Vanishing Policy

The notion of completely assimilating the Native American population into American society was grounded in a set of beliefs that were at the same time complex, confusing, and all too often conflicting. Old reformers like Richard Henry Pratt, Albert Smiley, and Henry L. Dawes, who more or less provided the theoretical basis for the vanishing policy, combined nationalism, Christian idealism and dogma, economic conservatism, and social Darwinism into a kind of mystical philosophy of Americanism. For the most part, they believed in brotherly love, charity, and human equality. On the other hand, they also held some strong convictions that relegated anything other than Euro-American culture to a position of inferiority. To them, Native Americans were not only a race but also a culture (although they did not fully understand the separation) that could be pictured in the most depreciating terms and singled out for deliberate extinction.

Despite their curious mixture of hatred for tribal cultures and apparent love for individual tribal members, none of their goals for Indians seemed to have been touched with ambiguity. The policies they formulated for dealing with Native Americans were straightforward and clearly articulated. Indians would no longer be treated as members of distinct polities with recognizable leaders and governments. Moreover, the old reformers essentially denied that the tribes were true states possessing autonomous structures of public authority, when in fact they did. Indians would be treated as atomized individuals having no links to kin, land, religion, or a political system other than that of the United States. So that Native Americans could become American citizens without stigma, each tribal state's basis in a sense of peoplehood was to be declared nonexistent and the "Indian" of old was to be put to death.

During the first twenty-five years of the twentieth century, the old Indian reform philosophy came under rough scrutiny from a group of new but no less ardent reformers. These new reformers in large part thought that the vanishing policy was, in fact, doing precisely what it was intended to do. The problem was that the policy was destroying cultures that possessed some admirable traits. The preservationists began to think that any modification of Native American customs would only make those customs less "Indian" and therefore contribute to their disappearance. Of the Native American cultures that were maintained or that had at least, in the minds of the preservationists, retained their "purity," they began to feel remarkably protective. To an old reformer, the decline of tribal cultures was a completely natural and anticipated occurrence. To a progressive reformer who sought to preserve the "best" of Indian life, the destruction of a lower civilization and a less sophisticated people was unworthy of America's greatness. Racism, too, cut across these new attitudes toward Native Americans.

The injection of this preservationist sentiment, however widespread, clouded white thinking about Indians. Perhaps this ambiguity was the glorious inconsistency of a nation coming of age. It could no longer justify its treatment of the original inhabitants of America, nor could it bring itself fully to admire them. It preferred, therefore, to hold completely conflicting views concerning alien identities and their relationship with the nation and to refuse steadfastly to give up either idea. In any case, the ambiguity in thought regarding Native Americans contributed to a decline in the influence of the old reformers, who had worked so industriously to make the vanishing policy work in principle and in reality.

As early as 1901, *Outlook* magazine carried an article that criticized the Indian assimilation movement for being so immersed in its own conception of civilization that it had indiscriminately destroyed some facets of Native American life deemed highly commendable and worthy of emulation and absorption by American society. The idea of a kind of reverse assimilation was anathema to the vanishing policy, but according to the author of the article, the arrogance shown by persons who believed that Native American cultures were valueless served only to make Indians perceive themselves as unworthy. The destruction of tribal life, statehood, ceremonies, kinship structures, and art led to Native American demoralization. According to the writer for *Outlook*:

> After one hundred and thirty years of dealing with the American [Indian] we may quite frankly admit that, so far from developing what was best in him, the methods hitherto followed had produced in the modern Indians on the reservation a lower type than the colonists found.[1]

From the viewpoint of this anonymous writer, the effort to destroy tribal life represented a completely misguided zeal on the part of the adherents to Indian assimilation. The author lashed out against the "home industry" of making lace that had been forced upon Native American women. "Did we try to learn what industries he [the Indian] already possessed?" the author asked. And the answer, of course, was a resounding "Not at all!" Lace, according to the author, was "a product evolved to meet the requirements of a European aristocracy," not suited to American ideals of beauty, and an affront to rugged individualism.[2] The article lamented that many Native American industries were rapidly disappearing because of a narrow cultural arrogance that did not reflect well on America's picture of itself.

A few months after these comments on Indian home industries were published, another article appeared in *Outlook* that was even more critical of the missionary spirit that had actually led to the assimilation policy. The writer, Walter C. Roe, was himself a missionary and vice president of the recently formed Indian Industries League of Boston. The league was founded primarily as an effort to instill in Indians what the old reformers habitually called "the dignity of labor." As an organization designed to aid in the development of industries on the reservations, it was given the full support of the assimilation movement. Its president, Colonel John S. Lockwood, and Roe were highly regarded members of the Lake Mohonk Conferences of the Friends of the Indian. In fact, when the conference established the Lake Mohonk Lodge for "Indian industrial development," Roe was appointed to oversee its functions.[3]

While at the Lake Mohonk Lodge in western Oklahoma, Roe began to reassess the attitudes underlying the vanishing policy. He became enamored with the "beautiful art of beadwork" and worked to ensure its survival among the Cheyenne and Arapaho of the area. Although Roe believed in integrating the Native American population into mainstream society, as well as in allotment in severalty as the method of solving the problems surrounding Native American land tenure, he also believed that Native Americans, as persons, should enter society on an equal basis with whites. As Roe understood it, the problem with rapid assimilation and the concomitant castigation of anything Indian was that it left Native Americans without even a modicum of self-pride. According to Roe, "the underlying mistake of our National policy toward the Indian has been the attempt to crush the Indian out of him."[4] Roe believed that Indians should feel themselves equal to whites through a renewed pride in their own heritages. With pride came dignity. Because he thought that the assimilation policy had deemed tribal cultures unworthy and had instilled into Native Americans a sense of self-hatred (a common theme in colonization), Roe believed that the Indian reform movement had transformed the "lofty type of savage" of one hundred years before into "a wretched type of civilized man."[5]

As Roe conceived of it, the Lake Mohonk Lodge was intended to become a kind of halfway house, "a link between the old and new," for Indians in western Oklahoma. It became a meeting place and social center for many of the Cheyenne and Arapaho living nearby. It also became a workshop for the production of very fine beadwork. By serving these functions, the Lake Mohonk Lodge was essentially keeping a sense of community intact and therefore working against the effort to individualize Native Americans. Roe, however, believed that centers like the Lake Mohonk Lodge would eventually aid in the process of integrating Native Americans because "the Indians are naturally and strongly social" and needed some form of community interaction to cope with the great changes being made in their lives. Roe argued that their "strong gregarious tendencies" kept Native Americans from immediately and wholeheartedly accepting the dictates of the vanishing policy and that these tendencies were "the greatest obstacles to the success of the allotment system."[6]

Roe was not the only person to point out the deleterious social effects of individualization, allotment, and Christian zealotry. A year after Roe's article appeared in *Outlook*, the well-known writer Hamlin Garland published his views on the "Indian Problem" in the *North*

American Review. Like Roe, Garland believed that the Native American "gregariousness of habit" made it extremely hard for Indians to "adopt the Dawes land theories." Garland commended Roe's work in Oklahoma and agreed also that the self-respect brought by the maintenance of Indian art forms "cannot be overestimated." Unlike Roe, however, Garland believed that the allotment policy should have been totally revamped. He suggested that families of each tribe be grouped together along the waterways of the reservations with lands outlying. After recounting his own apparent distaste for the "solitary life of western farming," Garland argued in favor of the Native American system of holding lands in common. In Garland's opinion, "The red man's feeling that the earth is for the use of all men, is right; he has always distinguished between the ownership of things and the ownership of land and water."[7]

Garland further argued that cultural biases must be eliminated from the doctrines of Indian policy as set forth by the old Indian reform movement. In Garland's view, those Indians who had accepted allotments and had thereby gained citizenship should have the full rights and privileges of every other American citizen. They should not be hampered in any regard from maintaining their cultural identities. Indians were to be made truly free, he intimated, to do as they pleased in "dress, dance and religion."[8]

The novelist and social commentator attacked Indian boarding schools for the very reason that they had been established in the first place. The boarding school essentially taught the Native American child, according to Garland, to "abhor his parents." Moreover, Garland thought that these schools were "monstrous" and, finally, "unchristian." In the end, Garland assaulted the very core of the assimilationist movement, the Christian missionary. Missionaries, in Garland's view, were mere "sojourners," leading solitary lives on the reservations. In their religious zeal, they failed to recognize the good in Native American cultures, and had nearly destroyed the traditional artistic and social accomplishments that gave Native Americans the basic dignity and self-pride that all people so badly need to cope with the complexity of modern living. Garland further argued that the missionaries did "not represent the culture and scholarship of our day," and hence they were not "good examples to send to Indian country."[9] The missionaries' lack of perception and modern thought could do nothing but cause harm.

Christian morality, zeal, and the notion of "Christian civilization" did little else but demoralize the Native American population.

Garland and Roe both very likely thought that Native Americans were racially inferior and would one day become amalgamated into white society as a result of intermarriage, or else simply vanish from the face of the earth. In either case, they believed that Native Americans had the right to save as much of their self-pride and self-reliance through the retention of some aspects of their cultures. With this notion of self-pride, Native Americans could win the respect of non-Indians. The dignity of Native Americans could be uplifted if they were allowed to celebrate identifiably Indian achievements. Garland, Roe, and the staff writer for *Outlook* who preceded them—all were of the opinion that the development of Indian art would instill in Indians the pride that they once felt from being a distinct people. Garland and Roe attempted to break down stereotypes and teach whites to respect Indians for being Indians. In their minds, Native American cultures were in a steep decline, not because they were primitive and incapable of producing something of value, but because of white arrogance, greed, and misdirected missionary zeal.

Missionary zealotry and the vanishing policy in general continued to come under attack in the print medium. Seven months after Garland's article was published, *Independent* magazine printed an exposé of missionary wrongs and some suggestions as to what should be done to correct them. Although the article was far less severe than Garland's tract, it did expand on one of the important questions Garland had raised. Garland had frankly stated that the missionaries did not possess enough knowledge about Native Americans to deal adequately with the problems on the reservations. But though Garland asserted that the missionaries did not represent the scholarship of the period, he was decidedly vague in identifying exactly who did have the knowledge required to work out solutions to the Indian question.

The *Independent* was not vague at all. Missionaries, according to the article, were failing because their religious and assimilationist passions bordered on maliciousness.[10] They had condemned to destruction, for being "heathenish," any "of the good which exists in the inferior." Indians, from the point of view expressed in the *Independent* article, were backward, simple, and racially inferior to whites, but they nevertheless possessed some good qualities, such as artistic excellence and athletic endurance. Indians, when pressed to change, duly conformed outwardly, yet retained the same "old convictions." "The net product," according to the *Independent*, "is a hypocrite." The missionaries had created more deeply entrenched problems than they had solved with the vanishing policy because they had been "ignorant of ethnological knowledge and of both the scientific and moral value of aboriginal traditions, customs and arts."

The *Independent* clearly and forcefully argued that Native Americans could be uplifted only after careful study of their ethnological backgrounds. According to the article, it was "only the trained student" who fully understood how closely in substance were "human customs and institutions" that differed "most widely in outward expression and how important, for the moral well-being of the lowly, the familiar forms of expression may be." The racist overtones of the article were obvious, but the writer was also outlining the essence of conservatism in the United States: that human beings often and irrationally cling to their communities and institutions and that change is a slow, painful process that cannot take place mechanically. The article announced that the time had come for the true "friends of the Indian" to adopt a more scientific approach to the solution of the "Indian problem" because sending "into the mission field teachers whose chief qualification is a religious zeal can only work cumulative mischief."[11] Clearly the author of the article for the *Independent* was leaning toward science, rather than religion, to provide solutions to persistent problems plaguing the United States. Objectivity and detached reasoning were needed rather than zealotry and dogma.

Throughout the period similar attacks were made on the missionary mentality that buttressed the vanishing policy. James Mooney, a prominent ethnologist for the Bureau of American Ethnology, intensely disliked missionaries. In 1903, testifying before a board investigating the pilfering of funds from the bureau, Mooney blamed the assimilation movement for turning one of his Kiowa friends into a "dilapidated tramp."[12] One writer for the conservation-oriented *Overland Monthly* magazine feared further interference in the lives of the Havasupai, and thus the end of the beauty of the natural life he found in their domain.[13] Another conservationist, Dillon Wallace, writing for *Outing* magazine, stated that the missionary mentality had been "misdirected," and famed photographer Edward S. Curtis spoke out against the "inhumanity" of the vanishing policy for *Hampton Magazine* in 1912.[14]

George Warton James, in his book *Indian Blankets and Their Makers*, continued the onslaught against the assimilationists. Because of missionary interference and the accumulative pressures of forced assimilation, James asserted, government policy had turned "the Indian" into a "peculiar nondescript, in whose life aboriginal superstitions linger side by side with the white man's follies, vices, customs and conventional ideas."[15] Most of the preservationists were convinced that Native Americans were rapidly disappearing, and duly set the blame for the decline on the Christian missionaries, in whose trust Indian policy had been placed. Natalie Curtis Burlin was more outspoken than even James. The policy of assimilation, in her opinion, was a supreme example of American arrogance that had forced upon Native Americans a "form of racial suicide."[16]

The ideas of people like Roe, Garland, Burlin, James, Curtis, and many others were outlined in the pages of some very popular magazines and books, and hence either reflected or influenced public opinion to a great degree. American opinion in regard to Native Americans was undergoing a change. Once conceived of as the barrier to the spread of American civilization, the Native Americans were now being viewed as peoples being destroyed by a misguided and, therefore, an inefficient and unscientific philanthropy. More and more people interested in Indian policy began to turn to scientific analyses from ethnology and anthropology for answers to the "Indian Problem" and to shun the high-minded, yet highly destructive, ambitious philosophies of the vanishing policy.

By 1901 the Christian friends of the Indian were very much aware of the criticism aimed at them. They had been the guiding spirit behind the assimilation movement and had provided the liberal sentiments that had justified allotment, the boarding schools, the ban on Native American ceremonies, and the relegation of the tribes to the status of nonstates. As a consequence of the changing attitudes toward Native Americans and the Indian policy, many missionaries toned down their assaults on "heathenism" and began to advocate the perpetuation of certain aspects of Native American cultures, especially in the area of arts and crafts. Their ambivalence, however, exacerbated rather than solved the vast number of problems that existed in Indian country. To many of them, criticism of their philanthropy and zeal was unjustified, and few recognized that they were caught between conflicting feelings of repugnance and admiration for Native Americans.

At the 1901 meeting of the Lake Mohonk Conference, the friends of the Indian reversed their previous stance on the perpetuation of tribal cultures and decided to support the retention of Native American artistic endeavors. The members of the conference adopted an unprecedented platform that was remarkably inconsistent with its previous staunch assimilationist sentiment. The importance of Indian industries, according to the new Lake Mohonk Conference platform, was such "that the Government, and all teachers and guides of the Indian, should cooperate in the endeavor to revive them." To Indians, it noted, arts and crafts were "valuable as a means of profitable occupation and natural expression." For the rest of the country, Indian crafts were "specimens of a rare and indigenous art, many of them artistically excellent, some of them absolutely unique." But the platform also suggested that even more important results would come from the maintenance of tribal art forms. The majority of people at the conference believed that Native American handicrafts would provide "congenial and remunerative employment at home" and "foster, in the Indian, self-respect, and in the white race, respect for the Indians."[17] Essentially, Roe's ideas about Indian art and the self-pride that it would engender in Native Americans were given some credit.

There was, however, another side to the question of preserving and fostering the perpetuation of Native American artisanship. Richard Henry Pratt, whose views had long been respected and followed at the conferences, was hardly favorable to the continuity of Native American craftsmanship or to the perpetuation of tribal identities in the manufacture of these crafts. He began to raise some objections to the "industry business." Although Pratt was certainly in favor of keeping Native Americans busily occupied, he did not like the idea of Native Americans sitting around working on "native" crafts. In 1903 at the Lake Mohonk Conference, Pratt adamantly stated that "If we insist on their staying in their tepees and working at the industries it is a hindrance."[18] Permitting Indians on reservations to do beadwork, weave blankets for white tourists, or build canoes for sportsmen was not, in Pratt's opinion, the proper method of making Native Americans vanish into mainstream American society.

But by 1903 neither Pratt nor the sentiment he expressed could stop the fostering and perpetuation of Native American arts and crafts. Nor could it alleviate the tension that resulted from the conflict between Pratt's views and the preservationist sentiment. The 1903 Lake Mohonk meeting was marked by a strained camaraderie among its guests. At first the members sat placidly through speeches that attacked the central beliefs of the vanishing policy. Alice M. Robertson, who was supervisor of the Creek Nation schools and a descendent of missionaries, supported the Creek traditionalists' hostility toward the assimilationists' demand that they give up their culture and autonomous government, turn their backs on their religion, reject their historical social arrangements, and accept allotment. In Robertson's opinion, the Snakes under Chitto Harjo were "as sincere in rising against the United States authorities as our people were in rising against taxation without representation."[19] She was also quite frank in her appraisal of the notion that Native American customs and cultures were in some way inferior or unworthy when compared with the white man's "civilization." In that vein she related to the conference an anecdote:

> The other day I took a New York college girl to an Indian cabin, and showed her their simple life, their simple furniture, and the beautiful white flour made from the particular kind of corn they raise. We had just taken her in to see one of the rented houses of the cotton people, and I said to her, "Which do you think is really the higher type of civilization to-day?" She said she thought the Indian was far beyond the white.[20]

As the meeting wore on, both understated and overt criticism of this kind leveled at the vanishing policy finally produced a series of defensive outbursts. In large part the clash centered on the usefulness, or lack thereof, of ethnology as a tool in the search for a solution to Indian affairs. This conflict directly confronted the old reformers who were theoreticians of the assimilation policy. Richard Henry Pratt, for one, looked upon anthropology as the principal culprit behind the perpetuation of Native American cultures and the maintenance of a sense of peoplehood among members of the various tribes. He evidently still held to the idea that Indians would naturally abandon their tribal values and ways when given the opportunity to enter American society. When he criticized the retention of tribalism, Pratt, instead of blaming Indians or arguing that they were mentally incapable of entering the white world, accused the anthropologists of hindering Indian development. He adamantly opposed tribalism in any form and dutifully attacked "an Indian agency where three tribes are located under one agent" for setting up a separate school system for each tribe. Pratt denounced the system in no uncertain terms, calling it "a kind of anthropologist and ethnologist arrangement to keep up tribal distinctions."[21]

Pratt's defensiveness became obvious, and it seemed as if he were fighting a final battle for everything he held dear. Indeed he was. He was a vigorous advocate of the idea that Native Americans should receive the basic skills necessary for competition with whites in white society. Given that opportunity, Native Americans would not only change their ways but also become contributing citizens of the United States. Then, they would no longer be "Indians." But in 1903 Pratt's ideas regarding the education of Native American youths were experiencing an unprecedented amount of criticism. The famous novelist Hamlin Garland had called Pratt's method of removing children from their families, sending them to faraway boarding schools, and essentially teaching them to oppose the views and ways of their parents no less than an "unchristian" approach to Indian education. Pratt's "outing system," which had placed Indian children in white homes during the summer months to teach them the values of Christian family life and American citizenship, was also under fire. The outing system, which had been touted only three years before as "a definite method—perhaps *the* method—of Americanizing Indians," was viewed by many whites as simply providing a few white households with Indian servants and farm laborers free of charge. In sum, the outing system was being looked upon as a form of Indian servitude that stopped just short of slavery.[22]

Apparently believing in the old military dictum that attack was the best defense, Pratt lashed out against the critics of his philosophy and focused his attention specifically on the ethnologists. In this case, Pratt's attack came at a perfect time. The previous July, an incident involving James Mooney of the Bureau of American Ethnology and George A. Dorsey of the Field Museum occurred at the Cheyenne

Sun Dance held near Colony, and the Lake Mohonk Lodge, in western Oklahoma. The incident seemed to support Pratt's contention that anthropologists were encouraging Indians to live in the past.

On the day that the Cheyenne ceremony ended and the campsite was being taken down, a Cheyenne man had skewers placed in the flesh of his back. He then had rawhide line strung with bits of buffalo skull attached to the skewers. After the lines were attached, the man walked in a complete circle around the large encampment, dragging the pieces of buffalo skull behind him. Mooney and Dorsey, who were in attendance, had observed the man's actions and hurried to a better vantage point from which they could watch the ritual. John H. Seger, the superintendent of the Cheyenne agency, had also observed the proceedings and had met Mooney and Dorsey at the point where the Cheyenne began his ceremonial encirclement of the campsite. According to the two ethnologists, Seger said absolutely nothing to the Cheyenne involved in the incident, nor did he comment to the two scientists about the strictly forbidden ritual. After the camp had been disbanded, however, Seger publicly accused Mooney and Dorsey of paying the Cheyenne man in question to undergo the "tortures" of the Sun Dance.[23]

Mooney and Dorsey denied the charge and issued a counteraccusation. According to Mooney, the Cheyenne headmen had asked him to attend their council meeting that immediately preceded the Sun Dance celebration. During the meeting one of the chiefs told Mooney that a pledger was "anxious to sacrifice himself in the old style." Mooney said he "strongly advised" against making a sacrifice of the flesh, even though the Cheyenne "had won all the ordinary rights of American citizens in religious matters." Mooney asserted that Seger was the real culprit in the matter because he allegedly told the Cheyenne that their Sun Dance was not "genuine" without the element of self-torture. The superintendent was said to have further incited the particular Cheyenne man's commitment to sacrifice his flesh by stating that if the ceremony was made "genuine" by the addition of the ritual of self-sacrifice, "he might think it worth while to attend." Dorsey supported Mooney's claims, as did most of the Cheyenne headmen.[24]

Pratt, despite a significant amount of testimony supporting Mooney's version of the incident, chose to believe Seger and attempted to turn the situation into an indictment of ethnological interference with government policy. Although Pratt was never mentioned in any of the accounts of the event, he nevertheless stated, "I was there, and I know it happened just about the way our good old Seegar [*sic*] said it did." Moreover, Pratt not only said that Mooney paid the Cheyenne man to undergo self-torture, but also implied that the ethnologist was currently occupied in the process of paying the entire Cheyenne tribal council to come to his defense against Seger. With that, Pratt declared that the "usefulness of the Bureau of Ethnology has gone in the way they hold people to the past."[25]

Other people at the conference of 1903 were far more cautious in their statements regarding anthropology. Although many of the conferees condemned any ceremonial that caused injury and any scientist who went among the tribes "simply . . . to delve in the past of the Indian," they were not ready to dismiss completely the entire profession as useless. One prominent member of the conference, Merrill E. Gates, thought, in fact, that the "whole Indian problem is a problem of ethnology." Another member stated that the discipline of ethnology had attracted him to the attempt to preserve Native American art because it "appealed to my sense of beauty" and in turn led him to devote himself "to the interest of the downtrodden people."[26]

Clearly the Lake Mohonk Conference membership favored only those ethnologists who believed in the cultural evolutionist school of anthropological theory. Alice C. Fletcher, for example, was cited at the 1903 meeting as "the best" that science had to offer. Gates, in his principal address to the assembled members, even cited Lewis Henry Morgan's concept of social evolution to prove how Indian problems were "deeply rooted" in the attempt to overcome the often torturous transition from barbarism to civilization. The Sun Dance, which was actually a continuing contemporary religious ceremony from the point of view of the Cheyenne living in western Oklahoma, was described as a part of the Indian past, a remnant of savagery yet to be overcome. It was obvious that the Christian reformers at Lake Mohonk respected science, but they also used a great deal of caution when dealing with individual ethnologists.[27]

Less clear were their attitudes concerning the goal of complete Native American assimilation. They were timorously beginning to back away from the vanishing policy. Complete Indian assimilation seemed less urgent. Some members of the conference thought that Native Americans were "backward" by nature and incapable of immediately blending into American society. Moreover, an "Indian" identity, especially one connected with the production of crafts, was entirely too popular with most conferees for the old reformers, save for Pratt, to attack directly. The old reformers at Lake Mohonk were already under fire for embracing and advocating the missionary philosophy that had nearly destroyed certain features of Native American life—features that most whites had only just begun to appreciate. As a result of these factors, the membership of the Lake Mohonk Conference of 1903 seemed ambivalent in thought and deed. Once the bastion of forceful and straightforward advocacy for the complete and speedy assimilation of Native Americans into white society, the conference began to reassess its ultimate purpose.

Perhaps the only person at the 1903 meeting at Lake Mohonk who was consistent in his theories concerning Indian assimilation was Richard Henry Pratt. His fervor in defending the Carlisle school system was never greater. In an impassioned speech to the conference, Pratt attacked those people who had accused his institution of attempting to make household servants and farm laborers out of Native American children and stated that Carlisle was merely following the government's policy of assimilation. He insisted that Native Americans' destiny was linked to the agricultural element of the American economy and that Indians were either to become farmers or farm wives. Teaching Indian children the manual arts and the rudiments of reading, according to Pratt, was the "best way to make the Indian a farmer, and at the same time enable him to realize what it is to be a citizen."

For Pratt, allowing Indians to maintain their tribal identities amounted to a denial of American greatness, and he insisted that the "melting pot" was the only method of keeping America great. The preservation of a culture that he considered antiquated was antithetical to Pratt's belief in the value of assimilation. Native Americans, like European immigrants, were, in Pratt's opinion, destined to become "Americanized." "I have said over and over again," he reiterated, "that putting a community of Italians in one of our greatest cities to settle by themselves in a mass will simply reproduce a little Italy in America."[28] Pratt firmly believed that the same idea should be applied to Native

Americans and to the making of Indian policy. Indians—as well as Italians, Balts, Jews, Slavs, and others—would never become Americanized without getting into the "swim of citizenship." Unfortunately for Pratt, he was maintaining his own sense of duty and mission by holding on to convictions that were rapidly becoming obsolete.

Despite Pratt's passion, some members of the conference began to treat his ideas rather lightly. He was chided several times for his attacks on ethnologists. Samuel J. Burrows talked about Pratt "putting on his war paint" and pursuing scientists fleeing his monumental wrath. Merrill E. Gates was a bit more caustic toward Pratt's outbursts. According to Gates, "we cannot help laughing here when Colonel Pratt lifts his tomahawk over the head of the ethnologist."[29] Pratt, one of the most earnest and militant of the nineteenth-century reformers and perhaps the least racist of the entire group, was treated like a crusty old uncle, to be heard but not taken too seriously.

This attitude prevailed outside the confines of the Lake Mohonk Conference as well. The very next year Pratt was forced to resign his position at his beloved Carlisle because of the position he took in advocating the dissolution of the Bureau of Indian Affairs. His assimilationist fervor eventually led to his undoing. Moreover, most of his colleagues in the assimilation movement timidly failed to come to his defense. Only Carlos Montezuma and Elaine Goodale Eastman remained strongly and actively supportive.

Chiding Pratt for his constancy served only to highlight the other members' of the Lake Mohonk Conference ambivalence. Lyman Abbott, the editor of *Outlook* and one of the conference's oldest members, became decidedly ambiguous in his editorial positions on Indian affairs. He printed Roe's article, for example, favoring the retention of Indian arts and strongly praising the Boston-based Indian Industries League.

But less than three years after Roe's article appeared, Abbott reprinted, and agreed editorially with, a reservation agent's letter attacking the idea of preserving Indian craftsmanship in the native arts. The letter, which Pratt had read to the Lake Mohonk Conference in 1903, told how the agent had been asked to help provide objects of Indian art for display at the St. Louis World's Fair. The agent, who remained anonymous, was proud to report that "the Indians in my charge" could not supply any of the materials requested because "I do not know of an old Indian in this district who can make a basket." He added that he would much rather have displayed crops and other "works of industry," and did so at a local fair. The agent then made a mild attack on the Boston headquarters of the Indian Industries League. "I did not," he wrote, "enter my exhibit any old time golf-belts or music rolls or the war club with which Captain John Smith was not killed." Instead, he left "that kind of exhibit to the frontiersmen from Boston and other frontier places."[30]

This agent's letter clearly demonstrated that there were men and women of the Pratt philosophy still active in Indian affairs. And it demonstrated that they would continue to raise their voices in protest against any hint of tribal ceremonialism. During World War I, several adherents of the assimilationist philosophy suggested that war would serve to civilize recalcitrant Indians. They believed that Native American troops would learn from and become like their white comrades in arms. When the war ended, however, they decried the fact that several of the Native American soldiers were welcomed home from the trenches with ceremonial dances and songs.[31] As late as 1920, an Indian agent was reported to have verbally attacked "a well-known archaeologist" who allegedly urged several tribal leaders in the Southwest to continue their rituals in spite of white admonishments against such activities. The Indian agent was reported to have told the archaeologist, "If it weren't for you damned scientists we'd soon have the Indians off the mesas and at work."[32]

The controversy over whether to preserve "the Indian" on the one hand or to assimilate "the Indian" on the other was not necessarily an argument between two distinct groups. Not all ethnologists supported the idea of freezing Native American cultures in time and place, and many of the staunch Christians in the Indian reform movement certainly favored the preservation of Native American cultures in so far as they stimulated the production of fine arts and crafts. Rather, it was as if each person interested in Indian affairs—except for Richard Henry Pratt—had internalized both positions and could wax supportive of one argument or the other as circumstances dictated.

This ambiguity was certainly evident among the members of the Board of Indian Commissioners for example. In 1905 the board, a group that perennially supported the vanishing policy, stated flatly that the "wisest friends of the Indian recognize with great delight and value highly the art impulse in certain Indian tribes," an impulse that had been demonstrated "in Indian music, in Indian art forms—such as the birchbark canoe, in Indian basketry and more rarely in Indian pottery." The board did not, however, think it right to keep Native Americans "out of civilization in order that certain picturesque aspects of savagery and barbarism may continue to be within reach of the traveler and the curious." The "savagery" that had spawned numerous works of art should not, according to the board, be allowed to continue, even for the benefit of the "scientific observer."[33]

Questions of race and culture seemed to baffle whites throughout the first twenty years of the twentieth century. They could firmly believe, for example, that "An Indian can no more resist the temptation to drink liquor, if it is accessible, than a two-year-old child can help taking a lump of sugar if it is within his reach."[34] Yet they also thought that Native Americans' spirituality and knowledge about the environment were important enough to be taught to white youngsters in the Boy Scout and Camp Fire Girl organizations. Several of Charles Eastman's best-selling books were written for children.

The inconsistency in white thought about Indians—whether the Indian of reality or the stereotype—was clearly demonstrated during World War I. Many whites argued persuasively that Native Americans should be integrated into all the white regiments and treated the same as any other soldier, without regard to race. And Native Americans were indeed signed up for or drafted into white regiments. At the same time, the assimilationist newsletter *The Indian's Friend* reported with pride that "Indians in the regiments are being used for scouting and patrol duty because of the natural instinct which fits them for this kind of work."[35] This kind of racial stereotype, coming as it did in the pages of one of the leading periodicals favoring Indian integration into the armed forces, would have been humorous had not the stereotype of the "Indian Scout" led the military to utilize Native Americans for these kinds of perilous and often lethal duties in no man's land.

Perhaps the best example of white confusion regarding Native Americans swirled around the belief that Indians were a "vanishing race." Some certainly thought the decline and eventual extinction of Native Americans were part of the natural biological process of evolution. Others, especially those fundamentalist Christians who did not believe in evolution by natural selection, very likely thought that Indians were dying simply because God had willed them to do so. Whatever the process, however, both the old reformers and the new preservationists sought to make Indian extinction less painful and brutal or to stop it altogether. Either way, they were attempting to defy "natural law" or usurp God's will. Both the scientists and the Christian philanthropists must have wrestled with this conundrum.[36]

Finally, in 1917 the commissioner of Indian Affairs announced that the Native American birthrate had finally started to exceed the death rate. This fact did not immediately dispel the myth of the vanishing Indian. Far from it: the myth remained intact for years, principally because many Americans continued to equate race with culture. In a way, Richard Henry Pratt's favorite and timeworn phrase, "kill the Indian and save the man," captured the essence of nineteenth-century Indian reform. If, through allotment and the boarding schools, one could Americanize Native Americans, then one could "save" the "Indian race." On the other hand, according to early twentieth-century progressives, "the Indian" could be saved only if one could salvage the supposedly superior Native American racial characteristics such as a propensity for creating objects of beauty, athleticism, a spiritual connection with the land, and an inherited knowledge of the environment. It must be remembered that the idea, as articulated by Franz Boas and his students, that culture determined human behavior was only in its earliest stages of development in the period. Most Americans in the early years of the twentieth century thought that race determined both culture and behavior. Perhaps Pratt and the other old reformers really were ahead of their time. Unfortunately, despite their rather liberal ideas concerning race, they nevertheless believed in the innate superiority of Euro-American culture.

The confusion in white thought regarding Native Americans could have been the product of the conflict that usually punctuated every phase of the relationship between the colonizer and the colonized. Although the phases in colonial relationships do not necessarily mark time periods—and are not signified by specific changes in colonial power differentials—they seem to fall into a well-described pattern. Additionally, the phases may overlap somewhat. First, there is the colonial occupation of lands used and usually held sacred by an indigenous group or groups. Next, the colonial power seeks to restrict the movements of indigenous people and gain clear title to these lands by drawing supposedly definitive boundaries between "settlers" and "natives." Treaties and reservations mark this particular phase. The third phase is usually an attempt on the part of the colonial power to assimilate or marginalize an indigenous population either to control it or to be able to utilize it as a work force. During the fourth phase, the colonial power seemingly admits that assimilation has failed and seeks to accommodate on a limited, structural basis the fact that the indigenous groups still maintain their distinct senses of peoplehood. Conflict not only punctuates each of these phases, but also leads to changes in colonial policies that bring on the next phase.

Historically, the United States fell into the same pattern of colonial relationships. After independence, Americans began to expand the boundaries of the new nation, displacing Native Americans and creating new conflicts. In order to quell the frontier violence and to draw boundaries that would promote orderly expansion, the United States made treaties, created reservations, and even removed many tribes from their homelands to other well-defined areas outside the jurisdiction of the various states. The pressure placed on Native Americans to change their cultures so that they could survive in these highly restricted "new lands" led to more conflict. In time, this conflict led to the attempt to dismantle the reservation system, end treaty making, and assimilate the Native American population. Perhaps the Progressive Era in Native American–white relations was the period of conflict that led, as we will examine, to the colonial phase of structural accommodation under the supervision of John Collier, commissioner of Indian Affairs in the 1930s.

Whatever the case, it appears that the conflict that punctuates each phase of this colonial model occurs not only between the colonizer and the colonized but also within both groups. In dealing with the United States government, each of the Native American tribal states had both their appeasers and their recalcitrants; their share of those willing to become allied with the United States and those who advocated war against the Americans. In a like manner, Americans fell into groups that were pro- and antitreaty, pro- and antireservation, pro- and antiallotment, and pro- and antiassimilation. Internal divisions, in short, perennially exist, and it is only when one side or the other gains the political upper hand that policies actually change. Before policies can change, however, the opposing sides go through a period of conflict.

A close look at the development of federal Indian policy shows that most policies were indeed formulated very early in the colonial relationship. The idea of allotting tribal lands in severalty was introduced as early as 1808; the notion of clearly delineating tribal boundaries and "civilizing" Native Americans through gifts of livestock, spinning wheels, and the services of blacksmiths was part of the Trade and Intercourse Act of 1802 and had been advocated as early as 1791 by President George Washington; the formula for removing Native Americans from within state boundaries to new lands in the public domain was an aspect of the Georgia Compact of 1802. Policy makers then have what might be called a grab bag of policies in which they can find a particular broad formula for a policy that can be implemented with modifications as the need arises.

Consequently, in different periods of time or under extenuating circumstances or because the conflict over a previous policy had reached a boiling point, policy makers have focused on different solutions to the "Indian Problem." Thus, policy makers focused on reservations and "civilization" in the early years of the federal government, on Indian removal in the 1830s, and on allotment in the post–Civil War period. The conflict and confusion seemingly always lay in deciding which policy would solve the problem at a given time or under a particular set of circumstances. A number of Americans in the early years of the twentieth century viewed the vanishing policy as an abject failure. They began to search in the policy grab bag for something different, and conflict and confusion necessarily ensued. This "colonial phase model" does seem to fit the historical development of American Indian policy.

On the other hand, whites' ambiguity regarding Native Americans and their place in America may have been a reflection of the greater inconsistencies in American social thought during the early years of the new century. American ideas about the function of persons in society changed little as the new century began. These ideas and the nature of reform itself in the United States were nevertheless in the process of change. Many Americans, concerned about social conditions, began to suggest that instead of absolute freedom to do what they wished, people had a responsibility to sublimate their personal goals, or idiosyncrasies, to the betterment of the larger society. This belief was in direct opposition to the traditional liberal notion that held sacrosanct an individualism equated with personal assertiveness, responsibility for one's actions, and liberty.

The public attitude toward corporate capitalism in the period was especially revealing. Americans began to attack "Big Business" for creating corporate behemoths that infringed upon the rights of free trade and competition. The trusts and monopolies were frightening because they were a burden on the American middle class, destroying free choice, gouging society for high profits, yet producing inferior goods. Americans could also resent Big Business because it was born out of the chaos of rampant and ruthless *laissez-faire* individualism. Men such as Rockefeller, Carnegie, and Morgan had utilized personal liberty to build corporate and financial empires that crushed the personal liberties of many people in American society. Individualism, in other words, could go too far; it could become oppressive and inimical to society if it grew large enough to rival or surpass other institutions or grew to control them. The American public's new concern for society was basically a quest for order, stability, and justice. Muckraking, trust-busting, and even Prohibition were efforts to impose order on an almost fanatical brand of American individualism.

The growing social conscience of the American middle class and the ideas it represented launched a new movement that promised to affect the lower classes as well. Laborers, immigrants, African Americans, and Native Americans were expected to conform to the values of mainstream middle-class American society in a manner that would not infringe upon the lives of the majority of the American populace. Because of their poverty, immigrants, blacks, and Indians could conceivably become rebellious, but in any event they were generally considered to be welfare burdens on the upper classes. Lower-class individualism, which was often perceived in criminal activity, could be rendered benign if it was encouraged to become more assimilated in American society and if it was confined to the framework of middle-class mores.

Ultimately, these beliefs should have produced effects on Native Americans in America like those of the Indian assimilation movement. Indians were expected to conform to American values and neither threaten, nor become burdens on, America's middle-class majority. But many important white intellectuals, artists, and scientists believed that Native American conservationist thought, athletic ability, and artistic accomplishment actually enhanced the quality of American life. According to these idealists, therefore, Native Americans should be granted the limited liberty to maintain those tribal cultural traits perceived positively by the American public.

Unlike the old assimilationists, who wanted Native Americans to become citizens by rejecting their tribal cultural identities, the new reformers sought to maintain an identifiable Indian presence in American society that nevertheless conformed to white values and institutions. As a consequence, Native Americans found themselves placed in a strange kind of confusion in the early years of the twentieth century. It was as if whites wanted Indians to exist in a perpetual limbo of marginality, becoming neither fully Indian in a traditional sense, nor full-fledged members of the American middle class in a cultural sense.

The new reformers, in their search for stability and order, could not fully condone the old assimilationist ideas about Native Americans. The vanishing policy did not create new citizens; it had created only a demoralized racial group living within the boundaries of the United States. The old assimilationists' emphasis on Christian reform seemed chaotic and lacking in efficient scientific thought. Because of their religious and cultural biases, the old reformers lost credibility in the minds of the progressive thinkers.

But the new reformers, although strongly secular and scientific in approach, seemed far more impersonal than the assimilationists. They lacked the old reformers' honesty and clarity, though perhaps not their bigotry, when establishing long-range goals for Indian policy. Policy makers found themselves without a strong philosophical or theoretical basis on which they could ground their Indian programs and policies. Little wonder that Fayette Avery McKenzie, the white "father" of the Society of American Indians and advocate of the ultimate assimilation of Native Americans into middle-class American society, wrote in 1910 that government officials, lacking a forceful direction, had produced a "great confusion in Indian policies."[37] That McKenzie was reviewing former Indian commissioner Francis Leupp's book, *The Indian and His Problem*, emphasized the notion that Indian policy had taken a wrong turn when professional bureaucrats had taken control of Indian affairs. To McKenzie, Leupp seemed to exemplify the secular, scientific approach to Indian policy that had been spawned as a result of conflict and confusion over the vanishing policy.

CHAPTER VII

THE "GREAT CONFUSION" IN INDIAN AFFAIRS

B Y 1910, WHEN MCKENZIE WROTE HIS REVIEW of *The Indian and His Problem*, the vanishing policy was under attack from all sides. The New Indians had outflanked it by refusing to give up their Native American roots and continuing to demand the rights their ancestors had fought for over the years. Native Americans on the reservations were fighting a cunning defensive action to maintain their spiritual connections with the land through syncretism and to preserve their communities by sustaining long-standing kinship systems. Scientists denounced the vanishing policy as an unscientific, inefficient, and unsuccessful attempt to create white people out of Native Americans, and demanded that Indians be left alone so that they could be studied more thoroughly. Without fully grasping what they were doing, white intellectuals, artists, and art connoisseurs recognized that Native American art was the product of complex societies and that it could not be "Indian art" without Native American spirituality or a tribal sense of peoplehood. Conservationists of the romantic stripe flayed the vanishing policy with a series of cutting articles that essentially branded it as an attempt to loot Native American lands and destroy a culture that possessed a knowledge of the environment that could renew America and counterbalance the deleterious effects of industrialization.

Between 1900 and 1920, federal Indian policy did indeed become a confusing bureaucratic attempt to find order in the midst of the philosophical debate over what "the Indian" was and what Native Americans in general could become. Ultimately, the philosophical conflict represented a clash between old notions of liberalism that stressed personal initiative and new, more conservative ideas of social control that led to the growth of the federal bureaucracy in social service areas. The old assimilationists believed that if their policies were followed in Indian education and in the allotment of tribal lands, Indians would abandon tribal cultures and would eventually be freed from the "cramping reservation yoke."[1] After Indians had been freed and Americanized, the federal government would then abandon its role as the final arbiter of Native Americans' future. Native Americans would then become masters of their own personal destinies. In any case, once the tribes were eliminated as distinctly identifiable peoples within American society, the Board of Indian Commissioners assured those interested in Indian affairs, there would follow "the speedy extinction of a separate bureau for Indians."[2]

But to attain the lofty goal of eliminating a federal bureaucracy, the old reformers actually promoted the imposition of increasingly greater controls over Indian affairs. Chief Justice John Marshall's ruling in *Worcester v. Georgia* in 1832, that Indians should be looked upon as "wards" in their relationship with the national government, was now taken literally and erroneously to mean that the United States had assumed guardianship over individual Native Americans. Likely as not, Marshall viewed individual Native Americans as members of tribal polities and those Indian polities as protectorates rather than wards. Whatever the case and whatever the Marshall court's intention, the Indian Office, at the instigation of the assimilation movement, assumed more and more discretionary authority over the lives of individual Native Americans, handing out allotments, abducting children to be placed in boarding schools, providing health care, distributing rations and the like. Tribal states could be bypassed as the Indian Office assumed more responsibilities in its role as the guardian of individual Indians' interests. The Dawes and Curtis Acts, the extension of federal jurisdiction over crimes committed on Indian lands, and the whole assimilation process could not have occurred without violating the provisions of treaties and trampling on personal rights, and these acts were all justified on the grounds that Indians were wards of the federal government.

In the early twentieth century the Indian Office was a constantly growing bureaucracy. Civil service reform in the late nineteenth century had ensured that low-level officials, with certain degrees of expertise, would be retained in the Indian Office despite changes of presidential administration. In 1913, Secretary of the Interior Franklin K. Lane ironically described the Indian Office as a "vanishing bureau," apparently without recognizing or understanding that the number of the office's employees had more than doubled since 1900.[3] The Indian service had taken on greater responsibility and consequently had grown enormously to perform its expanded functions and services.

Fayette McKenzie's review of Francis Leupp's *Indian and His Problem* was in reality more an evaluation of the course the government's relationship with Indians had taken since 1900. That Leupp, as commissioner of Indian Affairs from 1905 to 1909, had been the driving personality behind the growth of the Indian Office as well as behind the course of Indian-white relations in the period served only to make McKenzie's critique a sharper and more precise indictment of early twentieth-century Indian policy. Leupp, according to McKenzie, had effectively become the greatest barrier to the realization of complete assimilation for Native Americans and to the end of a special bureau for Indian affairs.[4]

Leupp, however, was simply an easy target for the old assimilationists. Although it was true that under Leupp's direction the Indian Service expanded, it was equally true that the quick assimilation of the Native American population had not indeed taken place. It was plainly clear that, even before Leupp took office, the movement to Americanize and assimilate Native Americans was hanging by a thread and holding on only because assimilation expressed a liberal and moral ideal. But three events during 1903 prophetically indicated that assimilation was less a moral and liberal crusade than it was an attempt to deny Native Americans their human, religious, and political rights and to purloin the tribal estate. The Cheyenne Sun Dance incident during the summer sparked the controversy at the Lake Mohonk Conference regarding the usefulness of ethnology and the value of preserving Indian art. This incident effectively demonstrated that the assimilation movement, mired in ambivalence, had reached an impasse regarding whether or not Native Americans should be fully assimilated and thus robbed of their special heritage. Even the assimilationists were drifting away from their clear-cut philosophical and theoretical positions.

The Supreme Court decision in a suit brought by a Kiowa leader named Lone Wolf against Secretary of the Interior Ethan Allen

Hitchcock confused the issue of Indian assimilation even more. Lawyers for Lone Wolf sought an injunction against the allotment of the Kiowa, Comanche, and Kiowa-Apache reservation in southwestern Oklahoma and the opening of its surplus lands to white settlers. Under the Treaty of Medicine Lodge, made in 1867, the tribes and the United States had agreed that any further land cessions would require three-fourths of the adult males of the signatory tribes to approve the cession for it to be considered legally binding.

After the passage of the General Allotment Act in 1887, the Kiowa were pressured into making another "agreement" with the government. In 1871, Congress had added a provision to the Indian Appropriations Act of that year stipulating that the federal government would make no further treaties with Native American tribes. In part, this action was taken for political reasons—the House objected to the Senate's exclusive power over the use or distribution of ceded Indian lands by treaty—and in part because making treaties with Native American tribes acknowledged that they were more than simple groupings of individuals to be absorbed into the American body politic. Indian assimilation would not be served by admitting through the treaty-making process that autonomous and sovereign Native American polities actually existed.

Since 1871, however, federal agents, government commissions, and Army officers had been negotiating with Native American leaders and signing "agreements" and "conventions" for all the same reasons that the federal government had made treaties with Indian tribes in the past. Although they certainly carried the weight of any kind of contractual arrangement made between the federal government and an Indian tribe, these "agreements" were no longer called "treaties," because treaties would, by definition, have acknowledged the tribes as sovereign nations.

In any case, the General Allotment Act included a provision stating that allotment would be carried out only under presidential direction. To accelerate this process, Congress established commissions authorized to seek agreements with particular tribes, essentially bypassing the executive branch and making it appear as if the tribes were petitioning the government for the allotment of their reservation lands. Congress would then ratify these agreements and allot the reservations, purchasing the surplus lands for white homesteaders.

The Kiowa agreement with the Jerome Commission was concluded in 1892 under rather dubious circumstances. Most conspicuously, the agreement lacked tribal ratification as described and required under the Treaty of Medicine Lodge. A ratified treaty was and is on the level of constitutional, as opposed to statutory, law. Despite Native Americans' accusations of fraud and duress, in 1900 Congress passed the Jerome Commission's agreement into law, although in a substantially amended version and without the consent of a Kiowa majority for the amended version. In short, the Jerome Commission and Congress broke a treaty provision that carried the weight of constitutional law.[5]

Lone Wolf, with legal assistance from the Indian Rights Association, brought suit against Secretary of the Interior Ethan Alan Hitchcock to enjoin him from proceeding with the congressional directive to allot the reservation. Lone Wolf's lawyers argued that the new agreement could not be binding because of the stipulations of the Treaty of Medicine Lodge. Though the Jerome Commission and Congress had clearly violated the treaty, the high court ruled against Lone Wolf. In the opinion of the majority of the justices, "plenary authority over the tribal relations of the Indians has been exercised by Congress from the beginning" and was "not subject to be controlled by the judicial department of the Government." Therefore, the power existed "to abrogate the provisions of an Indian treaty." This power, according to the court, should be exercised only when circumstances arose that would "not only justify the government in disregarding the stipulations of the treaty, but may demand, in the interest of the country and the Indians themselves, that it should do so."[6]

On the surface, the *Lone Wolf* decision should have brightened the outlook of the zealous assimilationists. The ruling made it possible to allot lands and destroy tribal relations without regard for former treaties. But many of the old Indian reformers were skeptical of the court's ruling. The Indian Rights Association openly contested the original Kiowa agreement as fraudulent and smacking of land speculation.[7] George Kennan, a writer for Lyman Abbott's *Outlook* magazine, had warned the year before the *Lone Wolf* decision that there was little or no protection for Native American land holdings.[8] In light of the ruling in *Lone Wolf*, Kennan believed that the Indians' only protection would be the moral principles of the majority of fair-minded Americans, "which the Court assumed that Congress would observe."[9] Kennan did not believe that Congress was following the dictates of civil rectitude and moral justice. The legal implications of *Lone Wolf* were indeed unsettling to the old reformers. They favored allotment as a way to free Indians from government entanglements; the decision actually served to extend government control over Indian matters. Once again, the old reformers were caught in a quandary that was actually of their own making.[10]

Within months of the *Lone Wolf* decision, another setback to the policy of complete Indian assimilation occurred. On August 16, 1903, the *New York Times* broke the story of an Indian Rights Association agent, Samuel M. Brosius, who had uncovered a scandal in the Indian Territory "in comparison with which most of the other recently reported scandals in Government departments are paltry."[11] Brosius had found that members of the commission to the Five Civilized Tribes, which had been formed in 1893 as the Dawes Commission and been set to work cajoling the tribes into accepting allotment, were defrauding Native American allottees of money and lands.

The *Times* story alleged that choice townsite lots and effective control of the allotments had fallen into the hands of such companies as Muskogee Title and Trust and the Canadian Valley Trust Company. Tams Bixby, who had replaced Henry Dawes as head of the commission, and George Wright, a representative of the secretary of the interior, were found to have had connections with the companies involved in speculating in allotted Indian land. According to Brosius, Indians leased their lands to whites, and then the lessees refused to pay rent to the Indians, leaving the rightful Indian owner, poor to begin with, without funds to seek legal action. Bixby was not only a stockholder in the Muskogee Title and Trust Company, but also president of the board of the Canadian Valley Trust Company. Wright was a board member of Muskogee. Both Bixby and Wright had clear conflicts of interest. The old reformers, indignant that a commission established to accomplish what they considered a noble undertaking had been accused of committing such improprieties, immediately called for a thorough investigation.

Two days after the *Times* revealed the story, the Justice Department was implicated in the scandal. The *Times* reported that Brosius's findings had been known for some time, but officials in the Department of Justice had failed to act on behalf of the Native American allottees', no doubt, as the paper intimated, because of sinister connections between Justice and members of the commission. The commissioner of Indian Affairs, W. A. Jones, and Secretary of the Interior Hitchcock initiated an investigation. Within two more days, however, Hitchcock was called upon to remove himself from the affair. A *Times* article stated that there was "a strong want of confidence . . . in the Secretary's ability to conduct an impartial investigation" because "large sums," supposedly from the sale of town lots in the Indian Territory, "have been deposited in St. Louis banks in which Mr. Hitchcock's friends are interested as stockholders." Ominously, the *Times* warned that the "secretary is a St. Louis man."[12]

The scandals reached such serious proportions that President Theodore Roosevelt sent his friends, Charles J. Bonaparte of Baltimore and Clinton Rogers Woodruff of Philadelphia, to investigate the situation in Indian Territory. Roosevelt responded out of sheer political expediency. His administration had already been accused of wrongdoing in the Postal Department, and the national press was giving the Indian Territory scandals full coverage.[13] *Literary Digest*, for example, suggested that the scandals might have grave effects on the outcome of the 1904 elections because the Democratic press was launching a crusade to "Turn the Rascals Out" as a consequence of the postal and Indian Territory investigations.[14] *Outlook*, under Lyman Abbott's editorship, was indignant about the apparent double-dealing going on between the members of the commission to the Five Civilized Tribes and the land speculation companies, and asked the rhetorical question "Who Will Guard the Guards?" Abbott was concerned primarily with what kinds of protections Indian allottees were receiving, if any, from the federal government.[15] Soon Roosevelt decreed that all members of the commission to the Five Civilized Tribes would either terminate their business relationships or resign from government work.

The effect of the scandals on the intellectual cohesion of the old reformers at the Lake Mohonk Conference of 1903 was at least as great as that created by the Cheyenne Sun Dance incident. In large part, the debate at Lake Mohonk centered on the issue of government regulation. Lyman Abbott spoke out in favor of tighter controls and even suggested that the Indian Office be turned over to the War Department "because it is the only direct, straightforward way of breaking up the spoils system." Merrill E. Gates argued that the whole intent of the assimilation program was to give the Native American freedom, not to "turn him over to the army 'to be governed.'" Richard Henry Pratt, although he thought that Abbott had made a "good point," agreed with Gates. In Pratt's opinion, "the Indian is to become free from Bureau control and from the clutches of this all-absorbing administration of his affairs and destiny, which is really the Indian problem." The conference seemed stalemated over the issue of regulation. Despite Pratt's arguments and the earlier goals it had established for Indians, the Indian Rights Association nevertheless opted for stricter controls and published Brosius's pamphlet. Brosius argued persuasively that government control had to be maintained and even enhanced in order for Native Americans to secure their allotments perpetually.[16]

Basically the debate over government regulation made two opposite points. Those who opposed more extensive controls, like Pratt, thought that Native Americans should be allowed to "sink or swim" in American society after they had been given the tools—the three "R's," manual training, allotments—to become full-fledged American citizens. Pratt and like-minded others thought that Indians needed to experience change and that constant government interference served only to create dependency and stagnation. Intelligent, hardworking Native Americans, from Pratt's viewpoint, would prosper in American society; less gifted, lazy Indians, or those who "cling to the past," would fail according to the "natural" law of social Darwinist thought.

The opposing line of thought, articulated by Lyman Abbott, Merrill E. Gates, the leaders of the Indian Rights Association, and, of course, Samuel Brosius, essentially believed that Indians, because of their limited experience with Euro-American culture, were doomed to be preyed upon by unscrupulous and immoral members of American society. Indians, to Abbott, were either incompetent or "backward" and were thus unable to handle their own affairs without proper management. Additionally, Indians needed protection in order to prevent the loss of what lands they still possessed.

In retrospect, both sides of the issue were dancing around the central point of the American colonization of Native Americans. The relatively quick expansion of American society across the continent had left in its wake numerous pockets of Native Americans who had been deprived of the experience of change on their own terms. Colonization, in other words, had shoved change down their throats and created dependency. Both sides of the regulation issue recognized that most Native Americans had been forced into a state of dependency; they were arguing over the proper method of eliminating it. Pratt's "sink or swim" mentality emphasized the idea of simply dropping all barriers that made Indians dependent on the colonizer. Abbott, on the other hand, argued that Indian dependency could not be eliminated in one fell swoop. Change had to come gradually, and perhaps even painfully, and it had to be accompanied by controls that would prevent further loss of land, poverty, and, thus, greater dependency on the larger society. Those who advocated more regulation did not seem to recognize that it had a snowball effect. Pratt, however, recognized that more regulation would simply lead to greater dependency.

In general, politicians, old and new reformers, and perhaps even the American population at large believed that Indians were competent in some areas—art, athletics, and knowledge of the environment—but were incapable of handling the basics of American life—the management of private property, finances, and business. Obviously, white Americans thought, at minimum, that Indians did not yet possess the acumen required to deal adequately with unscrupulous businessmen, land speculators, or avaricious politicians.

The land scandals showed the Roosevelt administration that Indian affairs were reaching a crisis. Roosevelt resolved questions about regulation in favor of management. Dealing with Indian problems required, it was thought, effective and efficient administration rather than missionary zeal. A more secular and scientific approach was needed, people believed, to bring expertise and order to the chaos brought on by the vanishing policy. Roosevelt thought he had found the right man to reform and manage Indian affairs in a former journalist and onetime agent for the Indian Rights Association, Francis E. Leupp. On December 7, 1904, the president appointed Leupp commissioner of Indian Affairs. In fact, Roosevelt chose Leupp "because he was an expert on the subject."[17]

Although he had been a journalist with solid credentials as a civil-service reformer, Leupp was an administrator rather than an impassioned Christian reformer of the old school. He immediately began to develop an Indian policy based on "improving" the Indian "instead of struggling vainly to convert him into a Caucasian." In short, Leupp thought that it was not his duty "forcibly to uproot his strong traits as an Indian, but to induce him to modify them."[18] He actively supported the perpetuation of Indian arts and crafts as a potential source of employment and economic gain. He immediately permitted many Indians, much to the dismay of the old reformers, to join the Wild West shows and later to act in motion pictures. Although Leupp did not consider these forms of employment "particularly exalting," they nevertheless provided some degree of gainful occupation and allowed Indians "to see the world."

Unlike the old reformers Leupp had no qualms about Native Americans' wearing their native dress. He wrote, "in the matter of costume, I never could see why we should not allow the Indian the same latitude we grant to members of other races." "If a white man," he continued, "preferred a suit of chain-armor to one of broadcloth, I suppose we should set it down to eccentricity." To Indians, however, there was granted "no such range of liberty." If an Indian wore his hair in braids or covered himself with a blanket instead of an overcoat, he was, according to Leupp "pronounced a savage without more ado, and every effort is made to change his habits in these regards."[19]

Leupp could be labeled a racist for his notion that assimilating the majority of Indians was basically a lost cause. He was convinced that most Native Americans were "fundamentally incapable of certain of our moral, social, and intellectual standards."[20] In consequence, he often disregarded those theoretical underpinnings of the vanishing policy asserting that Indians could indeed become like whites in morals, manners, and custom. He dispassionately determined that many Native Americans could be talented artists, gifted athletes, and that Indian knowledge of the land might indeed contribute to the overall benefit of American society. His support of the retention of Native American art led to the proposition in 1905 that a new building at Carlisle Indian School be named the Leupp Indian Art Studio.

Leupp also knew that the main feature of the vanishing policy, allotment, had actually led to an alarming decrease in Native American landholdings. During 1906 and 1907 a Senate select committee was sent to Indian Territory to investigate the many problems surrounding the allotment of lands to the Five Civilized Tribes. The committee's members took testimony that filled two volumes of the *Senate Reports*. To a great degree, the investigation dealt with the insecurity of Indian allotments.

To the committee's great surprise, a number of traditional or "full-blood" members of the tribes had petitioned the federal government to continue in its role as the guardian of Indian lands and, specifically, to deny them American citizenship. Not only did these traditional Creek, Cherokee, Choctaw, and Chickasaw believe that they would be swindled if the trust relationship with the government was canceled, but they also rejected American citizenship in the belief that it would destroy them as a people. Despite the forced removal of the 1830s, the subsequent cultural changes wrought by missionaries, and the allotment policy, they had not lost their distinct sense of peoplehood, and in essence they were asking, as a people, to be given the status of a protectorate of the United States.

"Mixed-blood" members of the same tribes, considered more "civilized" by the federal government, had apparently succumbed to the land speculators as well. D. W. C. Duncan, a Cherokee lawyer, stated that, prior to the allotment policy, the Cherokee had "more than enough to fill up the cup of our enjoyment." Duncan argued effectively for more regulation, for he, an educated man, had lost the major portion of his family estate.[21]

These reports, coming as they did from the Five Civilized Tribes, telegraphed the message that the vanishing policy was an ultimate failure and that the moralism of the old reformers was an unsound basis for conducting Indian affairs. Leupp, perhaps because he thought of himself as a pragmatist rather than as a Christian moralizer or romantic preservationist, began to shape a rather disjointed, opportunistic, and bureaucratic form of Indian policy. Lacking a coherent philosophy regarding the "Indian Problem," but maintaining a commitment to the overall economic development of the United States, he simply dealt with specific problems on the reservations as they arose. In Leupp's opinion, "tuberculosis, drunkenness and child labor" had unfortunately followed the missionaries. Indians needed, according to Leupp, jobs, health care, a degree of financial security, and educations suited to their particular locales. To accomplish these goals, Leupp attempted to replace the far-flung boarding schools with reservation day schools, started a program to find employment for Indians, and tried to promote the incorporation of a few tribes as joint-stock companies in order to bring all tribal assets under a single institution.[22]

Leupp's troubleshooting approach to Indian affairs—under the guise of economy and efficiency—was indeed confusing, as Fayette McKenzie pointed out in 1910. In an attempt to make sense of Leupp's policies, historian Frederick Hoxie found that the commissioner actually accelerated allotment and other nefarious land schemes that put more Native American lands under white control. According to Hoxie, Leupp believed that since Indians were incapable of handling their own affairs and using their lands productively, they should be rapidly dispossessed of their property and used as a labor force in their particular locales for white landlords. Essentially, Hoxie maintained, during the first twenty years of the twentieth century there emerged a distinctly colonial land policy under which Native Americans became marginalized, disinherited, and forgotten.[23]

Another scholar, Janet A. McDonnell, saw Leupp's approach to Indian policy as detestable, to be sure, but contended that Leupp was a gradualist regarding the assimilation of Native Americans. Leupp, according to McDonnell, thought that Indian property rights needed to be protected until individual Native American owners had either learned to operate their farms or ranches efficiently or had failed in their agricultural endeavors. If they failed, then whites had every right to purchase or otherwise acquire the land and make it productive. Leupp, in effect, was a social Darwinist of the first order.[24]

On the other hand, historian Lawrence C. Kelly, in his study of John Collier's Indian policy reforms, contended that Leupp had determined before he took office that allotment was a disastrous policy and that he consequently forbade its application to Indian lands in the New Mexico and Arizona territories.[25]

In all probability, Leupp was neither a master schemer nor much of a believer in any social theory. A colonial land policy had been in place long before Leupp took office, and his brand of social Darwinism was essentially the same as that of the old reformers. A secular approach to management was Leupp's real calling. And if he advocated protecting Indian allotments on the one hand and leased or sold them to whites on the other, he was very likely thinking in terms of "on the spot" management and a "troubleshooting" administrative style. Leupp certainly thought that Indians should become less dependent on the federal government, but until that time came, he advocated limitations on Indian citizenship. This seemingly incongruous attitude was reflected in Leupp's support of the Burke Act of 1906.

The Burke Act, named for its author, Charles H. Burke, was an amendment to section six of the Dawes general allotment law. Whereas the Dawes Act had granted citizenship to individual Native Americans upon the assignment of an allotment, under the Burke Act citizenship would be deferred for twenty-five years. More importantly, the bill allowed the secretary of the interior, "in his discretion," to grant certificates of citizenship to individual allottees if he deemed them competent to live in white society, that is, by demonstrating their ability to follow white social and political practices.

The measure was introduced, referred to the Indian committee (where Leupp himself urged its passage), reported on, debated, slightly amended, and passed in the House during late March and early April of 1906. The Senate also passed the bill with relative ease. On April 20, the measure was debated on the Senate floor. The only real objection to the bill came from a senator who was apparently disturbed that some Indians were already citizens under the Dawes Act and that the Burke measure would thus "create an aristocracy of citizenship." The bill passed in the Senate with minor amendments on April 25. President Roosevelt signed the new law on May 8, 1906.[26]

The Burke Act was a direct product of Leupp's attempts to deal with specific Indian problems, in this case the spread of alcoholism. After the Dawes Act was passed, many whites feared that citizenship would lead to universal Indian alcohol addiction. As free citizens, Indians could indulge in their presumed proclivity for drink. As early as 1893, ethnologist George Bird Grinnell warned of the necessity of maintaining strict laws forbidding liquor to Indians. Leupp, who was quite friendly with the ethnologist, agreed. The Board of Indian Commissioners, which normally supported Indian citizenship and personal liberty within the confines of white values, hoped that the new Indian citizens would not be tempted "to prove their freedom by ruining themselves through the use of alcohol."[27]

In 1905 their fears seemed to be realized. A whiskey trader name Albert Heff was arrested and convicted for selling liquor to Native American allottees in Kansas. Sentenced to a four-month jail term and a $200 fine, Heff and his lawyer appealed. In April the Supreme Court heard the case and decided in favor of Heff. Since the allottees were citizens of the United States, in the opinion of the court, they were subject only to state and local liquor laws. The federal marshals who made the arrest and the United States district court that had convicted Heff had overstepped their authority because Heff had committed no federal crime.[28]

In effect the Supreme Court ruled that citizen Indians were no longer wards of the federal government. Leupp, as head of the Indian office, heartily recommended that Congress find some method of preserving their wardship status in order to protect Indians from alcohol dealers like Heff. The Senate Committee on Indian Affairs agreed. Referring to the *Heff* case, the committee judged the Burke Act to be a feasible means of maintaining the wardship status of Indians and thus the power to enforce prohibition on all Native Americans who had not yet taken allotments. The Senate report noted that following the decision in *Heff* there had been widespread and increasing "demoralization" among the tribes because "most of them have taken allotments and liquor has been sold to them, regardless of the fact that they are Indians." Thus the Senate Committee on Indian Affairs thought it advisable "that all Indians who may hereafter take allotments be not granted citizenship during the trust period" and that they "shall be subject to the exclusive jurisdiction of the United States."[29]

The old reformers universally loathed the Burke Act. Despite its recommendation in favor of some form of regulation regarding Indian allotments, the Indian Rights Association resoundingly criticized government interference with personal liberties.[30] The Board of Indian Commissioners, which had the year before expressed its concern over the possibility that the grant of individual citizenship might add to the growth of the alcohol problem in Indian country, stated that "we regret this modification of the allotment law, designed to keep Indians out of citizenship for twenty-five years after they received their allotment." The commissioners were primarily concerned that the new law would create "a class of 'Indians untaxed and not citizens,'" to be perpetually under the jurisdiction of the Indian Office. The Board of Indian Commissioners wanted the Burke Act either amended or repealed, and its members began to support the idea of completely dismantling the Indian service.[31]

The conflicting issues of increased federal regulation versus personal liberty and civil rights were basic controversies surrounding the passage of the Burke Act. But no one in the controversy was seen to be clearly on one side or the other.[32] The Board of Indian Commissioners and the Indian Rights Association called for regulating liquor sales or placing strict controls on Native Americans to quell what they supposed to be an inherent trait of Indians to "crave stimulants," yet they balked when it came to denying Native Americans United States citizenship. The old reformers—so concerned were they with the outward trappings of American culture—opposed the wearing of traditional tribal dress and engaging in ceremonial dancing, and they steadfastly supported the establishment of strict regulations regarding these aspects of Indian life. At the same time, they enthusiastically recommended that Indians be granted the protection of citizenship under the Constitution. Commissioner Leupp, on the other hand, allowed Indians a substantial degree of latitude in regard to tribal dress and art, yet he and Congress denied citizenship to Native Americans on the assumption that they were incapable of dealing with the full array of civil liberties. It was a paradox seemingly built into the American ethos: the rights of the atomized person versus the need for social responsibility. And although the two need not conflict, they often do.

Perhaps the longest battle that reflected the intellectual turmoil and the inconsistency of American Indian policy during the Progressive era was the controversy over government funding of Catholic schools on reservations. The old reformers were primarily Protestant. But the influx of Irish and eastern European immigrants in the nineteenth century rapidly increased the number and influence of Catholics. During the 1880s, several Catholic schools were established on reservations under government contract. In the final decade of the nineteenth century, anti-Catholic sentiment, however, became rampant, especially among the ranks of the old Christian reform movement. Eventually the Protestants, arguing that Catholic education on government reservations violated the American principle of separation of church and state, were able to convince Congress to stop the direct funding of these church schools.[33]

The Catholics fought back, and between 1900 and 1912 the battle was particularly intense. Some government officials had, in 1900, taken the position that government funding for sectarian schools basically violated the constitutional position of the separation of church and state. Taking a position that echoed earlier Protestant arguments favoring missionary educational programs on the reservations, however, one supporter of the Catholic schools wrote that when "a race or tribe living under a government is in a state of wildness, and is a source of danger to the commonwealth, because it refuses to conform to the laws of the nations, it is the duty of the government" to civilize it. It was necessary, according to this particular writer, for religious instruction to be given to this "wild" race because "without religion there can be no morality." Since it was the duty of the government to transform Indians into "peaceful and intelligent members of this Christian nation," religious instruction was "not contrary" to the Constitution. It was, rather, "fully in conformity with it."[34]

Other Catholic supporters, using the print media to its fullest capacity, relied on the argument that Indians, as human beings, had the natural and civil rights of freedom of religion and education. If the money expended for Catholic schools came from trust and treaty funds, the Catholics argued, it was Indian money, and therefore the tribes should be allowed to spend it in anyway they saw fit. Sounding the Catholic battle cry, R. R. Elliot of the *American Catholic Quarterly*, wrote that the "autocratic control over the education of Indian youth" must be ended immediately.[35] Indians had First Amendment rights, but only if they wanted a Christian education.

In 1905 the controversy broke out again. Commissioner Leupp, with authorization from President Roosevelt, allocated over $100,000 of tribal trust monies to sectarian schools for Indian education. The old reformers generally were outraged. *Outlook* magazine, reflecting assimilationist Lyman Abbott's views on Indian policy, called the expenditure a "mischievous appropriation" and declared that it would set "Catholic Indian against Protestant Indian." Moreover, the periodical claimed, the allocation was in direct "violation of the first Amendment" (as if the bans on Native American ceremonies that Abbott advocated were not).[36]

Outlook continued to print the "main facts" in the case, and in a barrage of verbiage reviewed the controversy in a later edition:

> The sum of $102,000 has been or is to be, disbursed by the Indian Office to Catholic and Lutheran schools for the sectarian education of Indian children; the money comes from a trust fund belonging to the Indians; the Indians have not given their consent to the expenditure, because so far as we can learn, as many Indians have petitioned against this disbursement as have petitioned for it;

the Chairman of the Committee of Indian Affairs opposes the obtaining of this consent on the floor of the House, throws obstacles in the way of those who are earnestly, and we think wisely, working in Congress for non-sectarian Indian education, and dust in the eyes of Outlook readers who in the exercise of their perfectly proper rights as voters and citizens are trying to see into the somewhat dusky and unilluminating atmosphere of the Indian Committee Room.[37]

In less than a week the *Nation* entered the fray and settled itself ever so gently on the side of the Protestants.[38] Lyman Abbott and *Outlook*, however, remained in the forefront of the controversy and continued to represent the anti-Catholic standard-bearers. On February 11, 1905, the magazine reprinted Samuel M. Brosius's charges that Professor E. L. Scharf of Catholic University had threatened Congressman John H. Stephens with defeat by Catholic voters in the next election if Stephens did not immediately withdraw his opposition to the Catholic Indian schools.[39] In the next issue of *Outlook*, Abbott came out in favor of tighter controls on Indian funds. Arguing that the money was appropriated for the tribes, he stated that the money was therefore "public money" and should be subject to disbursement only with popular consent. Although Abbott maintained that "the same principles are to be applied to Indians and to Anglo-Saxons, to black men and white men," he rather inconsistently argued that Indians were wards of the federal government and that their trust funds should be managed for them. In Abbott's opinion, the government "cannot rid itself of that responsibility by saying that its wards want the money spent in some particular fashion."[40] In other words, everyone had First Amendment rights except Indians.

The Indian Rights Association did not remain neutral during the sectarian school conflict. In 1905 the organization published Matthew K. Sniffen's pamphlet entitled, aptly, *Indian Trust Funds for Sectarian Schools*. Sniffen, an old official of the IRA, opposed the "arbitrary use" of the trust funds and thought that some form of federal regulation should be utilized regarding the disbursement of the tribal monies. The pamphlet also contained a petition from some of the Lakota Protestants from the Rosebud reservation in South Dakota against the allocation of their trust funds to sectarian schools.[41] The

IRA next initiated a lawsuit in the name of Reuben Quick Bear of the Rosebud agency against Commissioner Leupp to enjoin the Indian Office from expending Indian trust funds for Catholic instruction. The IRA lawyers argued that such allocations violated the First Amendment and that in 1900 a congressional appropriation for sectarian education stipulated that it would be the final such allocation. In 1908 the Supreme Court ruled in *Quick Bear v. Leupp* that the trust funds were Indian tribal monies and that Congress had no right to restrict their disbursement. The Protestants lost the first round.[42]

The second round did not begin for another four years. In 1912 the entire issue flared up again, this time with a different twist. During that year Leupp's successor at the Indian Office, Robert G. Valentine, ordered that priests and nuns teaching in reservation schools either discard their clerical vestments or resign their positions. Again the anti-Catholicism was cloaked in the argument of separation of church and state. President William Howard Taft rescinded the order, thus rebuking Valentine, but asked both sides of the controversy to prepare arguments concerning the question.[43]

By the time of President Taft's intervention, the "nun's garb controversy" was making national news. *Literary Digest*, for example, carried several articles about the controversy. For the most part, the Catholic press urged that Valentine be forced to resign from office. According to the *Catholic Universe* of Cleveland, "only the most wanton and arrant bigotry could inspire a bureaucrat like Valentine to promulgate [such] an order." The Protestant media agreed with Valentine's contention that the wearing of religious dress in what were considered government schools was a violation of the doctrine of separation of church and state. The Protestants, however, requested that President Taft thoroughly investigate the matter and issue some kind of ruling. In the end, the president refused to support Valentine, which, according to the *Literary Digest*, would have amounted to a "discharge" had it not been for the civil service laws.[44]

The sectarian schools controversies, which could be attributed to bigotry or bureaucratic bungling, were symptoms of a much larger problem in federal–Native American relations. The "trust fund" and "religious garb" battles, although basically sectarian quarrels, produced results that greatly expanded the scope of federal regulation over Indian affairs. Protestants were clearly in favor of using the federal government to prevent Indians from coming into closer contact with Catholic missionaries and educators. Catholics, on the other hand, although they argued that Indians should have a free choice in the matter, simply wanted the government to support their efforts to promote civilization among the tribes. Neither side was willing to grant Native Americans the right, even under the First Amendment, and if they so desired, to continue their own time-honored tribal religious practices. The result of the religious controversy was a significant expansion of the discretionary powers of the federal government, a wholly secular institution, over the lives and properties of all Native Americans.

The controversies also signaled that the theories and ethos underlying the vanishing policy were on their last legs. The decision in *Quick Bear* essentially legitimized Leupp's discretionary authority over the distribution of Indian trust funds. The Indian bureau, which was supposed to "vanish" along with "the Indian," actually expanded its power. When Valentine attempted in 1912 to return authority, on a small scale, over Indian affairs to the old Protestant reform agenda, he was ultimately reminded that the old reformers were no longer in charge of Indian policy.

The federal government grappled with these kinds of unique problems throughout the period. To most Americans, citizenship meant almost unlimited personal liberty in a democratic society. Although citizenship for Indians was the avowed goal of federal Indian policy, there was a continuing demand by almost all interested parties for more government regulation of Native American institutions and individuals. As a consequence, perhaps, the federal bureaucracy grew larger, more powerful, and more despotic when developing regulations and guidelines in order to handle specific aspects of the "Indian Problem," which, in turn, was constantly being redefined. To the old assimilationists, this kind of political diversity implied confusion. But to a government bureaucrat, it seemed to be the most effective means of obtaining "efficient" control over the vast number of problems then plaguing the nation's Native American populations.

The annual reports of the Commissioners of Indian Affairs during the first twenty-five years of the twentieth century demonstrate an almost overwhelming concern with the number of Native Americans affected by specific policies and programs. In many instances the reports contain more pages devoted to tables and population figures than to the ideas of the various commissioners. The figures demonstrate bureaucratic efficiency in record keeping and in cost-benefit analysis, but make both the bureau and the annual reports considerably more impersonal. Indian policy, it seems, ceased to be a general but comprehensible blueprint for action, as it had been in the nineteenth century. The old reformers may have been wrong, but they were never ambiguous.

Once it had legitimized its discretionary authority, however, the Indian Office began to deal less with assimilation and citizenship as a general goal and more with specific policies in the fields of health, education, employment, alcoholism, water resources, and land. The assumption that these problems would be easily resolved by the rapid assimilation of Native Americans was quietly abandoned. The Indian Office, consequently, continued to treat symptoms produced by its inconsistent policies and programs without attempting to create a fundamental restatement of the ultimate goals of its Indian policy.

The vast "Indian Problem" had been redefined to mean Indian problems, none of which was greater than Indian education. Although the Indian education system, exemplified by the boarding schools, had been founded to provide manual—and a good deal of military—training, they were nevertheless coming under a good deal of criticism. The most important accusation during the early part of the twentieth century was that Indian education had become impractical. In 1906 a staff writer for the *American Review of Reviews* complained that in "contrast with the sane and sensible policy of negro education pursued by such institutions as Hampton and Tuskegee," the federal government was plagued with the "mistaken attempt of certain well-meaning philanthropists to give the American Indian an education of which he can make no possible use in actual life."[45] The same author suggested that "the rudiments of book learning" should be taught to the Indians, but the main emphasis should be placed on the manual arts for use in particular places.

The writer was apparently suggesting that the manual training at the boarding schools, as well as the boarding schools themselves, was far removed from the places and the economies to which the graduated students would return one day. There were two basic reasons behind the new demands for vocational training in the Indians schools. Many whites believed that Indians were in some way racially limited—despite the accomplishments of such Native Americans as Carlos Montezuma, Charles Eastman, Angel DeCora, and others—and therefore that Indians, in the interests of efficiency and economy, should receive only a limited education. The second reason lay in the nature of educational thinking in that era. There was a strong demand for practical instruction that would prepare students for jobs in their own regions. The old classical disciplines were being discarded in favor of new subjects believed to be relevant to contemporary life in particular locales. In other words, students should not be trained to raise peanuts in the South if they were going to find employment in northern Wisconsin, nor should they learn cattle ranching if they would be returning to the logging areas of Washington.

The Bureau of Indian Affairs generally followed these trends. Boarding schools began to be de-emphasized in favor of day schools on the reservations. Some of the schools also placed an emphasis on learning native arts that, according to the Indian commissioners of the day, demonstrated natural native creativity and served as a form of vocational training. From their training in the Indian school system, Indians could participate in the "curio" business and benefit from tourist dollars. Agricultural training became the norm, but it was tailored to those products deemed practical for particular regions. Carpentry, sewing and tailoring, and mechanical training were given special emphasis as well. Indian students were being prepared to find employment rather than to take back and teach the "civilized" skills they had learned in the boarding schools to others on their reservations.

In 1921 Cato Sells, commissioner of Indian Affairs from 1913 to 1921, argued that under his administration the Indian schools had essentially gone through a quiet revolution: they had finally introduced into their curricula lessons in American Indian culture and history. Although these lessons were Euro-American versions of Native American tribal heritages, they nevertheless were concessions to the notion that Native Americans indeed had cultures and histories. Although the Indian Office stressed "the utilitarian side of education," as was the focus of the day, Sells stated that the schools also had "a definite regard for the influences that foster spiritual and artistic aspiration." "We recognize," he wrote, "that in the Indian's tribal lore, his art, handicrafts, and some of his ceremonies were cultural elements of value which should be retained and encouraged."[46] This emphasis was in fact a tacit admission that complete assimilation was no longer an inevitable goal of federal Indian policy and programs.

Vocational training went hand in hand with employment, and the Indian Office responded. Matthew K. Sniffen of the Indian Rights Association called upon the bureau to "make the Indians the American Cattle King." Another writer, elaborating on Sniffen's idea to make Indians productive employees in businesses suitable for their remote rural locations, urged that the Navajo be instructed in how to raise sheep more profitably. He also suggested that the people of the woodlands be employed cutting timber because they "are lumbermen by instinct."[47]

Native American employment became identified as a specific but soluble problem, and in the manner of other bureaucracies, the Indian Office responded by establishing a subagency to investigate conditions and suggest remedies and solutions that would help alleviate the critical lack of employment among Indians. During his tenure as commissioner, Francis E. Leupp hired a Peoria Indian named Charles E. Dagenett to head the newly created office of Indian employment. In 1909 Robert G. Valentine, Leupp's successor, praised Dagenett for his activities in placing Indians as workers on railroads, on farms, and in "sundry employments for which their strength and abilities are equal."[48]

By 1924, Commissioner Charles H. Burke reported even greater successes. According to Burke, the year "marked a steady gain in the number of Indians finding remunerative employment." "The demand for Indian labor," he continued, "is greater than the supply and no shortage of good wages and food prevails for Indians willing to work." Burke reported that Native Americans were employed in agriculture, railroading, land reclamation, and the telegraph and telephone services. Automobile factories were hiring Indians and advancing them "as their skill and experience warrant." Burke counted migrant fruit, vegetable, and grain harvesting as "remunerative employment," but he took greater pride in reporting that "hundreds of Indian school graduates are giving excellent service in Government and commercial positions." The Indian Office itself employed approximately 2,000 Native Americans from all tribes.[49]

"Native" industries aided the Indian Office's quest for full Indian employment. Corporations were recruited to help Native Americans benefit from the tourist trade. The Santa Fe railroad, in its promotion of the Southwest as a place of "natural" health and beauty, exploited the image of the peaceful Indian artist and offered patronage to craftsmen. As Burke stated in 1921, the "railway system found it profitable to continue to provide attractive work rooms for families of Indian artisans at stations along the line, where their handiwork sells readily." Given the images of Indians during the period, it was relatively easy for the Indian Office to place numerous Native Americans in jobs connected with the production and sale of arts and crafts, in summer camps acting as guides, and in Boy Scout work. Native Americans also continued to "make good" in athletics and, when that failed, to work in shops selling athletic equipment.[50]

Certainly by 1921, when Burke took office as commissioner, the federal government was stepping discreetly into the fourth phase of colonial-colonized relations. Native Americans, whether landless, on reservations, or holding allotments—and whether or not they were American citizens—became the responsibility of the Indian Office. By way of its expanded operations and its greater discretionary authority in handling Indian affairs, the bureau was fast becoming a large and permanent part of the structure of public authority in the United States. Native Americans had not vanished, and the federal government began to accommodate itself to that fact and to perpetuate its presence among Native Americans. Essentially, the Indian Office became an "Indian" entity—it employed Native Americans and made policy exclusively for Indians (whether good or bad)—within the American state.

Perhaps the greatest demand placed on the Indian Office in the period, and the one that permanently established its exclusivity, was to provide more and better health care for Native Americans. Throughout the early twentieth century, tuberculosis plagued the tribes. Thought at the time to have originated during the Indians' "transformation" from "barbarian athletes" enjoying the "old life in the open" to demoralized wards confined to reservations and their "accumulation of filth," tuberculosis accounted for more Native American deaths in the period than the next two leading causes.

As early as 1907 the Indian Office, in cooperation with the Bureau of American Ethnology (an example of the marriage of anthropological expertise and government policy toward Indians), carried out a survey of the disease's effects. In some areas persons suffering from tuberculosis made up nearly 40 percent of the population. The demand for a solution was overwhelming. Nearly everyone who wrote on the subject agreed that the Indian Office should take a direct interest in Indian health and establish sanatoria, hire field nurses, institute a health education program, supervise the building of houses on the reservations, and guarantee a "rigid enforcement of proper sanitary conditions." The demand for services entailed a growth in the Indian Health Service that was unprecedented.[51]

The influence of the Indian Health Service also grew. In 1909, Commissioner Valentine stated that the reservation physician was "next to the superintendent in importance" within the Indian Office's hierarchy.[52] Eight years later Commissioner Cato Sells had expanded the government's health care programs to include every one of the improvements recommended for better Indian health. Sanatoria were built, nurses were hired, and inspections were frequently made of reservation homes. The Indian Health Service also became interested in trachoma (bacterial conjunctivitis), infant welfare, and contagious diseases such as measles and influenza. The campaign was extensive. Sells reported that pupils in the day and boarding schools all received "compulsory treatment for trachoma" and that all students were vaccinated against smallpox. One Sells innovation that emphasized infant health was the institution of annual baby contests at the various Indian fairs held throughout the country. The Indian Office printed hundreds of "standard score cards" that "will be carefully graded by the physicians and the cards of the babies having the highest scores will be sent to Washington, where suitable certificates will be issued to the parents."[53]

From the standpoint of the Indian Office's many tables and charts, Sells's programs were rather successful. In a letter to Redbird Smith, chief of the Cherokee Keetoowahs, Sells requested help from the Cherokee irreconcilable in the Indian Office's "Choctaw and Cherokee Health Drives." Sells wrote that "the first obligation of the government to the Indians is to exert itself to the uttermost to save the race—to perpetuate its life." All of his projects were designed to "give the Indian baby an equal chance with the white child to live and to the Indian father and mother an opportunity to enjoy the fruits of life in a manner equal to that of their white neighbors." Sells stated that this "vigorous effort" from 1914 to 1917 had made it possible to say "for the first time in more than 50 years, there were more Indians born than died from every cause." Accordingly, Sells saw himself as an Indian savior and proudly wrote "that the Indian is no longer a dying race."[54]

Alcoholism was another difficult health problem in Indian communities. Typically, the Indian Office launched a vigorous campaign to suppress liquor sales, and Congress was more than willing to provide financial support for the program. In 1909 Congress allowed $40,000 for the project, and by 1917 the annual appropriation had increased to $150,000. But in 1919 funding was cut to $100,000 (still a large sum of money in that period), and was further reduced to $65,000 in 1920. By then, however, national prohibition had made it "very much more difficult for Indians to obtain intoxicating liquors."[55] The Eighteenth Amendment to the Constitution applied the same kinds of prohibitions against liquor to the white citizenry as it had always placed on noncitizen Native Americans. In strict bureaucratic terms, the Indian Office was bringing in money, expanding its list of employees, and gaining more authority over the lives of Native Americans.

The Indian Office's policy of pragmatic problem solving could not, however, deal effectively with the difficulties involved in clarifying Native Americans' status under the law. Because its policies were essentially based upon the idea that Indians were wards and could not be trusted to direct their own affairs, the Indian Office was unable to either justify or meet the growing demands for Indian freedom in the form of American citizenship. Large numbers of Indians had already become citizens under the Dawes and Curtis acts. A few Indians had also been given certificates of citizenship under the provisions of the Burke Act of 1906.

All of those who had obtained citizenship, however, had done so as the federal government was developing into a larger and more unwieldy bureaucratic institution. Native Americans were placed in the nebulous position of having to accept a citizenship that was severely limited or else remain noncitizens. Some Indians desired citizenship even if it were restricted; others rejected the notion completely. Some Native Americans refused to become citizens on the grounds that American citizenship was irreconcilable with their own sense of peoplehood. Many others were arbitrarily denied citizenship under the "competency" provisions of the Burke Act. The actual national status of Native Americans living within American society and under some form of federal jurisdiction was confused and almost indefinable.[56]

Recognizing the incongruity of the Native American position in American life and portraying it as the result of bureaucratic ineptitude, several people interested in Indian affairs began to attack the Indian Office for not allowing the government's wards complete freedom. To many whites, but primarily the old assimilationists, reservations were little more than bureaucratically controlled concentration camps. The Indian Office was accused of confining, segregating, and regulating Indians merely to perpetuate itself as a government agency. Allotment had not worked, because commissioners had manipulated the program to the point that most of the land had fallen into the hands of whites.

Arthur C. Parker, the editor of the Society of American Indians journal, wrote eloquently on the subject and represented, although not as militantly as Carlos Montezuma, the anti–Indian Office stance. In 1917 he argued that in its abuse of Native American liberty, the "Indian Bureau is an un-American institution." "The fundamental errors of the Bureau are those of its attitude toward Indians," he stated. The Indian Office's errors were "paternalism, segregation, autocratic action, amounting to tyranny, politics." "Make the Indian a citizen," he admonished, and "demonstrate that America is a safe place for every American citizen . . . whether he happens to be the First American or of a later importation."[57]

As it happened, World War I neatly and effectively ended the confusion over American citizenship for Indians. When Congress declared war on Germany, thousands of Indians either were drafted into the military or volunteered for the armed services. A few tribes even declared war on Germany independently of the federal government. Many Indians entered the services as noncitizens, refusing to take advantage of their draft-exempt status. By 1918 there were over 10,000 Native Americans in the armed forces, 85 percent of whom, according to the *Indian's Friend*, volunteered for duty in the trenches. "Indians—men and women alike—are doing their bit to help make the world safe for democracy."[58] In 1920 Cato Sells stated that Indians had purchased over $60,000,000 in Liberty Bonds, amounting to a cash outlay of over $25,000,000.[59] To the surprise and delight of many whites, Indians were doing their utmost to prove that they warranted American citizenship and could stand shoulder to shoulder with the white man.

The war generated a tremendous outburst of nationalistic fervor and calls for unswerving loyalty and devotion to the nation and the federal government. In this atmosphere of rabid patriotism and imagined crisis, which extended into the 1920s as a result of the Red Scare, Americans became more amenable to the proposition that personal liberties could be subordinated to the public welfare and especially to national security as defined by the federal government. Congress, for example, was able to pass sedition and subversion acts with only token opposition. During the Red Scare, the government clearly violated the constitutional rights of many people, ostensibly to protect itself from being overthrown by subversive forces.

Given these reactionary attitudes, it became acceptable to think that government regulation of Indian affairs was not incompatible with Indians' personal freedom. But it was also not difficult for whites to overcome their qualms about conferring citizenship on the Native American "wards" who had served in the war. The bill granting citizenship to Indian soldiers and sailors was introduced into the House of Representatives on June 5, 1919, and referred to committee. Five months later it became law. The act provided that any Indian with an honorable discharge from one of the armed services could receive a certificate from an American court "with no other examination except as prescribed by said court." An Indian veteran could obtain citizenship if the court did not object. The law really did not change anything; courts could still require competency examinations.

In less than five years another bill was introduced in Congress to confer United States citizenship on all Native Americans who were not already citizens. The bill, entitled "an act to authorize the Secretary of the Interior to issue certificates of citizenship to Indians," quickly passed the House of Representatives. The Senate, slower to take action, did not return the bill with its amendments until mid-May. President Calvin Coolidge signed the law on June 2, 1924.[60]

These confirmations of Native American citizenship were hardly the measures the old reformers had dreamed of. The secretary of the interior, as head of a cabinet-level bureaucracy, still held actual power over Native Americans' lives. All of the regulations of the Indian Office remained in effect, and the bureau itself had grown to proportions that the old assimilationists could not possibly have conceived of several decades before. The new citizenship acts, like the Indian Office policies, were makeshift, opportunistic, and completely lacking in any broad theoretical framework. Citizenship did not confer upon Indians the ability to act as peoples or, for that matter, as individuals. In several states Native Americans were disenfranchised until the 1950s.

Allotment continued throughout the period, and with it the concomitant loss of tribally as well as individually owned land. Those Native Americans who worked their allotments found that farm prices remained low and rural poverty rampant. Few Indians owned as much arable land as their white neighbors, and even those whites who had leased Indian land were able to eke out only a meager existence. The Indian Office had become the sole arbiter of Indian policy, and Indians still had to rely on the bureau to conduct their business and legal affairs and to provide the health, housing, and education benefits that their ancestors had secured for them by treaty and agreement with the federal government. Clearly, something had to be done. The vanishing policy was dying a long, painful death, but there was no grand scheme to replace it. Bureaucratic regulation had become simply a series of stopgap measures without a broad philosophical basis or long-term goals.

But then again, citizenship even for whites no longer carried the same connotations as it had in the late nineteenth century. The federal government had effectively become the countervailing power to big business and big labor. The Department of the Interior effectively controlled the use of public lands. Prohibition was in effect, and although most whites broke the law continuously, it stood as a symbol of government regulation of the private lives of American citizens. During the Red Scare, Americans accepted Attorney General A. Mitchell Palmer's insidious tactics to rid the nation of communists, anarchists, and sundry other "un-American" ideologies and ideologues. The Progressive ethos truly was a search for order and stability, despite the costs, and it led to regulation and the growth of bureaucracy.

In spite of the emphasis the Indian Office placed on Indian employment, the vocational education programs, and American citizenship, Native Americans remained desperately poor throughout the 1920s. But Native American tribes were, above all, persistent peoples. Despite having been removed or otherwise disinherited from their native soil, Native Americans remained strongly connected with the land. Reservations had become homelands, and even those whose lands had been allotted remained connected to place. Ceremonies with a strong relationship to the landscape were still being conducted. Among some tribes, foreign religions had been filtered through the matrix of peoplehood and thereby "nativized." Native American languages were still being spoken: some just in connection with religious ceremonies, and many simply as the language of the household. The stories were still being told, thus preserving the sacred histories of the people. Indian art stood as a symbol of Native American survival. The "New Indians," refusing to be fully absorbed into mainstream America, had initiated a new feeling of Pan-Indian relationships. Native American individuals and societies had endured the assaults of the assimilation policy and watched as it collapsed in theory as well as practice. Equally, they had survived the confused conflict in the ideology and make-up of policy that characterized the period between 1900 and 1925 in the United States. Perhaps that was the greatest achievement of all.

CHAPTER VIII

EPILOGUE

John Collier and Indian Reform

BECAUSE IT LACKED A CLEAR THEORETICAL FOUNDATION, Indian policy in the first quarter of the twentieth century developed into a series of troubleshooting measures designed to deal with particular problems. Simply put, it was not a single, all-encompassing policy, and so it failed to satisfy nearly everyone interested in the conduct of Indian affairs. Native American peoples, placed in marginal political positions, continued in a steep economic decline.

There was an obvious need for direction in the formulation of a new Indian policy. Out of this search for another paradigm in Indian affairs, a new movement for Indian reform grew up in the early 1920s. Prophetically, the movement began in the artist-intellectual white community of Taos, New Mexico, and found its champion in John Collier.

Collier came to the forefront of a new Indian reform movement, bypassing Native American spokespersons and other whites who had a great deal more experience in Indian affairs, because he formulated a new philosophical basis for the direction of American Indian policy. He was also able to enlist a number of influential people in his cause. But most of all Collier was able to put his ideas, often in severely modified form, into action when he became commissioner of Indian Affairs in 1933.

Collier first cast himself into the turbulent waters of Indian affairs in 1922, when he became involved in the battle to stop the passage of the Pueblo Indian Land Act. On July 19 of that year, Senator Holm O. Bursum of New Mexico, with the full support of Secretary of the Interior Albert Bacon Fall, introduced the bill, as its supporters argued, to quell a series of disputes over Pueblo land titles.[1] Under the Treaty of Guadalupe Hidalgo that ended the Mexican War in 1848, Congress confirmed the ownership of certain lands to the various Pueblo peoples of the newly created territory of New Mexico. Additionally, the Pueblo people were individually recognized as citizens of the United States. As citizens, some of the people sold land to white settlers without hindrance from the federal or tribal governments. Additionally, there were numerous whites who had squatted on Pueblo Indian lands without the benefit of a legal sale or title. Between 1910 and 1920, a number of people involved in Indian affairs began to question the right of the Pueblo Indians, even as citizens of the United States, to sell parts of the tribal estate; they also examined white claims to what was Indian land. In 1913, the Supreme Court, in *U.S. v. Sandoval*, decided that the Pueblo peoples, regardless of their U.S. citizenship, were to be treated as wards of the federal government. They therefore had been incompetent since 1848 to negotiate the sale of their lands.[2] The Bursum bill essentially sought to end the problem by confirming not the Indian title but all non-Indian land claims.

Collier immediately launched a campaign to defeat the Bursum bill. He, along with Stella Atwood, who was chairperson of the General Federation of Women's Clubs' Indian Welfare Committee, wrote several articles for *Sunset* and *Survey* magazines protesting the bill.[3] They also enlisted several members of the Taos artist-intellectual community, including authors Witter Bynner and D. H. Lawrence, to write tracts in opposition to the proposed legislation.[4] Eventually public opinion was rallied to the Pueblo cause, and the bill was killed.[5]

The next piece of legislation that caught Collier's attention was even more insidious than the Bursum bill. On January 16, 1923, the Indian Omnibus Bill was introduced in the House of Representatives. The bill authorized the secretary of the interior to appraise tribal property, pay Native Americans the cash value of their assets, and terminate responsibility for all lands held in trust.[6] In essence, the bill was a logical conclusion to the crumbling vanishing policy. It would have immediately and irrevocably cancelled all treaties, court decisions, and laws relating to the protection of Native American landholdings. Native Americans, in theory, would then be free from government control and placed automatically in the white competitive world.

The bill floated through the House in fairly quick order and was sent to the Senate. There it met its demise in the hands of Senator Robert La Follette of Wisconsin. During the debate on the Senate floor, the old Progressive legislator demanded that the Indian Omnibus Bill be passed over. Since the sixty-seventh Congress was then in its last session, the Senate supporters of the legislation could ill afford its being tabled, which would have effectively killed it until the next congressional session. La Follette, who had been in contact with Collier, was adamant about passing over the bill. When told that the bill needed to go through more quickly because it had to do with the "welfare" of Native Americans, La Follette replied "it has to do with the 'wrongfare' of Indians, I think. I insist on the objection." The Indian Omnibus Bill of 1923 was officially killed.[7]

The next Indian issue that Collier became involved in was the "Indian Dance Imbroglio." The whites who advocated total assimilation had always had grave problems with the continuation of Native American ceremonies, especially those that involved dancing. To the old reformers, dancing was lascivious and savage behavior. Not only that, but it usually involved some form of ritualized gift giving, which, to an old reformer, Native Americans could ill afford to practice. The assimilationists had been defeated again and again over this particular question, but they nevertheless refused to admit or accept defeat.

Perhaps in frustration over the efforts of preservationists to salvage what was considered an Indian art form, they began a renewed campaign to bring an end to Native American ceremonial dances. In 1918 the Board of Commissioners for Indian Affairs took notice that a number of Native American groups across the country were still conducting ceremonies with much the same vigor as they had done before the advent of the vanishing policy. The board contended that the ceremonies were "revivals" of the old ways and constituted a "reversion" to paganism. Accordingly, the board warned that "we cannot see anything but evil in permitting these dances."[8]

To promote the idea that the ceremonies should be banned, the board played upon the fervent patriotism stimulated by America's entrance into World War I. Native American dancing, they inferred, was being done principally to subvert the will of the government. Dancing was not only "uncivilized" but also "un-American." In this completely narrow-minded vein, the board reported that there were "good reasons to believe that a considerable number of these Indians are covertly disloyal to the United States and have been victims of pro-German propaganda." The board further "endeavored to bring to bear such influence as we could upon them to point out the impropriety of such conduct on their part and the probability of its getting them into serious difficulty."

To breakup "this hotbed of sedition," the commissioners called upon the various Indian agents across the country to stop the dances and to keep a close watch on those whites who showed an interest in the preservation of Native American ceremonies. "The same persons among the Indians," according to the board's annual report, "who were active in trying to reintroduce the pagan dances are those who are apparently the leaders in sowing disloyalty."[9] Evidently, anthropology had become an un-American activity. Try as it might, however, the board was unable to discover a link between Native American ceremonialism, sedition, and pro-German propaganda.

Anticeremonial rhetoric such as the commissioners indulged in cropped up from time to time during the first quarter of the twentieth century. For the most part it was relegated to a low priority on the "Indian Problem" agenda. There were far greater problems to deal with, and, in addition, preservationist critics of the vanishing policy had pointed out several sound reasons why the government should allow tribal ceremonies to persist. The allegations of disloyalty during World War I could have been serious, but because of Native Americans' war records, the government refused to act upon the charges.

After the Native American veterans returned from the war, however, the ceremonies done to honor them for—or to purify them after—their combat experiences drew more criticism from the assimilationists. In 1920 the Indian Rights Association issued a scathing attack on "depraved and immoral" Native American dances. According to the association, the dances served only to demoralize Indians and act as a stumbling block to their eventual entrance into American society. In the end, the organization's leadership called upon the Indian Office to effect an immediate ban on all Native American ceremonies.[10]

Commissioner Charles H. Burke untypically rebuffed the association. In Burke's words: "it is not the policy of the Indian Office to denounce all forms of Indian dancing." The commissioner continued that he was "tolerant of pleasure and relaxation sought in this way, or of ritualism and tradition sentiment thus expressed." He also thought that dance united "art, refinement and healthful exercise" and thus was "not inconsistent with civilization." But perhaps to placate the growing storm of protest from the assimilationists, Burke issued orders that Native American ceremonies were to be suppressed if they featured self-torture, "immoral acts," or "reckless" giveaways; employed any kind of "harmful" drug or alcohol; or were so lengthy that Indians missed work or ignored their agricultural pursuits.[11]

Reaction to the attempt to suppress Native American ceremonies came swiftly and cut to the heart of the matter. Many of those who wanted to preserve Indian dancing argued that the dances were artistically valuable and that opposition to this form of self-expression was against all of the principles on which the nation was founded.[12] The eminent ethnologist F. W. Hodge took direct issue with the charges of immorality. He stated emphatically that the persons who had made these claims either were totally misinformed or had not taken the trouble to investigate any of the Native American ceremonies in question.[13]

But it was John Collier who framed the issue as a case of whether or not Native Americans had the right to enjoy religious freedom under the First Amendment. Late in 1923, Collier wrote to the *New York Times*, criticizing the suppression of Native American dances as a violation of constitutionally protected religious liberty. He argued that all Native American rituals were religious by nature and that those who sought to ban them were no less than tyrants seeking to rob Indians of their heritage, spiritual well-being, and basic human rights.[14] Eventually the attacks on tribal ceremonies lessened, and given the Indian Office's policy of noninterference, most opposition to dancing had ceased by 1930.

Religious freedom for Native Americans had not been fully regained, however, and there were continued agitation and court rulings against various aspects of Native American religious practices throughout the twentieth century. Dancing, on the other hand, had ceased to be an issue by the time Collier was appointed commissioner of Indian Affairs.[15]

The net effect of most of Collier's battles was a resurgence of public interest in Indian affairs. Popular magazines and newspapers of the 1920s devoted a great deal of space to the debates over Native American dancing, the Pueblo land issue, and the death of the Omnibus Bill at the hands of Robert La Follette. The rise in Indian popularity stimulated more and larger-scale scholarly studies of Native Americans. As a direct result of this renewed interest in Indians, in 1926 Secretary of the Interior Hubert Work requested that the privately funded Institute for Government Research undertake a thorough investigation of Native American issues. The study, a comprehensive survey of conditions among the tribes, was the work of a professional staff headed by Lewis Meriam, a member of the institute.

The Meriam Commission's report, published in 1928 under the title *The Problem of Indian Administration*, was a revelation to some and a confirmation of John Collier's belief that American Indian policy was in dire need of reform. In its total picture, the Meriam report was an attack on the vanishing policy. The report took the position that the suppression of Native American cultures served only to demoralize and degrade Indians. The Indian boarding schools not only were poorly administered and financed, but also served to break up and destroy Native American families. Meriam and his staff, including a former member of the Society of American Indians, Henry Roe Cloud, also attacked the allotment policy. Allotment was, to the members of the Meriam Commission, the primary factor underlying the grinding poverty found in Native American communities across the nation. It was obvious to anyone who acknowledged the validity of even some of the commission's research that the policy of allotting Indian lands in severalty had to be changed.[16]

The immediate result of the report's attack on allotment was a decline in the issuance of allotted lands. In the four fiscal years prior to the initiation of the study, 1922–1926, approximately 10,000 Native Americans were allotted over three million acres from their reservations. In comparison, during the fiscal years 1929 through 1932, the four years immediately following the publication of *The Problem of Indian Administration*, a little over 2,800 Native Americans were allotted less than 500,000 acres.[17] Although the numbers and acreage dropped considerably, the policy was nevertheless continued. But to most Americans interested in Indian affairs, allotment was an outmoded product of an outdated way of perceiving what it was to be an American citizen.

In 1929, the organization that had been most responsible for the development of the philosophical underpinnings of the vanishing policy met once more after a thirteen-year hiatus. The Lake Mohonk Conference of the Friends of the Indian had last met in 1916. The world war, and the relative lack of interest in Indian affairs that immediately followed it, interrupted the annual conferences. But with the renewed interest in Indian affairs and the publication of the Meriam report, Daniel Smiley, brother of the late Albert Smiley, the founder of the conferences, called another meeting.[18]

The shadow of the Meriam report hung heavily over the mid-October meeting. It was constantly referred to and quoted throughout the three-day convention, and most importantly it received no criticism during the open sessions. Lewis Meriam himself presided over a lengthy discussion concerning the organization of the Bureau of Indian Affairs, steadfastly advocating a policy of decentralization in its dealings with Indian problems.[19]

In large part the meeting reflected a changed viewpoint and a reshaping of the philosophical foundations of Indian affairs. One missionary, who had spent nearly forty years trying to convert Native Americans to Christianity, spoke eloquently against "the innate Anglo-Saxon snobbery which is convinced that anybody that does not look and talk just like us must therefore be inferior" and which had created the "Indian Problem" in the first place.[20] The members of the conference consistently urged patience and a less zealous approach toward changing Indians, not into ordinary citizens, but into "citizens of Indian descent."[21] Very little mention was made of allotment except within the context of attempting to find some method of reversing its disastrous effects. Finally, the conference adopted a resolution that called for the amendment of the allotment laws to make Native American landholdings "inalienable and non-taxable."[22]

Within five years allotment was abolished. On June 18, 1934, Franklin D. Roosevelt signed into law the Indian Reorganization Act. Collier, the new commissioner of Indian Affairs, had worked closely with the authors of the bill in supervising its several drafts. Although it did not contain all of Collier's wishes, it did indeed end allotment, permit tribes to organize governments, and allow them to incorporate—and partially consolidate—their trust lands. It provided for the establishment of a revolving fund "from which the Secretary of the Interior, under such rules and regulations as he may prescribe, may make loans to Indian-chartered corporations for the purpose of promoting the economic development of such tribes."[23] Although the law failed to immediately solve Native American poverty, it, at the very least, ended government ambivalence in relations with Native American people. Collier had partially won his twelve-year battle for Indian reform.

Collier's ideas concerning the management of Indian affairs were based on the notion of revitalizing historical intratribal relations and making them the basis for Native American organization. In this manner, Native Americans would be allowed to maintain certain aspects of their cultures that did not overtly conflict with the mores of American society. Thus, in Collier's mind, Native Americans would be saved from the degradation of being robbed of their separate, unique identities. Collier apparently understood the sense of peoplehood that every tribe knew, and he saw nothing improper in the maintenance of language, ceremonial cycles, sacred histories, and homelands.

Collier also believed that tribal reorganization would lead to economic uplift and serve to free Native Americans from the control of the Bureau of Indian Affairs. If the tribes were incorporated with advisory boards, somewhat in the manner of the National Recovery Act, they could control their natural resources and industrial output for their own benefit. Such reorganization would also aid in the program to decentralize the responsibilities of the bureau and remove it from further entanglements. It was a plan that seemingly combined the Progressive notions of collective management and personal liberty and at the same time extracted the government from its long-standing control over Native American lives.

The new commissioner's philosophies were rooted in the intellectual conflicts of the Progressive Era. In his youth he had been an outdoor enthusiast and an avid student of human relations. He became a social worker among immigrant populations in New York, a proponent of cultural preservation and community, and at the same time a firm believer in the protection of personal liberties as a method of maintaining cultural plurality.[24]

In 1920 he visited Mabel Dodge Luhan, his old friend from New York, in Taos, New Mexico, to investigate for himself her reports of the beauty and the social and artistic value of Pueblo Indian life. According to Collier, "the Taos experience . . . changed my life plan."[25] Among the Pueblo people he found exactly the type of communities he thought should be emulated by all Americans. To him, the tribal com-

munity at Taos represented a perfect example of *gemeinschaft* relationships, which combine communal living with individualism. The Taos
community was, to Collier, an escape from the "selfish individualism"
of white society.[26]

Collier, like many of his contemporaries in the New York bohemian community, thought himself alienated from mainstream American
life. He was decidedly critical of industrial and urban culture because
he thought it contradicted the basic tenets on which the nation was
founded. Urbanism essentially destroyed family life, and any kind of
cohesive communal life was nullified within the competitive structure
of American society.[27]

The Taos artist-intellectual community had been established as
early as 1900 when two young painters came to the New Mexico village. These artists attracted others, and the place itself became more or
less a haven for the radical subculture of New York. Mabel Dodge had
established a salon in Greenwich Village where a number of sophisticated but alienated intellectuals, artists, political activists, avowed
Marxists, and some relatively carefree celebrities of the stage met to
discuss books, art, politics, economics, and various other aspects of
American culture. Dodge, perhaps seeking solace away from the individualism and tawdry life of the big city, escaped to Taos in 1917. There
she met and married a Pueblo man, Antonio Luhan. Later she per-
suaded D. H. Lawrence and Collier to come to New Mexico to see for
themselves the beauty and serenity she had discovered.[28]

Even before Dodge or Collier came to New Mexico, members of
the Taos Society of Artists had sharply criticized the course of American Indian policy. Perhaps because of their own sense of alienation
from mainstream American culture, these artist-intellectuals felt a
basic kind of kinship with Native Americans. In any case, they became
dedicated to Native American cultural preservation, perhaps even to a
greater or more militant degree than the ethnologists who made their
living studying Native Americans. To the members of the Taos artist
community, Native Americans were "struggling against the mighty
white race that threatens to swallow them up and spit them out again,
servants with short hair and clad in overalls!"[29] From this protective
philosophy it was a short step to the Collier Indian policy.

The antiurban, aesthetic, and nostalgic aspects of the conservation
movement in the United States appealed to Collier. He found almost

everything in Native American life to be just as people such as Charles Eastman, Laura Cornelius, and Zitkala Sa purported it to be: ecological-minded, socially cohesive, spiritual, and balanced. He and the others who gravitated around Taos fought against the destruction of a worthy, though different, culture. And in their efforts to maintain Native American cultures, they became advocates of cultural pluralism. In this aspect of Collier's philosophy, he was supported by the latest trends in anthropological research.

The culture concept in anthropology began in the United States largely because of the research done by Franz Boas and his students at Columbia University. Trained in Germany as a physicist, Boas firmly believed in the value of empirical research. In America he ignored his own scholastic field of study and turned to ethnology. Once he entered the new discipline, he carried with him the devotion to empiricism normally associated with experimental scientific training. As a consequence, he stressed empiricism in his own work among the Eskimos and the tribes of the northwest coast. He also urged his students to make in-depth studies of particular cultures. He emphasized in the scientific study of peoples absolute objectivity by attempting to remove any racial or social bias the researcher might have. Conjecture concerning the superiority or inferiority of a group was to be eliminated.

The Boas school found out two very important things about human societies. The first was what has come to be known as cultural determinism. Essentially, Boas thought that culture, not race, determined human behavior. Second, his student Ruth Benedict, in her classic 1934 book, *Patterns of Culture*, realized that since all humans came from the same stock and were thus of the same age, it was an effort in futility to study so-called "primitives" in order to find an original human cultural form. This idea, at a minimum, dented the notions underlying social and cultural evolution. To the Boas school, cultures were neither higher nor lower; they were merely different, and all were the same age. They had simply developed along different lines.[30]

But scientific theory, especially concerning human behavior, is usually publicly accepted only when it generally corresponds with the public's already-formed notions of how and why phenomena occur. Social Darwinism was made acceptable because it more or less corresponded with the American ideals of individualism and competitive capitalism. The old Indian reformers readily accepted the theory of social evolution in much the same manner, even though it explained human behavior from a standpoint other than Christian dogma. Social evolution served to confirm the assimilationists' belief that Native Americans should be "uplifted" from savagery to civilization. Had Lewis Henry Morgan or John Wesley Powell developed a theory of cultural determinism in the 1870s or 1880s, the old reformers probably would have done without "scientific" support for their ideas regarding Indian assimilation. They were Christians, nationalists, and, by their lights, civilized persons already convinced of their cultural and moral superiority. They had conceived of Native Americans as savage and barbaric long before Morgan's book *Ancient Societies* outlined the idea that human societies advanced along Darwinian lines.

Although the Boas school was a development of the first decade or so of the twentieth century, it did not become widely acceptable until the late 1920s and early 1930s. By that time, however, many whites had already accepted the idea that several aspects of "primitive" human cultures were indeed valuable to white "civilized" society. The mere thought of preserving tribal cultures was logically antithetical to the totality of social evolutionism. Its "natural" progression should have already seen the demise of identifiable Native American art, ceremonies, and customs. The fact that tribal cultures survived the onslaught of white civilization in fact weakened the absolutism of evolutionist thought. The preservationists of the Progressive Era, probably without knowing it, had caught a glimpse of the cultural determinists' rising star. Collier, the new reformer, professed cultural pluralism just as the old reformers had acknowledged social evolutionary thought as being inherently correct or simply a "natural" occurrence in human history.

Strangely, Boas himself disapproved of Collier's programs. But Collier was a social scientist and a theorist in his own right. In addition, one of Boas's important and influential students, A. L. Kroeber—the scientist who had found Ishi—had joined Collier's Indian Defense Association, thus lending scientific credibility to Collier's cause.[31] Even though he might have been the father of cultural pluralism, Boas was not essential to the "Indian New Deal." But then again, Lewis Henry Morgan was hardly essential to the vanishing policy. It is probably the fate of scholars that their studies are consulted only when they more or less match the ideologies of policy makers or are politically advantageous

Although Collier has been considered an important social theorist, his ideas were not completely new. Laura Cornelius thought that tribal relationships could be utilized to solve Native American social and economic problems as early as 1911. Red Bird Smith, to whom she dedicated *Our Democracy and the American Indian*, attempted, through Cherokee cultural survival, to revitalize Cherokee society and renew his tribe's sense of peoplehood. Many other Native Americans held the line in this manner, if only to retain their concepts of balance and order. Collier was caught up not only with the idea of collective reform, but also in the anti-industrial, practical, yet romantic side of conservationism—a side that Charles Eastman had earlier written and spoken about so eloquently. Collier's particular mission was to attempt to preserve Native American cultures and at the same time use them as models for the restructuring of white society. He was a white man attempting to spread Native American knowledge of the intricacy of the environment and a philosophy of communal life based on shared relationships and experiences. Native American customs and ideas were worthy of emulation.

Collier's policies, although they did not particularly enhance the economic status of Native Americans, at least marked a clear watershed in the development of American Indian policy. There can be no doubt that the Indian New Deal was as grand a scheme as the vanishing policy had been. The assaults on Native American peoplehood ceased; allotment was given up; the boarding schools were de-emphasized; tribal quasi-states were allowed to exist; Indian art was officially patronized and protected; and the tribes gained some autonomy in managing the natural resources that they still possessed. For all his social and political experimentation and his ideas of cultural pluralism, Collier's policies were essentially based on the premise that Native Americans would become more productive members of the greater American nation if they were allowed to rejuvenate and take pride in their own institutions and heritage. Collier sought to "repair as far as possible, the incalculable damage done by the allotment policy and its corollaries."[32]

The Indian New Deal, however, did not mean for Native American peoples full autonomy or complete freedom of action. The Indian New Deal really marked the official entrance of the United States into the structural accommodation phase of its colonial relationship with

Native American peoples. The Indian Reorganization Act increased, legitimated, and, for all intents and purposes, made permanent the discretionary authority of the Department of the Interior and the Bureau of Indian Affairs. The Indian Office had become, in the sense of Max Weber's treatise on the subject, a legitimized bureaucracy that was here to stay. No longer was there even a notion that it would vanish along with "the Indian."

The discretionary authority of the secretary of the interior over Indian affairs grew well beyond its historic boundaries. The secretary was given the legal power to purchase or otherwise acquire lands for the purpose of restoring them to tribal ownership, to make rules for the management of Indian forestry and range units, and to proclaim new Indian reservations. The Interior Department also had the authority to issue charters of organization, call for elections to decide whether or not a tribe would organize under the Indian Reorganization Act, and utilize an appropriated $250,000 to help defray the costs of incorporating Native American tribes. A ten-million-dollar appropriation was made for the secretary to establish a "revolving fund" from which to make loans to chartered Indian tribes for the purpose of economic development.

Moreover, the secretary was given the authority to appoint Native Americans "without regard to civil-service laws, to the various positions maintained, now or hereafter, by the Indian Office, in the administration of functions or services affecting any Indian tribe."[33] The provisions of the Indian Reorganization Act were extended to include the tribes of Oklahoma under the Oklahoma Indian Welfare Act of 1936.[34] But even before the Oklahoma act, Collier and Congress acted to "promote the development of Indian arts and crafts" in acknowledgment of the art movement that had been so important in changing white attitudes toward Native Americans during the first quarter of the twentieth century.[35]

The provisions in the Indian Reorganization Act that authorized the secretary of the interior to extend credit to newly incorporated tribes, issue charters, and appoint Indians to positions within the Indian Office were perhaps the most important of all of its many sections for guaranteeing the permanence of the bureaucracy. In the first place, the line of credit from the ten-million-dollar appropriation could, according to the act, be extended only to "Indian-chartered corporations." Since the secretary of the interior held the power to issue charters, these provisions strongly bound "chartered" tribes to the federal government. Essentially, Congress had delegated the federal government's trust responsibility to Native American tribes to an executive branch, cabinet-level bureaucracy, thereby ensuring that the Department of the Interior's Indian Office would be in place as long as there were Indians.

And interestingly enough, although the tribes had the right to determine their own tribal members, the determination of who was and who was not an Indian—by the blood-quantum certification—also rested with the Indian Office bureaucracy. With the power to appoint Native Americans to positions within the Indian bureaucracy, the federal government could also offer "qualified Indians" the opportunity to become part of the structure of American public authority. The structural accommodation to the fact that Native Americans had not disappeared was complete.

The Indian New Deal was the legacy of the ambivalence in American Indian policy during the first quarter of the new century. Collier was able to select certain arguments and ideas that arose during the Progressive Era concerning Native Americans and Indian policy and mold them into a larger philosophy of Indian affairs. That the Indian Office bureaucracy grew in both size and authority was a direct outcome of Progressives' emphasis on management and the need for order. But the intellectual conflicts in Indian affairs of the Progressive period would not have arisen had Native Americans simply vanished into mainstream American society or as separate peoples.

Whether or not they legally possessed the territory on which they lived, or held it in trust, or lived on individual allotments, Native Americans remained strongly connected with the land. Native languages were still being utilized to tell the old stories and to conduct the ceremonies that renewed tribal bonds and a sense of place. Even though the "New Indians" had taken up new lives, none of them could forswear or forsake their tribal identities. Despite the widespread notion that Native Americans would vanish according to the laws of nature or as a result of the nineteenth-century Indian reformers' attempt to hurry nature along by way of the vanishing policy, Native Americans' and each tribe's sense of peoplehood survived.

That they had done so implied either that "natural law" had been

suspended or that the vanishing policy was based on a misinterpreta-
tion of natural law. During the Progressive Era, a number of people,
including most Native Americans, began to point out the flaws of the
vanishing policy. Policy makers, most especially the commissioners of
Indian Affairs, simply played a juggling act with the vanishing policy,
the newer ideas of preservation, and the specific management of particular problems. The theoretical basis of the vanishing policy had
crumbled, and as an example of the pattern of Indian affairs, it had
failed. John Collier recognized its failure and pieced together another
paradigm for Indian policy. Between Collier and Richard Henry Pratt,
the old reformer who fought against the rise of the bureaucracy in
Indian affairs, lie the conflict and confusion of the Progressive Era.

Collier's conception of how Indian policy should work set a pattern
in Native-white relations that lasted a good deal longer than the vanishing policy. Native nations continue to assert those sovereign rights
that were recognized under Collier's tenure. The tribes had the ability
to organize governments; they could determine their own membership; they held proprietorship over their own lands; and the Native
nations could levy taxes if they so desired. Under Collier's direction,
the Indian New Deal essentially accommodated the federal government to the fact of Native resiliency. Collier's attempt to decentralize
the Bureau of Indian Affairs did not prevent its rapid growth into
the permanent and preeminent Indian institution within the federal
government.

During the fifteen years after Collier left office, the federal government did indeed attempt to renew the vanishing policy. Under the
aegis of the Indian Claims Commission the government tried to settle
quickly, quietly, and cheaply all Indian suits, claims, or demands in
regard to Native losses of treasure and land. Native deaths from disease
and warfare could never have been either ascertained or compensated.
Also launched during this brief period were the termination and relocation programs. Termination was the effort to extract the federal government from its trust responsibility to certain Native nations. Relocation was the name given to the federal program to provide job training
and transportation to Indians so that they would leave the reservations
and take up residence in urban areas. The recrudescence of the vanishing policy after World War II caused a great deal of panic among

Native peoples, and the specific policy of termination created another round of land losses for the tribes.

But in the 1960s Native peoples once again worked to subvert the new vanishing policy. Additionally, the Bureau of Indian Affairs began to reassert the discretionary authority it had gained under John Collier. By the time the Indian Self-Determination and Education Act was enacted in 1975, the BIA was the federal government's structural accommodation to the fact of Indian survival. More important was the fact that Native nations had essentially maintained their particular relationship with the federal government. The fourth stage in the colonial relationship was still intact and, for better or worse, functioning as if unchanged, except for some modifications, since 1934.

It appears, however, that another round of conflict and confusion is on the horizon. Gaming on the reservations, although it has offered some financial benefits to several tribes located within driving distance of larger population centers, is becoming the focus of a renewed white complaint about the "special" status of American Indians. Essentially, non-Indians in the United States have difficulty understanding the notion of Native American sovereignty and the actuality of Native nation-states. This lack of understanding probably revolved around the European roots of the concept of sovereignty. "Sovereignty" is derived from the Old French *souverein*, which applied to the person (king, prince, or, in some cases, *comte*) who ruled, without higher council or authority, a particular place and the people within its boundaries, usually through the force of arms. In the European tradition, the state wielded the powers of sovereignty, and according to Niccolo Machiavelli, the "principal study and care and the especial profession" of a sovereign was "warfare and its attendant rules and discipline." Moreover, Machiavelli wrote, no (sovereign) "state is safe unless it has its own arms." A state without an armed force "is completely dependent on fortune, having no effectiveness to defend itself in adversity."[36] True sovereignty could not, therefore, exist in disarmed or conquered states, at least according to the Western political tradition.

Native American nation-states, however, have what has been called "limited sovereignty." This concept is exceptionally difficult to grasp, given that Indians are United States citizens and are members of polities that have accepted protectorate status under the federal government. Limited sovereignty also means that certain rights of the sovereign state are still invested, despite the protectorate status, in all indigenous American nations. Native nation-states can tax, determine their own memberships, remove undesired persons from their own lands, police misdemeanors and lesser crimes, control how their own natural resources are to be used, and, technically, coin money. Of course, neither the average American citizen nor even the sovereign states of the union possess all of these rights, powers, and privileges. Native American rights go beyond those of any other ethnic group as well.

Therein lies the seed for further conflict and confusion that potentially could lead to the collapse of the American state's structural accommodation to the existence of Native peoples. At some point, Washington policy makers will be forced to filter through their own cultural and political perspectives the notion that Native nation-states made specific arrangements with the American government to retain their sovereign status. Once they do so, then perhaps the decolonization of Native North America can begin and the final stage in the colonial relationship—indigenous self-determination—can be implemented.

NOTES

Chapter I. The Vanishing Policy

1. See especially Kenneth Fink, "Riding Behind with a Pillow Strapped On," in *A Good Cherokee, a Good Anthropologist: Papers in Honor of Robert K. Thomas*, ed. Steven Pavlik (Los Angeles: UCLA American Indian Studies Center, 1998), 121; Edward H. Spicer, *Cycles of Conquest: The Impact of Spain, Mexico, and the United States on the Indians of the Southwest* (Tucson: Univ. of Arizona Press, 1962); George Pierre Castile and Gilbert Kushner, eds. *Persistent Peoples: Cultural Enclaves in Perspective* (Tucson: Univ. of Arizona Press, 1981); Tom Holm, J. Diane Pearson, and Ben Chavis, "Peoplehood: A Model for the Extension of Sovereignty in American Indian Studies," *Wicazo Sa Review* 18 (2003): 7–24; and Tom Holm, "Sovereignty and Peoplehood," *Red Ink* 8 (Spring 2000): 41–44.

2. Policy Development Group, *The Government of Aboriginal Peoples* (Ottawa: Sub-Committee on Indian Self-Determination of the Canadian House of Commons Standing Committee on Indian Affairs and Northern Development, 1983). This study was commissioned to aid constitutional reform in Canada during the early 1980s. A general look at colonial phases, it uses as examples the relations between Native Americans and the United States and Canada, the Sami and Finland, the Aboriginals and Australia, the Ainu and Japan, and the Maori and New Zealand. *The Government of Aboriginal Peoples* outlines each phase in the colonial relationship succinctly and compellingly and offers a possible fifth phase, "Self-Determination," to follow "Structural Accommodation."

3. Albert Memmi, *The Colonizer and the Colonized*, trans. Howard Greenfeld (Boston: Beacon Press, 1967).

4. See Francis Paul Prucha, *American Indian Policy in the Formative Years: The Indian Trade and Intercourse Acts, 1790–1834* (Cambridge, Mass.: Harvard Univ. Press, 1962); Reginald Horsman, *Expansion and American Indian Policy, 1783–1812* (East Lansing: Michigan State Univ. Press, 1967); Bernard W. Sheehan, *Seeds of Extinction: Jeffersonian Philanthropy and the American Indian* (Chapel Hill: Univ. of North Carolina Press,

1973). An early compilation of Native American treaties with the United States is in Charles J. Kappler, ed., *Indian Affairs: Laws and Treaties*, vol. 2 (Washington, D.C.: Government Printing Office, 1904). For a history of Native American treaties and treaty making, see Francis Paul Prucha, *American Indian Treaties: The History of a Political Anomaly* (Berkeley and Los Angeles: Univ. of California Press, 1994). The most comprehensive compilation and study of Native American treaties, agreements, and conventions (ratified and unratified) with the United States and foreign nations is Vine Deloria, Jr., and Raymond J. DeMallie, eds., *Documents of American Indian Diplomacy: Treaties, Agreements, and Conventions, 1775–1979*, 2 vol. (Norman: Univ. of Oklahoma Press, 1999).

5. See Francis Paul Prucha's introduction to D. S. Otis, *The Dawes Act and the Allotment of Indian Lands* (Norman: University of Oklahoma Press, 1973), ix–x.

6. Quoted in Francis Paul Prucha, "Andrew Jackson's Indian Policy: A Reassessment," *Journal of American History* 56 (December 1969): 527–539.

7. This theme is presented in Robert A. Trennert, Jr., *Alternative to Extinction: Federal Indian Policy and the Beginnings of the Reservation System* (Philadelphia: Temple Univ. Press, 1975).

8. Roy Harvey Pearce, *The Savages of America: A Study of the Indian and the Idea of Civilization* (Baltimore: Johns Hopkins Univ. Press, 1953), 240.

9. Francis Paul Prucha, *American Indian Policy in Crisis: Christian Reformers and the Indian, 1865–1900* (Norman: Univ. of Oklahoma Press, 1976), 14.

10. Donald Chaput, "Generals, Indian Agents, Politicians: The Doolittle Survey of 1865," *Western History Quarterly* 3 (July 1972): 269–282.

11. U.S. Senate, *Senate Report* 159, 39th Cong., 2nd sess., serial 1279, 3–10.

12. For a history of the peace policy, see Henry E. Fritz, *The Movement for Indian Assimilation, 1860–1890* (Philadelphia: Univ. of Pennsylvania Press, 1963). Concerning Parker, see Prucha, *Indian Policy in Crisis*, 37, 44, 48, 66–67, and Arthur C. Parker, *The Life of General Ely S. Parker* (Buffalo, N.Y.: Buffalo Historical Society, 1919).

13. Prucha, *Indian Policy in Crisis*, 58–59.

14. A great deal has been written on outbreaks of war between Native Americans and the United States following the Civil War. Still the most popular is Dee Brown, *Bury My Heart at Wounded Knee: An Indian History of the American West* (New York: Holt, Rinehart and Winston, 1971). For a take on the wars for the Great Plains from a British military historian, see John Keegan, "Warfare on the Plains," *Yale Review* 84 (January 1996): 1–48.

15. For the most detailed account of the Modoc war, see Keith A. Murray, *The Modocs and Their War* (Norman: Univ. of Oklahoma Press, 1959).

16. Prucha, *Indian Policy in Crisis*, 87–88.

17. A staggering amount has been written about the Little Bighorn campaign. An interesting military account comparing the U.S.-Lakota war of 1876 with the Zulu-British war in 1879 is James O. Gump, *The Dust Rose like Smoke: The Subjugation of the Zulu and the Sioux* (Lincoln: Univ. of Nebraska Press, 1994). For the reformers' reaction to the war, see Prucha, *Indian Policy in Crisis*, 93–94.

18. For the Nez Percé war, see Mark H. Brown, *The Flight of the Nez Perce: A Histo-*

ry of the Nez Perce War (New York: G. P. Putnam's Sons, 1967); and Merrill D. Beal, *"I Will Fight No More Forever": Chief Joseph and the Nez Perce War* (Seattle: Univ. of Washington Press, 1963). For the Bannock outbreak, see George F. Brimlow, *The Bannock Indian War of 1878* (Caldwell, Idaho: Caxton Printers, 1938). For an account of the Cheyenne escape from Indian Territory, see Peter M. Wright, "The Pursuit of Dull Knife from Fort Reno in 1878–1879," *Chronicles of Oklahoma* 46 (Summer 1968): 141–154; and, of course, Mari Sandoz, *Cheyenne Autumn* (New York: McGraw-Hill, 1953).

19. Prucha, *Indian Policy in Crisis*, 114.

20. Ibid., 115–116.

21. Fritz, *Indian Assimilation*, 202.

22. Helen Hunt Jackson, *A Century of Dishonor: A Sketch of the United States Government's Dealings with Some of the Indian Tribes* (New York: Harper and Brothers, 1881).

23. Jackson's impact is dealt with in Prucha, *Indian Policy in Crisis*, 161–165.

24. Fritz, *Indian Assimilation*, 202.

25. Otis, *Dawes Act*, 36–37; Prucha, *Indian Policy in Crisis*, 143–147; U.S. Department of the Interior, Board of Commissioners for Indian Affairs, *Annual Report* 1883.

26. The reformers reached the conclusion that allotment was the key to Indian freedom. See Prucha, *Indian Policy in Crisis*; Fritz, *Indian Assimilation*; Otis, *Dawes Act*; Robert Winston Mardock, *The Reformers and the American Indian* (Columbia: Univ. of Missouri Press, 1971); Loring Benson Priest, *Uncle Sam's Stepchildren: The Reformation of United States Indian Policy, 1865–1887* (New Brunswick, N.J.: Rutgers Univ. Press, 1942). For the reformers' views, see Francis Paul Prucha, ed., *Americanizing the American Indian: Writings by the "Friends of the Indian," 1880–1900* (Cambridge, Mass.: Harvard Univ. Press, 1973). The campaign to assimilate Native Americans, especially its political ramifications, is covered fully in Frederick E. Hoxie, *A Final Promise: The Campaign to Assimilate the Indians, 1880–1920* (New York: Cambridge Univ. Press, 1989).

27. Angie Debo, *The Rise and Fall of the Choctaw Republic* (Norman: Univ. of Oklahoma Press, 1934), 55, 69, 73.

28. For a detailed study of the Oklahoma territorial bills, see Roy Gittinger, *The Formation of the State of Oklahoma, 1803–1906* (Berkeley and Los Angeles: Univ. of California Press, 1917).

29. U.S. House of Representatives, *House Journal*, 45th Cong., 3rd sess., serial 1841, 332, 685; U.S. Senate, *Senate Journal*, 45th Cong., 3rd sess., serial 1827, 227.

30. U.S. House of Representatives, 46th Cong., 1st sess., *A Bill . . . Allotment in Severalty* (HR 354), April 21, 1879, Cherokee–Federal Relations File 1879, Indian Archives, Oklahoma Historical Society.

31. U.S. Senate, 46th Cong., 2nd sess., *A Bill . . . Allotment in Severalty* (SR 989), January 12, 1880, Cherokee–Federal Relations File 1880, Indian Archives, Oklahoma Historical Society.

32. U.S. House of Representatives, *House Journal*, 46th Cong., 2nd sess., serial 1901, 725, 1228; U.S. House of Representatives, *House Report* 1576, 46th Cong., 2nd sess., serial 1938.

33. U.S. Senate, *Senate Journal*, 46th Cong., 3rd sess., serial 1940, 139.

34. *Congressional Record* 11, 46th Cong., 3rd sess., part 1.

35. Ibid., 970.

36. Ibid., 781.

37. U.S. Senate, *Senate Journal*, 48th Cong., 1st sess., serial 2161, 469; U.S. House of Representatives, *House Report* 2247, 48th Cong., 2nd session, serial 2328.

38. S. C. Armstrong, *Report of a Trip Made in Behalf of the Indian Rights Association to Some Indian Reservations of the Southwest* (Philadelphia: Indian Rights Association, 1884).

39. Joint Resolution of the Cherokee National Council . . . inviting the Senate Committee on Indian Affairs to Tahlequah, November 10, 1884, Cherokee–Federal Relations File 1884, Indian Archives, Oklahoma Historical Society.

40. Dawes's address to the Lake Mohonk Conference is in the "Third Annual Meeting of the Lake Mohonk Conference," included in Board of Commissioners, *Annual Report* 1885, 86–91.

41. U.S. House of Representatives, *House Report* 1835, 49th Cong., 1st sess., serial 2440; U.S. House of Representatives, *House Journal*, 49th Cong., 2nd sess., serial 2459, 99, 105, 130, 217, 222, 684.

42. *United States Statutes at Large* 24, 388–391.

43. Ibid., 391.

44. Quoted in Fritz, *Indian Assimilation*, 208. Also see Tom Holm, "Indian Lobbyists: Cherokee Opposition to the Allotment of Tribal Lands," *American Indian Quarterly* 5 (May 1979): 115–134.

45. *U.S. Stats.* 27, 645–646.

46. Charles F. Meserve, *The Dawes Commission and the Five Civilized Tribes* (Philadelphia: Indian Rights Association, 1896).

47. *U.S. Stats.* 27, 693–698.

48. *U.S. Stats.* 29, 339–340.

49. *U.S. Stats.* 30, 495–519.

50. "Exeunt the Five Civilized Tribes," *Independent* 54 (October 9, 1902), 2432.

51. Charles Moreau Harger, "The Indian's Last Stand," *Outlook* 70 (January 25, 1902), 222.

52. "The New Indian," *Nation* 79 (July 2, 1904), 48.

53. Quoted in Elaine Goodale Eastman, *Pratt: The Red Man's Moses* (Norman: Univ. of Oklahoma Press, 1935), 188–189.

54. Report of the Cherokee delegation to Washington, 1885, unclassified Cherokee Nation papers, Western History Collections, University of Oklahoma.

55. Most of the information concerning the liberal reformers of the Gilded Age can be found in John G. Sproat, *"The Best Men": Liberal Reformers in the Gilded Age* (New York: Oxford Univ. Press, 1968); and Mardock, *Reformers and the Indian*.

56. Herbert Spencer and the impact of Social Darwinism are discussed in Richard Hofstadter, *Social Darwinism in American Thought* (Boston: Beacon Press, 1955).

57. See the preface in Lewis Henry Morgan, *Ancient Society, or Researches in the Lines of Human Progress from Savagery through Barbarism to Civilization* (New York:

Meridian Books, 1967 [orig. pub. 1877]) and Hoxie's discussion of Morgan's ideas in *Final Promise*, 17–18.

58. Mardock, *Reformers and the Indian*, 100.

59. Edwin Lawrence Godkin, "A Good Field for Reform," *Nation* 46 (March 15, 1888), 210–211.

60. Prucha, *Indian Policy in Crisis*, 209.

61. Quoted in Prucha, *Americanizing the Indians*, 39.

62. Biographical material on Pratt can be found in Elaine Goodale Eastman's uncritical and frankly obsequious book, *Pratt: The Red Man's Moses*. See also Hoxie, *Final Promise*, 54–57.

63. Quoted in Prucha, *Americanizing the Indians*, 270.

64. Richard Henry Pratt, "Indian No Problem," *Missionary Review* 33 (November 1910): 851, 856.

65. Quoted in Prucha, *Americanizing the Indians*, 270.

66. Elaine Goodale Eastman, "A New Method of Indian Education," *Outlook* 64 (January 27, 1900), 222.

67. John Keegan, *A History of Warfare* (New York: Vintage Books, 1993), 14–15.

68. Ibid., 15.

69. *Proceedings of the Lake Mohonk Conference 1888*, 6.

70. Elaine Goodale Eastman, "The Education of Indians" *Arena* 24 (October 1900), 414; on lace making, see Jane W. Guthrie, "Lace-Making among the Indians" *Outlook* 66 (September 1, 1900), 59–62.

71. *Lake Mohonk Proceedings 1897*, 115.

72. See F. Crissey "Renaming the Indians," *World To-Day* 10 (January 1906), 84–90. For a more modern account of the renaming program, see Daniel F. Littlefield, Jr., and Lonnie E. Underhill, "Renaming the American Indian, 1890–1913," *American Studies* 12 (Fall 1971): 33–45. A number of Native Americans in the early part of the twentieth century told stories about how they were essentially abducted by being promised something new and exciting. Angel DeCora, a Winnebago, told of how "a strange white man" asked her if she wanted to take a ride in a "steam car." She agreed, and the next day she was taken to a railroad station and shipped off to the Hampton Institute. She did not see home again for three years. See Angel DeCora, "Angel DeCora: An Autobiography," *Red Man* (March 1911), 280. Gertrude Bonnin (Zitkala Sa) was enticed away from her South Dakota home at age eight to White's Indian Manual Labor Institute in Wabash, Indiana, by the promise of "red, red apples." See P. Jane Hafen, "Zitkala Sa (Gertrude Bonnin)," in *Encyclopedia of North American Indians*, ed. Frederick E. Hoxie (New York: Houghton Mifflin, 1996), 708.

73. U.S. Congress, *Annual Report of the Secretary of War*, 1891, 14.

74. *Lake Mohonk Proceedings 1891*, 114.

75. See Vine Deloria, Jr., *Spirit and Reason: The Vine Deloria, Jr., Reader* (Golden, Colo.: Fulcrum Publishing, 1999), 223–229, 354–368.

76. R. L. Owen to J. D. C. Atkins, in Commissioner of Indian Affairs, *Annual Report 1887*, 112.

Chapter II. Persistent Peoples

1. Quoted in Otis, *Dawes Act*, 45.

2. Ernest L. Schusky, ed., *Political Organization of Native North Americans* (Washington, D.C.: Univ. Press of America, 1981), vii–viii.

3. See especially Angie Debo, *And Still the Waters Run: The Betrayal of the Five Civilized Tribes* (Princeton, N.J.: Princeton Univ. Press, 1972).

4. Statement of John Redbird Smith, Indian-Pioneer Papers, v. 85, 173, Western History Collections, University of Oklahoma; G. P. Horsefly, *A History of the True People: The Cherokee Indians* (Detroit: Rick Smith, 1979), 101; Debo, *Still the Waters Run*, 54.

5. Owens's statement is in Commissioner of Indian Affairs, *Annual Report* 1887, 113.

6. U.S. Senate, Senate Miscellaneous Documents 24, *Report of the Commission to the Five Civilized Tribes*, 53rd Cong., 3rd sess., Western History Collections, University of Oklahoma; Cherokee and Creek Delegates to Members of Congress, December 1894, Cherokee–Federal Relations File 1894, Oklahoma Historical Society, Indian Archives.

7. Debo, *Still the Waters Run*, 34.

8. See especially the *New York Times*, January 24, 25, 27, 28, 29, 1901, and February 4, 1901; Debo, *Still the Waters Run*, 53.

9. Chitto Harjo and his attorneys argued that allotment was in violation of Creek treaties and the Creek Nation's political sovereignty. This argument was repeated in the 1976 case, *Harjo v. Kleppe*, 420 F. Supp. 1110 (1976). Also see David H. Getches, Charles F. Wilkinson and Robert A. Williams, Jr., *Cases and Materials on Federal Indian Law* (St. Paul, Minn.: West Group, 1998), 185–190. For Chitto Harjo's own thoughts, see U.S. Senate, *Senate Report* 5013, v. 2, serial 5063, 1245–1255. The comment about Chitto Harjo and his attorneys is in L. Crane, "A Man Ruined by an Idea," *Harper's Weekly* 53 (June 26, 1909), 15.

10. The best analysis of the 1909 Creek War is Daniel F. Littlefield, Jr., and Lonnie E. Underhill, "The 'Crazy Snake Uprising' of 1909: A Red, Black or White Affair?" *Arizona and the West* 20 (Winter 1978): 307–324. An older account is Mel H. Bolster, "The Smoked Meat Rebellion," *Chronicles of Oklahoma* 31 (Spring 1953): 37–55. Also see Debo, *Still the Waters Run*, 295.

11. Louis H. Roddis, "The Last Indian Uprising in the United States," *Minnesota History Bulletin* 3 (February 1920): 272–290.

12. Davidson B. McKibbin, "Revolt of the Navajo, 1913," *New Mexico Historical Review* 29 (October 1954): 259–289; Matthew K. Sniffen, *The Meaning of the Ute "War"* (Philadelphia: Indian Rights Association, 1915).

13. See especially Robert K. Thomas, "The Redbird Smith Movement," in *Symposium on Cherokee and Iroquois Culture*, ed. William N. Fenton and John Gulick (Bureau of American Ethnology Bulletin 180, 1961); Horsefly, *True People*, 95–105; Statement of John Redbird Smith, Indian-Pioneer Papers, v. 85, 180–181; Morris L. Wardell, *A Political History of the Cherokee Nation, 1838–1907* (Norman: University of Oklahoma Press, 1938), 327–329; James Mooney and Frans M. Olbrechts, *The Swimmer Manuscript: Cherokee Sacred Formulas and Medical Prescriptions* (Bureau of American Ethnology

Bulletin 99, 1932), 27; Raymond D. Fogelson, "Change, Persistence and Accommodation in Cherokee Medico-Magical Beliefs," in Fenton and Gulick (see above), 216.

14. John Redbird Smith, Indian-Pioneer Papers, v. 85, 190.

15. Emmett Starr, *History of the Cherokee Indians and Their Legends and Folk Lore* (Oklahoma City: Warden, 1921), 481–483.

16. Thomas, "Redbird Smith Movement," 161–166.

17. Commissioner of Indian Affairs, *Annual Report* 1885, 11.

18. Prucha, *Indian Policy in Crisis*, 210.

19. Robert H. Lowie, *Indians of the Plains* (Garden City, N.Y.: National History Press, 1963), 197–199. See also George A. Dorsey to Major George W. H. Stouch, September 14, 1903, James Mooney–Cheyenne Sun Dance File, National Anthropological Archives, Smithsonian Institution.

20. Ruth Underhill, *Red Man's Religion: Beliefs and Practices of the Indians North of Mexico* (Chicago: Univ. of Chicago Press, 1965), 142–153; Peter J. Powell, *Sweet Medicine: The Continuing Role of the Sacred Arrows, the Sun Dance, and the Sacred Buffalo Hat in Northern Cheyenne History* (Norman: Univ. of Oklahoma Press, 1969), 300.

21. Reginald and Gladys Laubin, *Indian Dances of North America: Their Importance to Indian Life* (Norman: Univ. of Oklahoma Press, 1977), 275.

22. Powell, *Sweet Medicine*, 319–320; Margot Liberty, "Suppression and Survival of the Northern Cheyenne Sun Dance," *Minnesota Archaeologist* 27 (1965): 121–143.

23. Powell, *Sweet Medicine*, 320–338.

24. Ibid., 338–339.

25. Ibid., 340–341.

26. Donald J. Berthrong, *The Cheyenne and Arapaho Ordeal: Reservation and Agency Life in the Indian Territory, 1875–1907* (Norman: Univ. of Oklahoma Press, 1976), 217; James Mooney to W. H. Holmes, chief, Bureau of American Ethnology, August 24, 1903, Mooney–Sun Dance File.

27. *New York Times*, August 15, 1903; *Lake Mohonk Proceedings* 1903, 73; Berthrong, *Cheyenne and Arapaho Ordeal*, 294–295. See also the affidavit of the Darlington, Watonga, and Kingfisher Cheyenne, September 1, 1903, and of the Colony Cheyenne and the Cheyenne in the Arapaho District, Oklahoma Territory, September 1, 1903, Mooney–Sun Dance File.

28. Mooney to Holmes, August 24, 1903; Dorsey to Stouch, September 14, 1903, Mooney–Sun Dance File. See also Joseph G. Jorgensen, *The Sun Dance Religion: Power for the Powerless* (Chicago: Univ. of Chicago Press, 1972).

29. O. P. Phillips, "Moki Indians and their Snake Dance," *Era* 11 (February 1903), 115–129.

30. Thomas, "Redbird Smith Movement," 164.

31. Keith H. Basso, *The Gift of Changing Woman* (Bureau of American Ethnology Bulletin 196, 1966). Basso, *The Cibecue Apache* (New York: Holt, Rinehart and Winston, 1970), 53–72.

32. Robert F. Spencer, Jesse D. Jennings, et al., *The Native Americans: Prehistory and Ethnology of the North American Indians* (New York: Harper and Row, 1965), 330–331.

33. Harold E. Driver, *Indians of North America* (Chicago: Univ. of Chicago Press,

1975), 357, 522; Spencer and Jennings, *Native Americans*, 390–391.

34. Julia F. A. Frather, "Fourth of July at the Klamath Reservation," *Overland* 42 (July 1903), 116–123; Board of Commissioners, *Annual Report* 1918, 78–80.

35. Laubin and Laubin, *Indian Dances*, 42, 73, 81, 455.

36. Underhill, *Red Man's Religion*, 262–264.

37. DeKoven Brown, "Indian Workers for Temperance: The New Faith that Came from the Vision of Old John Slocum, Drunkard," *Collier's* 45 (September 3, 1910), 24; "Indian Shakers," *Literary Digest* 48 (March 7, 1914), 496; Sarah Endicott Ober, "New Religion among the West Coast Indians," *Overland* 56 (December 1910), 594.

38. For a concise treatment of the potlatch see Spencer and Jennings, *Native Americans*, 180–193.

39. Brown, "Indian Workers for Temperance," 24.

40. Driver, *Indians of North America*, 112–114.

41. James S. Slotkin, *The Peyote Religion: A Study in Indian-White Relations* (Glencoe, Ill.: Free Press, 1956), 70–75.

42. Driver, *Indians of North America*, 525.

43. Among the best sources on the development of a syncretic reservation culture are anthropologist Clark Wissler's memoirs of his many trips to the reservations during the 1890s and early 1900s: *Red Man's Reservations* (New York: Collier Macmillan, 1971 [orig. pub. 1919]).

44. Gordon MacGregor, "Changing Society: The Teton Dakotas," in *The Modern Sioux*, ed. Ethel Nurge, 98 (Lincoln: Univ. of Nebraska Press, 1975).

45. See Ben Chavis, "All-Indian Rodeo: A Transformation of Western Apache Tribal Warfare and Culture," *Wicazo Sa Review* 9 (Spring 1993): 4–11.

46. See Driver, *Indians of North America*, 516. See also P. Bion Griffin, Mark P. Leone, and Keith Basso, "Western Apache Ecology: From Horticulture to Agriculture," 69–72, and William Y. Adams and Gordon V. Krutz, "Wage Labor and the San Carlos Apache," 116–117, both essays in *Apachean Culture and Ethnology*, ed. Keith Basso and Morris E. Opler (Tucson: Univ. of Arizona Press, 1971).

47. Wissler, *Red Man's Reservations*, 115.

48. Mooney and Olbrechts, *Swimmer Manuscript*, 124; Sister M. Inez Hilger, *Arapaho Child Life and Its Cultural Background* (Bureau of American Ethnology Bulletin 148, 1952), 16–17.

49. Edward T. Dozier, "Hano: A Tewa Indian Community in Arizona," in *Native North American Cultures: Four Cases*, ed. George and Louise Spindler (New York: Holt, Rinehart and Winston, 1977), 68–69.

50. Hilger, *Arapaho Child Life*, 15.

51. Quoted in George and Louise Spindler, "The Menominee," in *Native North American Cultures*, ed. Spindler and Spindler, 443.

52. Commissioner of Indian Affairs, *Annual Report* 1882, 11; "Extracts from Personal Letters by the Commissioner—I. Indian Dances," *The Indian Craftsman* 1 (June 1909), 3.

53. "The New Indian," *Nation* 79 (July 2, 1904), 47–48.

Chapter III. The New Indians

1. Robert F. Berkhofer, Jr., *The White Man's Indian* (New York: Knopf, 1978), 5.
2. Ibid., 3–4.
3. Neil L. Whitehead and R. Brian Ferguson, "Deceptive Stereotypes about 'Tribal Warfare,'" in *Talking about People: Readings in Contemporary Anthropology*, ed. William A. Haviland and Robert J. Gordon (Mountain View, Calif.: Mayfield, 1996), 191; also see Whitehead and Ferguson, eds., *War in the Tribal Zone: Expanding States and Indigenous Warfare* (Santa Fe, N.Mex.: School of American Research Press, 2000).
4. Hazel Hertzberg, *The Search for an American Indian Identity: Modern Pan-Indian Movements* (Syracuse, N.Y.: Syracuse Univ. Press, 1971), 58.
5. Arthur C. Parker, "Making a White Man out of an Indian Not a Good Plan," *American Indian Magazine* 5 (April–June 1917): 85. Also see Parker's comments in "Editor's Viewpoint," *Quarterly Journal of the Society of American Indians* 2 (July–September 1914): 168.
6. Numerous books have effectively dealt with the many aspects of the imagery of Native Americans among Euro-Americans. See Berkhofer, *White Man's Indian*; Brian W. Dippie, *The Vanishing American: White Attitudes and U.S. Indian Policy* (Middleton, Conn.: Wesleyan University Press, 1982). For interpretations of the stereotypes in American literature, see Albert Keiser, *The Indian in American Literature* (New York: Oxford Univ. Press, 1933) and Leslie Fiedler, *The Return of the Vanishing American* (New York: Stein and Day, 1968). On Thoreau, see Frederick W. Turner's introduction to *Geronimo: His Own Story*, ed. S. M. Barrett (New York: Ballantine, 1971 [orig. pub. 1906]) and Lawrence Willson, "Thoreau: Student of Anthropology," *American Anthropologist* 61 (April 1959): 100–109.
7. See especially Keith Basso, *Wisdom Sits in Places* (Albuquerque: Univ. of New Mexico Press, 1996).
8. Underhill, *Red Man's Religion*, 49–50, 116–126.
9. Ohiyesa (Charles A. Eastman, M.D.), "First Impressions of Civilization," *Harper's Monthly* 108 (March 1904), 592.
10. Eastman, *The Indian To-day* (Garden City, N.Y.: Doubleday, Page, 1915), 177.
11. For the details of Eastman's life, consult Raymond Wilson, *Ohiyesa: Charles Eastman, Santee Sioux* (Urbana: Univ. of Illinois Press, 1983) and David Reed Miller, "Charles Alexander Eastman, 'the Winner': From Deep Woods to Civilization," in *American Indian Intellectuals*, ed. Margot Liberty, 61–70 (St. Paul, Minn.: West, 1978). See also Eastman's *Indian Boyhood* (New York: Dover, 1971 [orig. pub. 1902]) and *From the Deep Woods to Civilization: Chapters in the Autobiography of an Indian* (Boston: Little, Brown, 1917).
12. Miller, "Charles Alexander Eastman," 61.
13. Ibid., 62.
14. Publisher's note in Eastman, *Indian To-day*, viii–ix. Eastman's writings were reviewed favorably very early on. See E. L. Cory, "Recent Writings by American Indians," *Book Buyer* 24 (February 1901): 20–25.
15. Hertzberg, *American Indian Identity*, 59–78; Wilcomb E. Washburn, "The Soci-

ety of American Indians," *Indian Historian* 3 (Winter 1970): 21–23.

16. Parker, "Editor's Viewpoint," 168.

17. Eastman, "The Indian and the Moral Code," *Outlook* 97 (January 7, 1911), 31.

18. Eastman, *Indian Boyhood*, 43.

19. Eastman, *Indian To-day*, 177.

20. Eastman, "The Indian's Health Problem," *American Indian Magazine* 4 (April–June 1916): 141, 143.

21. Charles M. Harvey, "The Indians of To-day and To-morrow," *American Review of Reviews* 33 (June 1906): 703.

22. See Eastman's comments on Native American art in *Report of the Executive Committee on the Proceedings of the First Annual Conference of the Society of American Indians* (Washington D.C., 1912), 88; and ch. 10 of his *Indian To-day*, 148–163.

23. Eastman, *Indian To-day*, 177–178.

24. Eastman, *Red Hunters and the Animal People* (New York: Harper and Brothers, 1904), iv–v.

25. Eastman, *Woods to Civilization*, 167, 176, 188.

26. Wilson, *Ohiyesa*, 151.

27. Ibid., 189.

28. For the details of Montezuma's life, see Peter Iverson, *Carlos Montezuma and the Changing World of American Indians* (Albuquerque: Univ. of New Mexico Press, 1982) and his "Carlos Montezuma," in *American Indian Leaders: Studies in Diversity*, ed. R. David Edmunds (Lincoln: Univ. of Nebraska Press, 1980). Also see Neil M. Clark, "Dr. Montezuma, Apache Warrior in Two Worlds," *Montana: The Magazine of Western History* 23 (Spring 1973), 56; and Spicer, *Cycles of Conquest*, 530–531.

29. Carlos Montezuma, "Justice to the Indian," *To-morrow* (August 6, 1906), 62, Carlos Montezuma Papers (microfilm), University of Arizona.

30. Montezuma to Pratt, June 29, 1904, Carlos Montezuma Papers (microfilm), University of Arizona.

31. Montezuma to Roosevelt, June 29, 1904, Carlos Montezuma papers (microfilm), University of Arizona.

32. Choteau to Montezuma, August 3, 1904, Carlos Montezuma papers (microfilm), University of Arizona.

33. Choteau to Montezuma, August 13, 1904, Carlos Montezuma papers (microfilm), University of Arizona.

34. Montezuma, "Criticism of the *Indian Arrow*," February 8, 1907, Carlos Montezuma papers (microfilm), University of Arizona.

35. "The Future of Our Indians," *New York Tribune* clipping, April 9, 1905, Carlos Montezuma papers (microfilm), University of Arizona.

36. "A Review of Commissioner Leupp's Interview," April 9, 1905, Carlos Montezuma papers (microfilm), University of Arizona.

37. Iverson, *Carlos Montezuma*, 177.

38. Iverson, "Carlos Montezuma," 216–218.

39. See especially *Wassaja* 1 (May 1916), 2; *Wassaja* 1 (October 1916), 1; and Iverson, "Carlos Montezuma," 212–214.

40. Hertzberg, *American Indian Identity*, 71–75; *Proceedings of the Society of American Indians*, 54–55, 88.

41. Laurence M. Hauptman, "Kellogg, Minnie," in *Encyclopedia of North American Indians*, ed. Hoxie, 313–314.

42. See especially Daniel K. Richter, "War and Culture: The Iroquois Experience," *William and Mary Quarterly* 40 (October 1983): 528–559.

43. Morgan, *Ancient Society*.

44. Hoxie, *Final Promise*, 22.

45. *Proceedings of the Society of American Indians*, 54–55.

46. Laura Cornelius Kellogg (Wynnogene), *Our Democracy and the American Indian: A Comprehensive Presentation of the Indian Situation as It Is Today* (Kansas City: Burton, 1920), 41–42, 61–65, 89.

47. Ibid., 82.

48. Ibid., 37.

49. Hertzberg, *American Indian Identity*, 65, 71.

50. Publisher's preface to Kellogg, *Democracy and the Indian*, 9–10.

51. Dedication in *Democracy and the Indian*.

52. Hertzberg, *American Indian Identity*, 24, 80; Margot Liberty, "Francis LaFlesche: The Osage Odyssey," in *American Indian Intellectuals*, ed. Liberty, 45–54.

53. Hertzberg, *American Indian Identity*, 59–78; Washburn, "Society of American Indians," 21–23.

54. Editorial Comment, *Quarterly Journal of the Society of American Indians* 3 (January–March 1915): 2–3; Hertzberg, *American Indian Identity*, 101–102, 167–168, 302.

55. Editorial Comment, *American Indian Magazine* 5 (April–June 1917): 84; Parker, "Making a White Man out of an Indian," 86; Hazel Hertzberg, "Arthur C. Parker," in *American Indian Intellectuals*, ed. Liberty, 132–136.

56. Editor's Viewpoint, *Quarterly Journal of the Society of American Indians* 2 (April–June 1914): 100, 111.

57. Reprinted under the title, "The Indian Must Assume Responsibility if He Demands Rights," *Quarterly Journal of the Society of American Indians* 2 (July–September 1914): 44.

58. Editorial Comment, *American Indian Magazine* 4 (April–June 1916): 108.

59. Editorial Comment, *Quarterly Journal of the Society of American Indians* 2 (July–September 1914): 167.

Chapter IV. Symbols of Native American Resiliency

1. *Proceedings of the Society of American Indians*, 86–88.

2. Norman Feder, *American Indian Art* (New York: Abrams, 1971), 32; Robert Ashton and Jozefa Stuart, *Images of American Indian Art* (New York: Walker, 1977), 48.

3. Feder, *American Indian Art*, 16–17; Clara Lee Tanner, *Southwest Indian Painting* (Tucson: Univ. of Arizona Press, 1973), 35–36.

4. Spencer and Jennings, *Native Americans*, 191.

5. *Lake Mohonk Proceedings* 1890, 19–20.

6. *Lake Mohonk Proceedings* 1894, 71–72.

7. *Lake Mohonk Proceedings* 1897, 53; *Lake Mohonk Proceedings* 1899, 79; Walter C. Roe, "The Lake Mohonk Lodge: An Experiment in Indian Work," *Outlook* 68 (May 18, 1901), 176–178.

8. *Lake Mohonk Proceedings* 1901, 29.

9. George Warton James, "Indian Blanketry," *Outing* 39 (March 1902), 684–693.

10. Edwin L. Sabin, "Indian Weaver: A Poem," *Craftsman* 13 (March 1908), 643; Sabin, "The Navajo Blanket," *Red Man* 2 (February 1910): 17.

11. George Warton James, *Indian Blankets and Their Makers* (Chicago: A. C. McClurg, 1911), 202–208.

12. For a biography of the famous potter, see Alice Marriott, *Maria: The Potter of San Ildefonso* (Norman: Univ. of Oklahoma Press, 1948).

13. "American Indian Basket-work," *International Studio* 20 (August 1903): 144–146.

14. *Lake Mohonk Proceedings* 1901, 29.

15. F. Roberts, "How to Make the Indian Beadwork," *Ladies' Home Journal* 20 (August 1903), 24.

16. Clark Wissler, *Indian Beadwork: A Help for Students of Design* (New York: American Museum Press, 1919).

17. *Lake Mohonk Proceedings* 1901, 29.

18. Ashton and Stuart, *Images of American Indian Art*, 34.

19. Richard A. Van Orman, *A Room for the Night: Hotels of the Old West* (Bloomington: Indiana Univ. Press, 1966), 118–123.

20. Frank McNitt, *The Indian Traders* (Norman: Univ. of Oklahoma Press, 1972), 210–211; Lewis S. Deitch, "The Impact of Tourism upon the Arts and Crafts of the Indians of the Southwestern United States," in *Hotels and Guests: The Anthropology of Tourism*, ed. Valene L. Smith (Philadelphia: Univ. of Pennsylvania Press, 1977), 176–177.

21. McNitt, *Indian Traders*, 154–155; Deitch, "Impact of Tourism," 177.

22. Theodore Roosevelt, "A Layman's Views of an Art Exhibition," *Outlook* 103 (March 29, 1913), 719.

23. Karen Daniels Peterson, *Plains Indian Art from Fort Marion* (Norman: Univ. of Oklahoma Press, 1971), 261.

24. Ibid., 90–91.

25. Ibid., 264–265. See also Dorothy Dunn, *American Indian Painting of the Southwest and Plains Areas* (Albuquerque: Univ. of New Mexico Press, 1968), 173–176.

26. Pratt's views were made evident in his "Indian No Problem," 851, 856.

27. "Indians to Foster their Native Art," *Indian Craftsman* 1 (April 1909): 19.

28. *Proceedings of the Society of American Indians*, 86.

29. Ibid., 87.

30. DeCora, "An Autobiography," 279–285.

31. Indian Arts and Crafts Board, *Contemporary Sioux Painting* (Rapid City, S.Dak.: IACB Pamphlet, 1970), 30; Jamake Highwater, *Song from the Earth: American Indian Painting* (Boston: New York Graphic Society, 1976), 44.

32. "How Art Misrepresents the Indian," *Literary Digest* 44 (January 27, 1912), 160–161.

33. E. L. Martin, "The Story of Two Real Indian Artists," *Red Man* 5 (February 1913). Reprinted under *home.epix.net/~landis/Nartists.html*, 1–3.

34. Barbara Landis, "Some of the Names," Carlisle Indian School Research Pages, *home.epix.net/~landis/couples.html*, 3–4.

35. Martin, "Two Real Indian Artists," 1.

36. "How Art Misrepresents the Indian," 161.

37. Indian Arts and Crafts Board, *Contemporary Indian Artists: Montana, Wyoming, Idaho* (Rapid City, S.Dak.: IACB Pamphlet, 1972), 23.

38. Ibid., 24.

39. Tanner, *Southwest Indian Painting*, 64; Driver, *Indians of North America*, 35; J. J. Brody, *Indian Painters and White Patrons* (Albuquerque: Univ. of New Mexico Press, 1971), 76–77.

40. J. Walter Fewkes, "Hopi Katchinas, Drawn by Native Artists" (Bureau of American Ethnology, Twenty-first Annual Report, 1903): 3–126.

41. Driver, *Indians of North America*, 185.

42. Tanner, *Southwest Indian Painting*, 66; Highwater, *Song from the Earth*, 41–42.

43. Dunn, *American Indian Painting*, 199–217; Highwater, *Song from the Earth*, 44–45. See also the following three essays from *Native American Art in the Twentieth Century*, ed. W. Jackson Rushing III (New York: Routledge, 1999): Joseph Traugott, "Fewkes and Nampeyo: Clarifying a Myth-Understanding," 7–20; David W. Penney and Lisa Roberts, "America's Pueblo Artists: Encounters on the Borderlands," 21–38; and Bruce Bernstein, "Contexts for the Growth and Development of the Indian Art World in the 1960s and 1970s," 57–71.

44. Walter Pach, "The Art of the American Indian," *Dial* 68 (January 1920), 62–63.

45. Pach, "Notes on the Indian Water-Colours," *Dial* 68 (March 1920), 343.

46. *New York Times*, September 6, 1925.

47. Tanner, *Southwest Indian Painting*, 67; Highwater, *Song from the Earth*, 44.

48. Brody, *Indian Painters*, 120; Dunn, *American Indian Painting*, 218–223; Highwater, *Song from the Earth*, 61.

49. Peterson, *Plains Indian Art*; Brody, *Indian Painters*, 124–126.

50. Brody, *Indian Painters*, 126.

51. Hoxie, *Final Promise*, 25–28; "Alice Cunningham Fletcher," *American Anthropologist* 25 (April–June 1923): 254.

52. Liberty, "Francis LaFlesche," in *American Indian Intellectuals*, ed. Liberty, 46–47; *Lake Mohonk Proceedings* 1903, 79.

53. Fletcher's comment on "Indian Work" is quoted from the *Washington Times*, July 14, 1911. The clipping is in the Fletcher papers (miscellaneous), National Anthropological Archives, Smithsonian Institution. For the comment on her work in Native American music, see "Alice Cunningham Fletcher," 255. Concerning her efforts to collect Indian goods, record language, etc., see B. S. Baker, "Preserving the Indian," *Current Literature* 33 (December 1902): 735–737.

54. "The Music of the American Indian," *Literary Digest* 27 (September 5, 1903), 283.

55. "Review of Frederick R. Burton's *American Primitive Music*," *Nation* 90 (February 24, 1910), 196.

56. "Indian and Negro in Music," *Literary Digest* 44 (June 29, 1912), 1347.

57. Ibid.; Ralph E. and Natasha A. Friar, *The Only Good Indian: The Hollywood Gospel* (New York: Drama Book Specialists, 1972), 17–18.

58. *The New Grove Dictionary of Music and Musicians*, ed. Stanley Sadie (London: Macmillan, 1980), s.v. "Skilton, Charles Sanford" (17:365–366).

59. Friar and Friar, *Only Good Indian*, 17.

60. "Recording the Indian's Music," *Literary Digest* 46 (April 26, 1913), 951.

61. Marsden Hartley, "Tribal Esthetics," *Dial* 65 (November 16, 1918), 399–400.

62. Howard Fremont Stratton, "The Place of the Indian in Art," *Red Man* 2 (February 1910), 5.

63. W. G. Constable, "Indigenous American Art," *Living Age* 306 (July 24, 1920), 247.

Chapter V. Preserving the "Indian"

1. For the best synthesis of white attitudes toward Native Americans, see Berkhofer, *White Man's Indian*.

2. *Lake Mohonk Proceedings* 1896, 87.

3. Honore Willsie, "We Die! We Die! There is No Hope," *Everybody's Magazine* 26 (March 1912), 337–344.

4. Harvey, "Indians of To-day and To-morrow," 697.

5. Even though he was the father of cultural determinism, Boas evidently believed that some aspects of human behavior were genetically transmitted. In short, he still had the notion that race might be a factor in cultural development. Many of his students rejected the idea of "blood," race, and the whole eugenics movement of the period. See Boas's testimony in the hearing before the Special Committee on Administrative Affairs of the Bureau of American Ethnology, June 29–July 28, 1903 (typescript), National Anthropological Archives, Smithsonian Institution. Also see Franz Boas, "Making the Red Faces White," *World Outlook* 4 (January 1918), 6.

6. Albert Ernest Jenks, *Indian-White Amalgamation: An Anthropometric Study* (Minneapolis: Univ. of Minnesota Studies in the Social Sciences, 1916).

7. For an excellent examination of "scientific racism," see Reginald Horsman, "Scientific Racism and the American Indian in the Mid-Nineteenth Century," *American Quarterly* 27 (May 1975): 152–168. For Huntington's commentary, see his *Red Man's Continent: A Chronicle of Aboriginal America* (Temecula, Calif.: Best Books, 1921). Also see Hoxie, *Final Promise*, 126–129, for a discussion of the idea of "backwardness" as associated with Native Americans.

8. William Willard, "Zitkala Sa: A Woman Who Would Be Heard," *Wicazo Sa Review* 1 (Spring 1985): 11–16; and Hafen, "Zitkala Sa," 708–710.

9. Zitkala-Sa, "Why I Am a Pagan," *Atlantic Monthly* 90 (1902), 803.

10. See especially Samuel P. Hays, *Conservation and the Gospel of Efficiency, 1890–1920* (Cambridge: Harvard Univ. Press, 1959).

11. For the various aspects of conservationism in the early twentieth century, see

Arthur A. Ekirch, Jr., *Man and Nature in America* (New York: Columbia Univ. Press, 1963), 81–99.

12. Roderick Nash, *Wilderness and the American Mind* (New Haven, Conn.: Yale Univ. Press, 1967), 141–160.

13. Columbus is quoted in Wilcomb E. Washburn, ed., *The Indian and the White Man* (Garden City, N.Y.: Anchor Books, 1964), 5.

14. Samuel Cole Williams, ed., *Adair's History of the American Indians* (New York: Promontory Press, 1930), 5.

15. See George F. Spaulding's introduction to *On the Western Tour with Washington Irving* (Norman: Univ. of Oklahoma Press, 1968), 19.

16. Thomas C. Moffett, *The Indian on the New Trail* (New York: Methodist Book Concern, 1914), 9.

17. Friar and Friar, *Only Good Indian*, 80–81.

18. George Warton James, *What the White Race May Learn from the Indian* (Chicago: Forbes, 1908). The 1917 edition was published by Radiant Life Press of Pasadena, California.

19. Ibid., 28.

20. Ibid., 39.

21. Ibid., 11–12.

22. William Inglis, "Buffalo Bill's Last Trail," *Harper's Weekly* 54 (May 14, 1910), 382.

23. Friar and Friar, *Only Good Indian*, 92–92, 95.

24. Edward Wagenknecht, *The Movies in the Age of Innocence* (Norman: Univ. of Oklahoma Press, 1962), 87.

25. *Vinita Weekly Chieftain*, January 12, 1905.

26. Hartley, "Tribal Esthetics," 400.

27. James, *Learn from the Indian*, 241.

28. Warren K. Moorhead, "Indian Arts and Industries," *Indian Craftsman* 2 (January 1910): 9. For a solid short history of the effort to preserve Native American art, see the first chapter, entitled "Harbingers," in Robert Fay Schrader, *The Indian Arts and Crafts Board: An Aspect of the New Deal Indian Policy* (Albuquerque: Univ. of New Mexico Press, 1983), 3–21.

29. Roosevelt's comment is in Natalie Curtis, "Perpetuating of Indian Art," *Outlook* 105 (November 22, 1913), 624.

30. Marius DeZayas, Commentary, *Camera Work* 41 (January 1913), 17.

31. "A Museum of the American Indian," *Outlook* 114 (October 11, 1916), 301.

32. A. J. Fynn, "The Preservation of Aboriginal Arts," National Education Association, *Journal of Proceedings and Addresses, 1909*, 947, 950.

33. Ernest L. Blumenschein, "The Taos Society of Artists," *American Magazine of Art* 8 (September 1917), 445–451. Also see Arrell M. Gibson, *The Santa Fe and Taos Colonies: Age of the Muses, 1900–1942* (Norman: Univ. of Oklahoma Press, 1983) and W. Jackson Rushing III, *Native American Art and the New York Avant-Garde: A History of Cultural Primitivism* (Austin: Univ. of Texas Press, 1995).

34. Blumenschein, "Taos Society," 451; H. Chadwick Hunter, "The American Indi-

an in Painting," *Art and Archaeology* 8 (March–April, 1919): 96.

35. For more about these painters, see Doris Ostrander Dawdy, *Artists of the American West* (Chicago: Sage Books, 1974), 21–22, 27, 56–57, 109. On Hartley, see "Marsden Hartley Exhibition," *Camera Work* 38 (April 1912), 36. See also *The Britannica Encyclopedia of American Art* (New York: Encyclopedia Britannica, n.d.): 271.

36. Edward S. Curtis, "Vanishing Indian Types: The Tribes of the Northwest Plains," *Scribner's Magazine* 39 (June 1906), 657–671; "Photos by Curtis," *World's Work* 12 (August 1906), 7913–7914; "Karl Moon's Portraits of Southwest Indians," *Century Magazine* 75 (October 1907), 923–927; Karl Moon, "In Search of the Wild Indian," *Outing* 69 (February 1917), 533–545; Joseph K. Dixon, *The Vanishing Race* (Glorietta, N. Mex.: Rio Grande Press, 1973 [orig. pub. 1913]). The photography mania was certainly dehumanizing: witness Moon's search for the "Wild Indian," and E. S. Meany, "Hunting Indians with a Camera," *World's Work* 15 (March 1908), 10004–10011.

37. Barrett, *Geronimo*; "War Chiefs in Peace," *Nation* 81 (September 28, 1905), 255–256. Several of these "mug shot" photographs from the early twentieth century are in the author's possession.

38. See Theodora Kroeber, *Ishi in Two Worlds: A Biography of the Last Wild Indian in America* (Berkeley and Los Angeles: Univ. of California Press, 1961).

39. Fynn, "Preservation of Aboriginal Arts," 947; *Congressional Record* 38, pt. 2, 58th Cong., 2nd sess., 1651, 1872, 2000; ibid., pt. 3, 2712.

40. Natalie Curtis to Franz Boas, August 15, 1903, Franz Boas Papers (microfilm), National Anthropological Archives, Smithsonian Institution.

41. Boas to Alice C. Fletcher, February 15, 20, and 26, 1904; Boas to Nicholas Butler, February 19 and March 7, 1904, Boas Papers (microfilm), National Anthropological Archives, Smithsonian Institution.

42. Dick Schaap, *An Illustrated History of the Olympics* (New York: Ballantine, 1976), 76.

43. Curtis, "Perpetuating Indian Art," 624.

44. "Music of the American Indian," 283.

Chapter VI. Progressive Ambiguity

1. "Indians and Industrial Development," *Outlook* 67 (January 12, 1901), 101.
2. Ibid., 101–102.
3. *Lake Mohonk Proceedings* 1899, 79.
4. Roe, "Lake Mohonk Lodge," 176.
5. Ibid., 178.
6. Ibid., 177.
7. Hamlin Garland, "The Red Man's Present Needs," *North American Review* 174 (April 1902), 479–482.
8. Ibid., 485.
9. Ibid., 484.
10. "Ethnologists and Missionaries," *Independent* 54 (November 6, 1902), 2663–2665.
11. Ibid., 2664–2665.

12. Hearings before the Special Committee on Administrative Affairs of the Bureau of American Ethnology, June 29–July 28, 1903 (typescript), National Anthropological Archives, Smithsonian Institution, 975.

13. Arthur Inkersley, "Cataract Canyon, the Havasupais," *Overland* 4 (November 1903), 382–390.

14. Dillon Wallace, "Saddle and Camp in the Rockies: Across the Navajo Desert," *Outing* 57 (January 1911), 407; Edward S. Curtis, "The Vanishing Red Man: Inhumanity of the White Man toward the Indian," *Hampton Magazine* 28 (May 1912), 245–253, 308.

15. James, *Indian Blankets*, vi–vii.

16. Natalie Curtis Burlin, *The Indian's Book* (New York: Harper and Brothers, 1907): xxxviii.

17. *Lake Mohonk Proceedings* 1901, vi.

18. *Lake Mohonk Proceedings* 1903, 73–74.

19. Ibid., 79.

20. Ibid., 24.

21. Ibid., 51.

22. Pratt addressed these accusations in *Lake Mohonk Proceedings* 1903, 51–52. See also Elaine Goodale Eastman's laudatory article on the outing system, "New Method of Indian Education," 222.

23. Mooney to Holmes, August 24, 1903; Dorsey to Stouch, September 14, 1903; W. A. Jones, Commissioner of Indian Affairs, to Bureau of American Ethnology, September 23, 1903; all in Mooney Files, National Anthropological Archives, Smithsonian Institution. See also *New York Times*, August 15, 1903.

24. Affidavit of the Darlington, Watonga, and Kingfisher Cheyenne Indians, September 1, 1903; affidavit of the Colony Cheyenne Indians and Cheyenne at Arapaho District, Oklahoma Territory, September 1, 1903; Mooney–Sun Dance File, National Anthropological Archives, Smithsonian Institution. See also *New York Times*, August 26, 1903.

25. *Lake Mohonk Proceedings* 1903, 73.

26. Ibid., 60, 79, 105.

27. Ibid., 79, 106.

28. Ibid., 51, 73–74.

29. Ibid., 79, 105.

30. Correspondence, *Outlook* 75 (October 31, 1903), 519–520.

31. Commissioner of Indian Affairs, *Annual Report* 1919, 8–9.

32. Pach, "Art of the American Indian," 60.

33. Board of Commissioners, *Annual Report* 1905, 17.

34. George Bird Grinnell, *The Enforcement of the Liquor Laws a Necessary Protection to the Indians* (Philadelphia: Indian Rights Association, 1893), 10.

35. *Indian's Friend*, July 1918.

36. The idea that Native Americans were physically disappearing was occasionally rebutted, but never completely erased from popular belief. See J. Worden Pope, "The North American Indian: The Disappearance of the Race a Popular Fallacy," *Arena* 16

(November 1896), 945–959; Commissioner of Indian Affairs, *Annual Report* 1917, 20; Glenn Frank, "A Vanishing Race Comes Back," *Century Magazine* 99 (April 1920), 800. For more on the idea, see Dippie, *Vanishing American.*

37. Fayette Avery McKenzie, "The Indian and His Problem," *Dial* 49 (October 1, 1910), 230.

Chapter VII. The "Great Confusion" in Indian Affairs

1. Frances Campbell Sparhawk, "The Indian's Yoke," *North American Review* 182 (January 1906), 61.

2. Board of Commissioners, *Annual Report* 1900, 5.

3. "A Plan to Free the Indian," *Literary Digest* 47 (August 9, 1913), 196. For the numbers of Indian Office employees, see Commissioner of Indian Affairs, *Annual Report* 1920, 63. Table 1 gives the number of office employees for each year beginning in 1899. To demonstrate the bureau's efficiency, all of the *Annual Reports* of the period contained figures for the number of employees and their work output. The interesting point about the profusion of tables in the reports is that they differed greatly from the prosy and often abstract philosophical reports of the previous century. Clearly there was a change in administrative styles.

4. McKenzie, "The Indian and His Problem," 228–230.

5. Kappler, *Laws and Treaties*, 2:758; Deloria and Demallie, *American Indian Diplomacy*, 1:250, 1:355–358; Getches, Wilkinson, and Williams, *Federal Indian Law*, 182–185; Prucha, *American Indian Treaties*, 355–358; Hoxie, *Final Promise*, 154–156.

6. 187 U.S. 553–556.

7. Indian Rights Association, *Annual Report* 1903, 20–24.

8. George Kennan, "Have Reservation Indians Any Vested Rights?" *Outlook* 70 (March 29, 1902), 759–765.

9. Kennan, "Indian Lands and Fair Play," *Outlook* 76 (February 27, 1904), 498.

10. "A Trust Not Trustworthy," *Independent* 56 (February 25, 1904), 450–451.

11. *New York Times*, August 16, 1903.

12. Ibid., August 18, 20, 1903.

13. "The Interior Department and the Indians," *Outlook* 76 (March 19, 1904), 679; *New York Times*, August 21, 25, 1903; "Land Scandal in Indian Territory," *Independent* 55 (August 20, 1903), 1951.

14. "Government Scandals as an Issue," *Literary Digest* 27 (September 12, 1903), 309–310.

15. "Who Will Guard the Guards?" *Outlook* 74 (August 29, 1903), 1020–1021.

16. *Lake Mohonk Proceedings* 1903, 43–50. Abbott was convinced that the War Department, as a bureaucracy that was in theory relatively free of the spoils system, could once again handle Indian affairs. He became quite insistent on the point. See "The Indian Question," *Outlook* 75 (September 19, 1903), 149–151, and "Our 'Subject' Races," *Outlook* 75 (October 31, 1903), 482–485. For a more complete picture of Brosius's views, see his *Need of Protecting Indian Allotments* (Philadelphia: Indian Rights Association, 1904).

17. Quoted in Hoxie, *Final Promise*, 163.

18. Ibid.

19. Francis E. Leupp, *The Indian and His Problem* (New York: Charles Scribner's Sons, 1910), 53, 324–325; Leupp, *In Red Man's Land* (New York: Fleming H. Revell, 1914), 93; Commissioner of Indian Affairs, *Annual Report* 1905, 12.

20. McKenzie, "The Indian and His Problem," 229.

21. U.S. Senate, *Senate Reports*, serial 5062, 59th Cong., 2nd sess., 186; Debo, *Still the Waters Run*, 141, 202.

22. Leupp, "Back to Nature for the Indian," *Charities and the Commons* 20 (June 6, 1908): 338–340; Leupp, "Four Strenuous Years," *Outlook* 92 (June 5, 1909), 328–331.

23. Hoxie, *Final Promise*, 114–187.

24. Janet A. McDonnell, *The Dispossession of the American Indian, 1887–1934* (Bloomington: Indiana Univ. Press, 1991), 1–2, 6–7.

25. Lawrence C. Kelly, *The Assault on Assimilation: John Collier and the Origins of Indian Policy Reform* (Albuquerque: Univ. of New Mexico Press, 1983), 149.

26. *Congressional Record* 40, 59th Cong., 1st sess., 1110, 2812, 3598, 3602, 4153, 5605–5606, 5805, 5980; *U.S. Stats.* 34, 183.

27. Board of Commissioners, *Annual Report* 1905, 18. See also Grinnell, *Enforcement of Liquor Laws.*

28. 197 U.S. Reports 488.

29. U.S. Senate, *Senate Report* 1998, serial 4904, v. 1, 59th Cong., 1st sess., 2.

30. Indian Rights Association, *Annual Report* 1906, 45–48.

31. Board of Commissioners, *Annual Report* 1906, 8, 18.

32. "Congressional Guardianship," *Nation* 82 (June 21, 1906), 503–504.

33. For a full account of the parochial-school controversies, see Francis Paul Prucha, *The Churches and the Indian Schools, 1888–1912* (Lincoln: Univ. of Nebraska Press, 1980).

34. M. P. Casey, "Indian Contract Schools," *Catholic World* 71 (August 1900), 629, 637.

35. Richard R. Elliot, "Government Secularization of the Education of Catholic Indian Youth," *American Catholic Quarterly* 25 (January 1900): 163.

36. "The Week: A Mischievous Appropriation," *Outlook* 79 (January 21, 1905), 150.

37. "Unfair Indian Fighting," *Outlook* 79 (February 4, 1905), 264–265.

38. "Trust Funds for Indian Catholic Schools," *Nation* 80 (February 9, 1905), 106.

39. "The State, the Church and the Indian," *Outlook* 79 (February 11, 1905), 371.

40. "The President and the Indian: A Step Backward," *Outlook* 79 (February 18, 1905), 417–419. Interestingly, this article was preceded by an editorial entitled "The President and the Negro: A Step in Advance." See also "Indian Funds for Sectarian Schools," *Independent* 63 (December 19, 1907), 1507–1508.

41. Matthew K. Sniffen, *Indian Trust Funds for Sectarian Schools* (Philadelphia: Indian Rights Association, 1905).

42. 210 U.S. Reports 50.

43. "Religious Garb in Indian Schools," *Literary Digest* 44 (February 24, 1912), 379.

44. Ibid., 380; "Critics of Religious Garb in Indian Schools," *Literary Digest* 44

(February 24, 1912), 428; "The Nun's Garb Question," *Literary Digest* 45 (October 12, 1912): 626.

45. "The Failure of the Educated American Indian," *American Review of Reviews* 33 (May 1906): 629–630.

46. Cato Sells, "The Indian Bureau and Its Schools," *Saturday Evening Post* 193 (April 9, 1921), 42.

47. Matthew K. Sniffen, *A Man and His Opportunity* (Philadelphia: Indian Rights Association, 1914). "Failure of the Educated Indian," 630.

48. Commissioner of Indian Affairs, *Annual Report* 1909, 4.

49. Commissioner of Indian Affairs, *Annual Report* 1924, 15.

50. Commissioner of Indian Affairs, *Annual Report* 1921, 14–15.

51. Commissioner of Indian Affairs, *Annual Report* 1909, 2; Board of Commissioners, *Annual Report* 1908, 17; Delorme W. Robinson, "Tuberculosis among the Sioux," *American Review of Reviews* 33 (March 1906): 341; Ales Hrdlicka, "Tuberculosis in the Indian," *Charities and the Commons* 21 (November 7, 1908): 245–247; John M. Oskison, "Making an Individual of the Indian," *Everybody's Magazine* 16 (June 1907), 723; F. Shoemaker, "Tuberculosis: The Scourge of the Red Man," *Indian Craftsman* 1 (June 1909): 23–31; Eastman, "Indian's Health Problem," 141–145; U.S. Department of the Interior, *Tuberculosis among Indians* (Washington D.C.: Government Printing Office, 1917).

52. Commissioner of Indian Affairs, *Annual Report* 1909, 2.

53. Ibid., 16–17.

54. Ibid., 20.

55. Ibid., 10; Commissioner of Indian Affairs, *Annual Report* 1917, 25; Commissioner of Indian Affairs, *Annual Report* 1920, 46–47.

56. See especially Carl E. Grammer, *Responsibility for Indian Management* (Philadelphia: Indian Rights Association, 1914); and F. A. Cleveland, "An Analysis of the Indian Bureau," *American Indian Magazine* 4 (April–June 1916): 154–159.

57. Arthur C. Parker, Editor's Views, *American Indian Magazine* 5 (October–December 1917): 213–214.

58. *Indian's Friend*, November 1917, January 1918, March 1918, and January 1919.

59. Commissioner of Indian Affairs, *Annual Report* 1920, 8.

60. *Congressional Record* 58, pts. 1, 3, and 68, 66th Cong., 1st sess., 720, 2977, 5463, 6017, 7505; *Congressional Record* 65, pts. 2, 3, 5, 7, and 9, 68th Cong., 1st sess., 1665, 2977, 4446, 4477, 6753, 8621–8622, 9303–9304; 41 *U.S. Stats.*, 350; 43 *U.S. Stats.*, 253.

Chapter VIII. Epilogue

1. *Congressional Record* 61, pt. 4, 67th Cong., 1st sess., 2274.

2. 231 U.S. Reports 28–49. See also Felix S. Cohen, *Handbook of Federal Indian Law* (Albuquerque: Univ. of New Mexico Press, 1972), 383–390.

3. John Collier, "The Red Atlantis," *Survey* 48 (October 1922), 15–20, 63, 66; Collier, "Plundering the Pueblo Indians," *Sunset* 50 (January 1923), 21–25, 56; Collier, "The Pueblos' Last Stand," *Sunset* 50 (February 1923), 19–22, 65–66; Collier, "Our Indian Pol-

icy," *Sunset* 50 (March 1923), 13–15, 89–93; Collier, "No Trespassing," *Sunset* 50 (May 1923), 14–15, 58–60; Collier, "The Pueblos' Land Problem," *Sunset* 51 (November 1923), 15, 101. See also Stella M. Atwood, "The Case for the Indian," *Survey* 49 (October 1922), 7–11, 57.

4. Witter Bynner, "'From Him That Hath Not,'" *Outlook* 133 (January 17, 1923), 125–127. See also *New York Times*, November 26 and December 24, 1922.

5. Kenneth R. Philp, *John Collier's Crusade for Indian Reform, 1920–1954* (Tucson: Univ. of Arizona Press, 1977), 26–54; and Kelly, *Assault on Assimilation*.

6. *Congressional Record* 64, pt. 2, 67th Cong., 4th sess., 1866.

7. Ibid., pts. 3, 5, and 6, 2972–2997, 3027, 4831, 5083.

8. Board of Commissioners, *Annual Report* 1918, 79.

9. Ibid., 80. The Board of Commissioners for Indian Affairs was very influential in the formulation of Indian policy in the early twentieth century, despite the decline of the vanishing policy. For example, the board began to see the strengths of community inherent in tribal societies. But as Henry E. Fritz has pointed out, the board was the "last hurrah" of the old Christian Indian reform movement. See Henry E. Fritz, "The Last Hurrah of Christian Humanitarian Indian Reform: The Board of Indian Commissioners, 1909–1918," *Western Historical Quarterly* 16 (1985): 147–162.

10. Indian Rights Association, *Annual Report* 1920, 25–27.

11. *Indian's Friend*, July 1921.

12. John Sloan, "The Indian Dance from an Artist's Point of View," *Arts and Decoration* 20 (January 1924): 17.

13. *New York Times*, December 20, 1923, and October 26, 1924.

14. *New York Times*, December 16, 1923.

15. Philp, *Collier's Crusade*, 55–70.

16. Lewis Meriam et. al., *The Problem of Indian Administration*, Institute for Government Research, Studies in Administration (Baltimore: Johns Hopkins Univ. Press, 1928).

17. Commissioner of Indian Affairs, *Annual Report* 1923, 8; *Annual Report* 1924, 8; *Annual Report* 1925, 10; *Annual Report* 1926, 9; *Annual Report* 1929, 9; *Annual Report* 1930, 15; *Annual Report* 1931, 36; *Annual Report* 1932, 28.

18. *Lake Mohonk Proceedings* 1929, 13–14.

19. Ibid., 25, 39, 53, 91, 97, 127–128, 133, 156. For Meriam's address, see 128–132.

20. Ibid., 17.

21. Ibid., 15.

22. Ibid., 12.

23. 48 *U.S. Stats.* 984.

24. Philp, *Collier's Crusade*, 5–25. See also Stephen J. Kunitz, "The Social Philosophy of John Collier," *Ethnohistory* 18 (Summer 1971): 213–229, and Randolph C. Downes, "A Crusade for Indian Reform," *Mississippi Valley Historical Review* 32 (December 1945): 331–354.

25. John Collier, *The Indians of the Americas* (New York: Norton, 1947), 20.

26. Collier, "Our Indian Policy," 13; Collier, "Red Atlantis," 15.

27. Philp, *Collier's Crusade*, 1–4, 24.

28. Christopher Lasch, *The New Radicalism in America, 1889–1963* (New York: Vintage, 1965), 104–140.

29. Blumenschein, "Taos Society," 448.

30. See Berkhofer, *White Man's Indian*, 62–69.

31. John Collier, *From Every Zenith* (Denver: Sage Books, 1963), 216–217.

32. Commissioner of Indian Affairs, *Annual Report* 1934, 78.

33. 48 *U.S. Stats.*, 984–988.

34. 49 *U.S. Stats.*, 1967–1968.

35. Ibid., 891–893. Also see Schrader, *Indian Arts and Crafts Board*, 77–123.

36. Niccolo Machiavelli, *The Prince*, trans. and ed. T. G. Bergin (New York: Appleton-Century-Crofts, 1947), 14.

BIBLIOGRAPHY

Manuscript and Special Collections

Indian Archives, Oklahoma Historical Society, Oklahoma City, Oklahoma
  Cherokee–Federal Relations File
  Foreman Collection
  Miscellaneous Documents
National Anthropological Archives, Smithsonian Institution, Washington, D.C.
  Franz Boas Papers (microfilm)
  Alice C. Fletcher Files
  Hearings before the Special Committee on Administrative Affairs of the Bureau of American Ethnology, 1903 (typescript)
  Indian Rights Association Papers (microfilm)
  James Mooney Files (James Mooney–Cheyenne Sun Dance File)
Rare Book Collection, University of Wisconsin, Madison
University of Arizona Special Collections, Tucson
  Carlos Montezuma Papers (microfilm)
Western History Collections, Bizzell Memorial Library, University of Oklahoma, Norman
  Cherokee Nation Papers
  Indian-Pioneer Papers
  Frank Phillips Collection

NEWSPAPERS

Cherokee Advocate, 1880–1895
New York Times, 1898–1930
Vinita Weekly Chieftain, 1898–1905
Wassaja, 1916–1922

U.S. GOVERNMENT DOCUMENTS

Kappler, Charles J., ed. *Indian Affairs: Laws and Treaties*. Vol. 2. Washington, D.C.: Government Printing Office, 1904.

U.S. Congress. *Biographical Directory of the American Congress, 1774–1971*. Washington, D.C.: Government Printing Office, 1971.

U.S. Congress. *Congressional Record*. 46th Cong., 3rd sess.

———. *Congressional Record*. 58th Cong., 2nd sess.

———. *Congressional Record*. 59th Cong., 1st sess.

———. *Congressional Record*. 66th Cong., 1st sess.

———. *Congressional Record*. 67th Cong., 1st sess.

———. *Congressional Record*. 67th Cong., 4th sess.

———. *Congressional Record*. 68th Cong., 1st sess.

U.S. Department of the Interior. *Annual Report of the Board of Commissioners for Indian Affairs*, 1883–1930.

———. *Annual Report of the Commissioner of Indian Affairs*, 1880–1925.

———. *Annual Report of the Secretary of the Interior*, 1930–1934.

———. *Tuberculosis among Indians*. Washington, D.C.: Acme Printing, 1917.

U.S. Department of War. *Annual Report of the Secretary of War*, 1891.

U.S. House of Representatives. *House Journal*. 45th Cong., 3rd sess.

———. *House Journal*. 46th Cong., 2nd sess.

———. *House Journal*. 49th Cong., 2nd sess.

———. *House Report 1576*. 46th Cong., 2nd sess.

———. *House Report 2247*. 48th Cong., 2nd sess.

———. *House Report 1835*. 49th Cong., 1st sess.

U.S. Senate. *Senate Journal*. 45th Cong., 3rd sess.

———. *Senate Journal*. 46th Cong., 3rd sess.

———. *Senate Journal*. 48th Cong., 1st sess.

———. Senate Miscellaneous Documents 24. *Report of the Commission to the Five Civilized Tribes*. 53rd Cong., 3rd sess. Western History

Collections, University of Oklahoma.

———. *Senate Report* 159. 39th Cong., 2nd sess.

———. *Senate Report* 1998. 59th Cong., 1st sess.

———. *Senate Report* 5013. 59th Cong., 2nd sess.

United States Statutes at Large. Vols. 24, 27, 29, 30, 34, 41, 43, 48.

U.S. Supreme Court. *U.S. Supreme Court Reports.* Vols. 187, 197, 210, 231.

ORGANIZATION PUBLICATIONS, 1884–1929

American Indian Magazine, 1915–1917.

Armstrong, S. C. *Report of a Trip Made in Behalf of the Indian Rights Association to Some Indian Reservations of the Southwest.* Philadelphia: Indian Rights Association, 1884.

Brosius, Samuel M. *The Need of Protecting Indian Allotments.* Philadelphia: Indian Rights Association, 1904.

Grammer, Carl E. *Responsibility for Indian Management.* Philadelphia: Indian Rights Association, 1914.

Grinnell, George Bird. *The Enforcement of Liquor Laws: A Necessary Protection to the Indians.* Philadelphia: Indian Rights Association, 1893.

Indian Rights Association. *Annual Report*, 1900–1924.

Indian's Friend, 1910–1922.

Meserve, Charles F. *The Dawes Commission and the Five Civilized Tribes of Indian Territory.* Philadelphia: Indian Rights Association, 1896.

Proceedings of the Lake Mohonk Conference of the Friends of the Indian, 1888–1916, 1929.

Quarterly Journal of the Society of American Indians, 1913–1915.

Report of the Executive Committee on the Proceedings of the First Annual Conference of the Society of American Indians. Washington, D.C.: 1912.

Sniffen, Matthew K. *Indian Trust Funds for Sectarian Schools.* Philadelphia: Indian Rights Association, 1905.

———. *A Man and His Opportunity.* Philadelphia: Indian Rights Association, 1914.

———. *The Meaning of the Ute "War."* Philadelphia: Indian Rights Association, 1915.

PERIOD LITERATURE

"Alice Cunningham Fletcher." *American Anthropologist* 25, no. 2 (April–June 1923): 254–258.

"American Indian Basket-Work." *International Studio* 20 (August 1903): 144–146.

Atwood, Stella. "The Case for the Indian." *Survey* 49 (October 1922): 7–11, 57.

Baker, B. S. "Preserving the Indian." *Current Literature* 33 (December 1902): 736–737.

Barrett, S. M., ed. *Geronimo: His Own Story*. New York: Ballantine, 1971 (orig. pub. 1906).

Blumenschein, Ernest L. "The Taos Society of Artists." *American Magazine of Art* 8 (September 1917): 445–451.

Boas, Franz. "Making the Red Faces White." *World Outlook* 4 (January 1918): 6.

Brown, DeKoven. "Indian Workers for Temperance: The New Faith That Came from the Vision of Old John Slocum, Drunkard." *Collier's* 45, no. 24 (September 3, 1910): 23–24.

Burlin, Natalie Curtis. *The Indian's Book*. New York: Harper and Brothers, 1907.

Burton, Frederick R. *American Primitive Music*. New York: Moffat, Yard, 1909.

Bynner, Witter. "'From Him That Hath Not.'" *Outlook* 133 (January 17, 1923): 125–127.

Casey, M. P. "Indian Contract Schools." *Catholic World* 71 (August 1900): 629–637.

Cleveland, F. A. "An Analysis of the Indian Bureau." *American Indian Magazine* 4 (April–June 1916): 154–159.

Collier, John. *From Every Zenith*. Denver: Sage Books, 1963.

———. *The Indians of the Americas*. New York: Norton, 1947.

———. "No Trespassing." *Sunset* 50 (May 1923): 14–15, 58–60.

———. "Our Indian Policy." *Sunset* 50 (March 1923): 13–15, 89–93.

———. "Plundering the Pueblo Indians." *Sunset* 50 (January 1923): 21–25, 56.

———. "The Pueblos' Land Problem." *Sunset* 51 (November 1923): 15, 101.

———. "The Pueblos' Last Stand." *Sunset* 50 (February 1923): 19–22, 65–66.

———. "The Red Atlantis." *Survey* 48 (October 1922): 15–20, 63, 66.

"Congressional Guardianship." *Nation* 82 (June 21, 1906): 503–504.

Constable, W. G. "Indigenous American Art." *Living Age* 306 (July 24, 1920): 245–247.

Cory, E. L. "Recent Writings by American Indians." *Book Buyer* 24 (February 1901): 20–25.

Crane, L. "A Man Ruined by an Idea." *Harper's Weekly* 53 (June 26, 1909): 15–16.

Crissey, F. "Renaming the Indians." *World To-day* 10 (January 1906): 84–90.

"Critics of Religious Garb in Indian Schools." *Literary Digest* 44 (March 2, 1912): 428.

Curtis, Edward S. "Vanishing Indian Types: The Tribes of the Northwest Plains." *Scribner's Magazine* 39 (June 1906): 657–671.

———. "The Vanishing Red Man: Inhumanity of the White Man toward the Indian." *Hampton Magazine* 28 (May 1912): 245–253, 308.

Curtis, Natalie. "Perpetuating of Indian Art." *Outlook* 105 (November 22, 1913): 623–631.

DeCora, Angel. "Angel DeCora: An Autobiography." *Red Man* (March 1911): 279–285.

DeZayas, Marius. Commentary. *Camera Work* 41 (January 1913): 16–17.

Dixon, Joseph K. *The Vanishing Race*. Glorietta, N.Mex.: Rio Grande Press, 1973 (orig. pub. 1913).

Eastman, Charles A. (Ohiyesa). "First Impressions of Civilization." *Harper's Monthly* 108 (March 1904): 587–592.

———. *From the Deep Woods to Civilization: Chapters in the Autobiography of an Indian*. Boston: Little, Brown, 1917.

———. "The Indian and the Moral Code." *Outlook* 97 (January 7, 1911): 30–34.

———. *Indian Boyhood*. New York: Dover, 1971 (orig. pub. 1902).

———. "Indian Handicrafts." *Craftsman* 8 (August 1905): 659–662.

———. *Indian Heroes and Great Chieftains*. Boston: Little, Brown, 1918.

———. *Indian Scouts Talks*. Boston: Little, Brown, 1914.

———. *The Indian To-day*. Garden City, N.Y.: Doubleday, Page, 1915.

————. "The Indian's Health Problem." *American Indian Magazine* 4 (April–June 1916): 139–145.

————. *Red Hunters and the Animal People*. New York: Harper and Brothers, 1904.

————. *The Soul of the Indian*. Boston: Houghton Mifflin, 1911.

Eastman, Elaine Goodale. "The Education of Indians." *Arena* 24 (October 1900): 412–414.

————. "A New Method of Indian Education." *Outlook* 64 (January 27, 1900): 222–224.

————. *Pratt: The Red Man's Moses*. Norman: Univ. of Oklahoma Press, 1935.

Elliott, Richard R. "Government Secularization of the Education of Catholic Indian Youth." *American Catholic Quarterly* 25 (January 1900): 148–168.

"Ethnologists and Missionaries." *Independent* 54 (November 6, 1902): 2663–2665.

"Exeunt the Five Civilized Tribes." *Independent* 54 (October 9, 1902): 2431–2432.

"Extracts from Personal Letters by the Commissioner—I. Indian Dances." *Indian Craftsman* 1 (June 1909): 3–4.

"The Failure of the Educated American Indian." *American Review of Reviews* 33 (May 1906): 629–630.

Fewkes, J. Walter. "Hopi Katchinas, Drawn by Native Artists." Bureau of American Ethnology. *Twenty-first Annual Report*, 1903.

Frank, Glenn. "A Vanishing Race Comes Back." *Century Magazine* 99 (April 1920): 800–801.

Frather, Julia F. A. "Fourth of July at the Klamath Reservation." *Overland* 42 (July 1903): 116–123.

Fynn, A. J. "The Preservation of Aboriginal Arts." National Education Association. *Journal of Proceedings and Addresses*, 1909.

Garland, Hamlin. "The Red Man's Present Needs." *North American Review* 174 (April 1902): 476–488.

Godkin, Edwin Lawrence. "A Good Field for Reform." *Nation* 46 (March 15, 1888): 210–211.

"Government Scandals as an Issue." *Literary Digest* 27 (September 12, 1903): 309–310.

Guthrie, Jane W. "Lace-Making among the Indians." *Outlook* 66 (September 1, 1900): 59 62.

Harger, Charles Moreau. "The Indian's Last Stand." *Outlook* 70 (January 25, 1902): 217–222.

Hartley, Marsden. "Tribal Esthetics." *Dial* 65 (November 16, 1918): 399–400.

Harvey, Charles M. "The Indians of To-day and To-morrow." *American Review of Reviews* 33 (June 1906): 696–705.

"How Art Misrepresents the Indian." *Literary Digest* 44 (January 27, 1912): 160–161.

Hrdlicka, Ales. "Tuberculosis in the Indian." *Charities and the Commons* 21 (November 7, 1908): 245–247.

Hunter, H. Chadwick. "The American Indian in Painting." *Art and Archaeology* 8 (March–April 1919): 81–96.

Huntington, Ellsworth. *The Red Man's Continent: A Chronicle of Aboriginal America.* Temecula, Calif.: Best Books, 1921.

"Indian and Negro in Music." *Literary Digest* 44 (June 29, 1912): 1346–1347.

"Indian Funds for Sectarian Schools." *Independent* 63 (December 19, 1907): 1507–1508.

"Indian Industrial Development." *Outlook* 67 (January 12, 1901): 101–102.

"The Indian Question." *Outlook* 75 (September 19, 1903): 149–151.

"Indian Shakers." *Literary Digest* 48 (March 7, 1914): 496.

"Indians to Foster Their Native Art." *Indian Craftsman* 1 (April 1909): 19–20.

Inglis, William. "Buffalo Bill's Last Trail." *Harper's Weekly* 54 (November 1903): 382–390.

Inkersley, Arthur. "Cataract Canyon, the Havasupais." *Overland* 42 (November 1903): 382–390.

"The Interior Department and the Indians." *Outlook* 76 (March 19, 1904): 679–680.

Jackson, Helen Hunt. *A Century of Dishonor: A Sketch of the United States Government's Dealings with Some of the Indian Tribes.* New York: Harper and Brothers, 1881.

James, George Warton. "Indian Blanketry." *Outing* 39 (March 1902): 684–693.

———. *Indian Blankets and Their Makers.* Chicago: McClurg, 1911.

———. *What the White Race May Learn from the Indian.* Chicago: Forbes, 1908.

Jenks, Albert Ernest. *Indian-White Amalgamation: An Anthropometric Study*. Minneapolis: Univ. of Minnesota Studies in the Social Sciences, 1916.

"Karl Moon's Portraits of Southwest Indians." *Century Magazine* 75 (October 1907): 923–927.

Kellogg, Laura Cornelius (Wynnogene). *Our Democracy and the American Indian: A Comprehensive Presentation of the Indian Situation as It Is Today*. Kansas City: Burton, 1920.

Kennan, George. "Have Reservation Indians Any Vested Rights?" *Outlook* 70 (March 29, 1902): 759–765.

———. "Indian Lands and Fair Play." *Outlook* 76 (February 27, 1904): 498–501.

"Land Scandal in Indian Territory." *Independent* 55 (August 20, 1903): 1951.

Leupp, Francis E. "Back to Nature for the Indian." *Charities and the Commons* 20 (June 6, 1908): 336–340.

———. "Four Strenuous Years." *Outlook* 92 (June 5, 1909): 328–331.

———. *In Red Man's Land*. New York: Revell, 1914.

———. *The Indian and His Problem*. New York: Charles Scribner's Sons, 1910.

McKenzie, Fayette Avery. "The Indian and His Problem." *Dial* 49 (October 1, 1910): 228–230.

"Marsden Hartley Exhibition." *Camera Work* 38 (April 1912): 36.

Martin, E. L. "The Story of Two Real Indian Artists." *Red Man* 5 (February 1913). Reprinted under *home.epix.net/~landis/Nartists. html*, 1–3.

Meany, E. S. "Hunting Indians with a Camera." *World's Work* 15 (March 1908): 10004–10011.

Meriam, Lewis, et al. *The Problem of Indian Administration*. Institute for Government Research, Studies in Administration. Baltimore: Johns Hopkins Univ. Press, 1928.

Moffett, Thomas C. *The Indian on the New Trail*. New York: Methodist Book Concern, 1914.

Moon, Karl. "In Search of the Wild Indian." *Outing* 69 (February 1917): 533–545.

Moorehead, Warren K. "Indian Arts and Industries." *Indian Craftsman* 2 (January 1910): 9–16.

Morgan, Lewis Henry. *Ancient Society, or Researches in the Lines of*

Human Progress from Savagery through Barbarism to Civilization.
New York: Meridian, 1967 (orig. pub. 1877).

"A Museum of the American Indian." *Outlook* 114 (October 11, 1916):
301.

"The Music of the American Indians." *Literary Digest* 27 (September 5,
1903): 283.

"The New Indian." *Nation* 79 (July 2, 1904): 47–48.

"The Nun's Garb Question." *Literary Digest* 45 (October 12, 1912): 626.

Ober, Sarah Endicott. "New Religion among the West Coast Indians."
Overland 56 (December 1910): 583–594.

Oskison, John M. "Making an Individual of the Indian." *Everybody's
Magazine* 16 (June 1907): 723–733.

"Our 'Subject' Races." *Outlook* 75 (October 31, 1903): 482–485.

Outlook. Vol. 75, October 31, 1903. Correspondence [letter from an Indian agent with commentary]. 519–520.

Pach, Walter. "The Art of the American Indian." *Dial* 68, no. 1 (January 1920): 57–65.

———. "Notes on the Indian Water-Colours." *Dial* 68, no. 3 (March
1920): 343–345.

Parker, Arthur C. *The Life of General Ely S. Parker.* Buffalo, N.Y.: Buffalo Historical Society, 1919.

———. "Making a White Man Out of an Indian Not a Good Plan."
American Indian Magazine 5 (April–June 1917): 85–86.

Phillips, O. P. "Moki Indians and Their Snake Dance." *Era* 11 (February 1903): 115–129.

"Photos by Curtis." *World's Work* 12 (August 1906): 7913–7914.

"A Plan to Free the Indian." *Literary Digest* 47 (August 9, 1913):
196–197.

Pope, J. Worden. "The North American Indian: The Disappearance of
the Race a Popular Fallacy." *Arena* 16 (November 1896): 945–959.

Pratt, Richard Henry. "Indian No Problem." *Missionary Review* 33
(November 1910): 851–856.

"The President and the Indian: A Step Backward." *Outlook* 79 (February 18, 1905): 417–419.

"Recording the Indian's Music." *Literary Digest* 46 (April 26, 1913): 951.

"Religious Garb in Indian Schools." *Literary Digest* 44 (February 24,
1912): 379–380.

"Review of Frederick R. Burton's *American Primitive Music.*" *Nation* 90

(February 24, 1910): 196.

Roberts, F. "How to Make the Indian Beadwork." *Ladies' Home Journal* 20 (August 1903): 24.

Robinson, Delorme W. "Tuberculosis among the Sioux." *American Review of Reviews* 33 (March 1906): 340–341.

Roddis, Louis H., "The Last Indian Uprising in the United States." *Minnesota History Bulletin* 3 (February 1920): 272–290.

Roe, Walter C. "The Lake Mohonk Lodge: An Experiment in Indian Work." *Outlook* 68 (May 18, 1901): 176–178.

Roosevelt, Theodore. "A Layman's Views of an Art Exhibition." *Outlook* 103 (March 29, 1913): 718–720.

Sabin, Edwin L. "Indian Weaver: A Poem." *Craftsman* 13 (March 1908): 643.

———. "The Navajo Blanket." *Red Man* 2 (February 1910): 17.

Sells, Cato. "The Indian Bureau and Its Schools." *Saturday Evening Post* 193 (April 9, 1921): 40–45.

Shoemaker, F. "Tuberculosis: The Scourge of the Red Man." *Indian Craftsman* 1 (June 1909): 23–31.

Sloan, John. "The Indian Dance from an Artist's Point of View." *Arts and Decoration* 20 (January 1924): 17.

Sparhawk, Frances Campbell. "The Indian's Yoke." *North American Review* 182 (January 1906): 50–61.

Starr, Emmet. *History of the Cherokee Indians and Their Legends and Folk Lore.* Oklahoma City: Warden, 1921.

"The State, the Church, and the Indian." *Outlook* 79 (February 11, 1905): 370–372.

Stratton, Howard Fremont. "The Place of the Indian in Art." *Red Man* 2 (February 1910): 3–7.

Taft, William Howard. "The Indian Must Assume Responsibility if He Demands Rights." *Quarterly Journal of the Society of American Indians* 2 (July–September 1914): 44.

"Trust Funds for Indian Catholic Schools." *Nation* 80 (February 9, 1905): 106.

"A Trust Not Trustworthy." *Independent* 56 (February 25, 1904): 450–451.

"Unfair Indian Fighting." *Outlook* 79 (February 4, 1905): 264–265.

Wallace, Dillon. "Saddle and Camp in the Rockies: Across the Navajo Desert." *Outing* 57 (January 1911): 390–412.

"War Chiefs in Peace." *Nation* 81 (September 28, 1905): 255–256.

"The Week: A Mischievous Appropriation." *Outlook* 79 (January 21, 1905): 150.

"Who Will Guard the Guards?" *Outlook* 74 (August 29, 1903): 1020–1021.

Willsie, Honore. "We Die! We Die! There is no Hope!" *Everybody's Magazine* 26 (March 1912): 337–344.

Wissler, Clark. *Indian Beadwork: A Help for Students of Design.* New York: American Museum Press, 1919.

———. *Red Man's Reservations.* New York: Macmillan, 1971 (orig. pub. 1919).

Zitkala-Sa (Gertrude Bonnin). "Why I Am a Pagan." *Atlantic Monthly* 90 (1902): 801–803.

Secondary Sources

Ashton, Robert, and Jozefa Stuart. *Images of American Indian Art.* New York: Walker, 1977.

Basso, Keith. *The Cibecue Apache.* New York: Holt, Rinehart and Winston, 1970.

———. *The Gift of Changing Woman.* Bureau of American Ethnology Bulletin 196, 1966.

———. *Wisdom Sits in Places.* Albuquerque: Univ. of New Mexico Press, 1996.

Basso, Keith and Morris E. Opler, eds. *Apachean Culture and Ethnology.* Tucson: Univ. of Arizona Press, 1971.

Beal, Merrill D. *"I Will Fight No More Forever": Chief Joseph and the Nez Perce War.* Seattle: Univ. of Washington Press, 1963.

Berkhofer, Robert F., Jr. *The White Man's Indian.* New York: Knopf, 1978.

Berthrong, Donald J. *The Cheyenne and Arapaho Ordeal: Reservation and Agency Life in the Indian Territory, 1875–1907.* Norman: Univ. of Oklahoma Press, 1976.

Bolster, Mel H. "The Smoked Meat Rebellion." *Chronicles of Oklahoma* 31 (Spring 1953): 37–55.

Brimlow, George F. *The Bannock Indian War of 1878.* Caldwell, Idaho: Caxton Printers, 1938.

Brody, J. J. *Indian Painters and White Patrons.* Albuquerque: Univ. of

New Mexico Press, 1971.

Brown, Dee. *Bury My Heart At Wounded Knee*. New York: Holt, Rinehart and Winston, 1971.

Brown, Mark H. *The Flight of the Nez Perce*. New York: G. P. Putnam's Sons, 1967.

Castile, George Pierre, and Gilbert Kushner, eds. *Persistent Peoples: Cultural Enclaves in Perspective*. Tucson: Univ. of Arizona Press, 1981.

Chaput, Donald. "Generals, Indian Agents, Politicians: The Doolittle Survey of 1865." *Western History Quarterly* 3 (July 1972): 269–282.

Chavis, Ben. "All-Indian Rodeo: A Transformation of Western Apache Tribal Warfare and Culture." *Wicazo Sa Review* 9 (Spring 1993): 4–11.

Clark, Neil M. "Dr. Montezuma, Apache Warrior in Two Worlds." *Montana: The Magazine of Western History* 23 (Spring 1973): 56–65.

Cohen, Felix. *Handbook of Federal Indian Law, with Reference Tables and Index*. Albuquerque: Univ. of New Mexico Press, 1972.

Dawdy, Doris Ostrander. *Artists of the American West*. Chicago: Sage Books, 1974.

Debo, Angie. *And Still the Waters Run: The Betrayal of the Five Civilized Tribes*. Princeton, N.J.: Princeton Univ. Press, 1972.

———. *The Rise and Fall of the Choctaw Republic*. Norman: Univ. of Oklahoma Press, 1934.

Deloria, Philip J. *Playing Indian*. New Haven, Conn.: Yale Univ. Press, 1998.

Deloria, Vine, Jr. *Spirit and Reason*. Golden, Colo.: Fulcrum Publishing, 1999.

Deloria, Vine, Jr., and Raymond J. DeMaille. *Documents of American Indian Diplomacy: Treaties, Agreements, and Conventions, 1775–1979*. 2 vols. Norman: Univ. of Oklahoma Press, 1999.

Dippie, Brian. *The Vanishing American: White Attitudes and U.S. Indian Policy*. Middleton, Conn.: Wesleyan Univ. Press, 1982.

Downes, Randolph C. "A Crusade for Indian Reform." *Mississippi Valley Historical Review* 32 (December 1945): 331–354.

Driver, Harold E. *Indians of North America*. Chicago: Univ. of Chicago Press, 1975.

Dunn, Dorothy. *American Indian Painting of the Southwest and Plains Areas*. Albuquerque: Univ. of New Mexico Press, 1968.

Edmunds, R. David, ed. *American Indian Leaders: Studies in Diversity.* Lincoln: Univ. of Nebraska Press, 1980.

Ekirch, Arthur A. *Man and Nature in America.* New York: Columbia Univ. Press, 1963.

Feder, Norman. *American Indian Art.* New York: Abrams, 1971.

Fiedler, Leslie. *The Return of the Vanishing American.* New York: Stein and Day, 1968.

Fogelson, Raymond D. "Change, Persistence, and Accommodation in Cherokee Medico-Magical Beliefs." In *Symposium on Cherokee and Iroquois Culture,* edited by William N. Fenton and John Gulick. Bureau of American Ethnology Bulletin 180, 1961.

Friar, Ralph E., and Natasha A Friar. *The Only Good Indian: The Hollywood Gospel.* New York: Drama Book Specialists, 1972.

Fritz, Henry E. "The Last Hurrah of Christian Humanitarian Indian Reform: The Board of Indian Commissioners, 1909–1918." *Western Historical Quarterly* 16 (1985): 147–162.

———. *The Movement for Indian Assimilation, 1860–1890.* Philadelphia: Univ. of Pennsylvania Press, 1963.

Getches, David H., Charles F. Wilkinson, and Robert A. Williams, Jr. *Cases and Materials on Federal Indian Law.* St. Paul, Minn.: West, 1998.

Gibson, Arrell M. *The Santa Fe and Taos Colonies: Age of the Muses, 1900–1942.* Norman: Univ. of Oklahoma Press, 1983.

Gittinger, Roy. *The Formation of the State of Oklahoma, 1803–1906.* Berkeley and Los Angeles: Univ. of California Press, 1917.

Gump, James O. *The Dust Rose like Smoke: The Subjugation of the Zulu and Sioux.* Lincoln: Univ. of Nebraska Press, 1994.

Hays, Samuel P. *Conservation and the Gospel of Efficiency, 1890–1920.* Cambridge, Mass.: Harvard Univ. Press, 1959.

Hertzberg, Hazel. *The Search for an American Indian Identity: Modern Pan-Indian Movements.* Syracuse, N.Y.: Syracuse Univ. Press, 1971.

Highwater, Jamake. *Song from the Earth: American Indian Painting.* Boston: New York Graphic Society, 1976.

Hilger, Sister Inez M. *Arapaho Child Life and Its Cultural Background.* Bureau of American Ethnology Bulletin 148, 1952.

Hofstadter, Richard. *Social Darwinism in American Thought.* Boston: Beacon Press, 1955.

Holm, Tom. "Indian Lobbyists: Cherokee Opposition to the Allotment of Tribal Lands." *American Indian Quarterly* 5 (May 1979): 115–134.

———. "Sovereignty and Peoplehood." *Red Ink* (Spring 2000): 41–44.

Holm, Tom, J. Diane Pearson, and Ben Chavis. "Peoplehood: A Model for the Extension of Sovereignty in American Indian Studies." *Wicazo Sa Review* 18 (2003): 7–24.

Horsefly, G. P. *A History of the True People: The Cherokee Indians.* Detroit: Rick Smith, 1979.

Horsman, Reginald. *Expansion and American Indian Policy, 1783-1812.* East Lansing: Michigan State Univ. Press, 1967.

———. "Scientific Racism and the American Indian in the Mid-Nineteenth Century." *American Quarterly* 27 (May 1975): 152–168.

Hoxie, Frederick E., ed. *Encyclopedia of North American Indians.* New York: Houghton Mifflin, 1996.

———. *A Final Promise: The Campaign to Assimilate the Indians, 1880–1920.* New York: Cambridge Univ. Press, 1989.

Indian Arts and Crafts Board. *Contemporary Indian Artists: Montana, Wyoming, Idaho.* Rapid City, S.Dak.: IACB Pamphlet, 1972.

———. *Contemporary Sioux Painting.* Rapid City, S.Dak.: IACB Pamphlet, 1970.

Iverson, Peter. *Carlos Montezuma and the Changing World of American Indians.* Albuquerque: Univ. of New Mexico Press, 1982.

Jorgensen, Joseph G. *The Sun Dance Religion: Power for the Powerless.* Chicago: Univ. of Chicago Press, 1972.

Keegan, John. *A History of Warfare.* New York: Vintage, 1993.

———. "Warfare on the Plains." *Yale Review* 84 (January 1996): 1–48.

Keiser, Albert. *The Indian in American Literature.* New York: Oxford Univ. Press, 1933.

Kelly, Lawrence C. *The Assault on Assimilation: John Collier and the Origins of Indian Policy Reform.* Albuquerque: Univ. of New Mexico Press, 1983.

Kroeber, Theodora. *Ishi in Two Worlds: A Biography of the Last Wild Indian in America.* Berkeley and Los Angeles: Univ. of California Press, 1961.

Kunitz, Stephen J. "The Social Philosophy of John Collier." *Ethnohistory* 18 (Summer 1971): 213–229.

Landis, Barbara. "Some of the Names." Carlisle Indian School Pages, *home.epix.net/~landis/conples.html:* 3–4.

Lasch, Christopher. *The New Radicalism in America, 1889–1963*. New York: Vintage, 1965.

Laubin, Reginald, and Gladys Laubin. *Indian Dances of North America: Their Importance to Indian Life*. Norman: Univ. of Oklahoma Press, 1977.

Liberty, Margot, ed. *American Indian Intellectuals*. St. Paul, Minn.: West, 1978.

———. "Suppression and Survival of the Northern Cheyenne Sun Dance." *Minnesota Archaeologist* 27 (1965): 121–143.

Littlefield, Daniel F., and Lonnie E. Underhill. "The 'Crazy Snake Uprising' of 1909: A Red, Black, or White Affair?" *Arizona and the West* 20 (Winter 1978): 307–324.

———. "Renaming the American Indian, 1890-1913." *American Studies* 12 (Fall 1971): 33–45.

Lowie, Robert H. *Indian of the Plains*. Garden City, N.Y.: Natural History Press, 1963.

McDonnell, Janet A. *The Dispossession of the American Indian, 1887–1934*. Bloomington: Indiana Univ. Press, 1991.

McKibbin, Davisdson B. "Revolt of the Navajo, 1913." *New Mexico Historical Review* 29 (October 1954): 259–289.

McNitt, Frank. *The Indian Traders*. Norman: Univ. of Oklahoma Press, 1972.

Mardock, Robert Winston. *The Reformers and the American Indian*. Columbia: Univ. of Missouri Press, 1971.

Marriot, Alice. *Maria: The Potter of San Ildefonso*. Norman: Univ. of Oklahoma Press, 1948.

Memmi, Albert. *The Colonizer and the Colonized*. Translated by Howard Greenfeld. Boston: Beacon Press, 1967.

Mooney, James, and Frans M. Olbrechts. *The Swimmer Manuscript: Cherokee Sacred Formulas and Medical Prescriptions*. Bureau of American Ethnology Bulletin 99, 1932.

Murray, Keith A. *The Modocs and Their War*. Norman: Univ. of Oklahoma Press, 1959.

Nash, Roderick. *Wilderness and the American Mind*. New Haven, Conn.: Yale Univ. Press, 1967.

Nurge, Ethel, ed. *The Modern Sioux*. Lincoln: Univ. of Nebraska Press, 1975.

Otis, D. S. *The Dawes Act and the Allotment of Indian Lands*. Norman:

Univ. of Oklahoma Press, 1973.

Pavlik, Steve, ed. *A Good Cherokee, a Good Anthropologist: Papers in Honor of Robert K. Thomas.* Los Angeles: Univ. of California, American Indian Studies Center, 1998.

Pearce, Roy Harvey. *The Savages of America: A Study of the Indian and the Idea of Civilization.* Baltimore: Johns Hopkins Univ. Press, 1953.

Peterson, Karen Daniels. *Plains Indian Art from Fort Marion.* Norman: Univ. of Oklahoma Press, 1971.

Philp, Kenneth R. *John Collier's Crusade for Indian Reform, 1920–1954.* Tucson: Univ. of Arizona Press, 1977.

Policy Development Group. *The Government of Aboriginal Peoples.* Ottawa: Sub-Committee on Indian Self-Determination of the Canadian House of Commons Standing Committee on Indian Affairs and Northern Development, 1983.

Powell, Peter J. *Sweet Medicine: The Continuing Role of the Sacred Arrows, the Sun Dance, and the Sacred Buffalo Hat in Northern Cheyenne History.* 2 vols. Norman: Univ. of Oklahoma Press, 1969.

Priest, Loring Benson. *Uncle Sam's Stepchildren: The Reformation of United States Indian Policy, 1865–1887.* New Brunswick, N.J.: Rutgers Univ. Press, 1942.

Prucha, Francis Paul. *American Indian Policy in Crisis: Christian Reformers and the Indian, 1865–1900.* Norman: Univ. of Oklahoma Press, 1976.

———. *American Indian Policy in the Formative Years: The Indian Trade and Intercourse Acts, 1790–1834.* Cambridge, Mass.: Harvard Univ. Press, 1962.

———. *American Indian Treaties: The History of a Political Anomaly.* Berkeley and Los Angeles: Univ. of California Press, 1994.

———, ed. *Americanizing the American Indians: Writings by the 'Friends of the Indian,' 1880–1900.* Cambridge, Mass.: Harvard Univ. Press, 1973.

———. "Andrew Jackson's Indian Policy: A Reassessment." *Journal of American History* 56 (December 1969): 527–539.

———. *The Churches and the Indian Schools, 1888–1912.* Lincoln: Univ. of Nebraska Press, 1980.

———. *The Great Father: The United States Government and the American Indians.* 2 vols. Lincoln: Univ. of Nebraska Press, 1984.

Richter, Daniel K. "War and Culture: The Iroquois Experience."

William and Mary Quarterly 40 (October 1983): 528–559.

Rushing, W. Jackson. *Native American Art and the New York Avant-Garde: A History of Cultural Primitivism.* Austin: Univ. of Texas Press, 1995.

———, ed. *Native American Art in the Twentieth Century.* New York: Routledge, 1999.

Sandoz, Mari. *Cheyenne Autumn.* New York: McGraw-Hill, 1953.

Schaap, Dick. *An Illustrated History of the Olympics.* New York: Ballantine, 1976.

Schrader, Robert Fay. *The Indian Arts and Crafts Board: An Aspect of the New Deal Indian Policy.* Albuquerque: Univ. of New Mexico Press, 1983.

Schusky, Ernest L., ed. *Political Organization of Native North Americans.* Washington, D.C.: Univ. Press of America, 1981.

Sheehan, Bernard W. *Seeds of Extinction: Jeffersonian Philanthropy and the American Indian.* Chapel Hill: Univ. of North Carolina Press, 1973.

Slotkin, James S. *The Peyote Religion: A Study in Indian-White Relations.* Glencoe, Ill.: Free Press, 1956.

Smith, Valene L., ed. *Hosts and Guests: The Anthropology of Tourism.* Philadelphia: Univ. of Pennsylvania Press, 1977.

Spaulding, George F., ed. *On the Western Tour with Washington Irving.* Norman: Univ. of Oklahoma Press, 1968.

Spencer, Robert F., Jesse D. Jennings, et. al. *The Native Americans.* New York: Harper and Row, 1965.

Spicer, Edward H. *Cycles of Conquest: The Impact of Spain, Mexico, and the United States on the Indians of the Southwest.* Tucson: Univ. of Arizona Press, 1962.

———. *The Yaquis: A Cultural History.* Tucson: Univ. of Arizona Press, 1980.

Spindler, George, and Louise Spindler, eds. *Native North American Cultures: Four Cases.* New York: Holt, Rinehart and Winston, 1977.

Sproat, John G. *"The Best Men": Liberal Reformers in the Gilded Age.* New York: Oxford Univ. Press, 1968.

Tanner, Clara Lee. *Southwest Indian Painting.* Tucson: Univ. of Arizona Press, 1973.

Thomas, Robert K. "The Redbird Smith Movement." In *Symposium on Cherokee and Iroquois Culture*, edited by William N. Fenton and

John Gulick. Bureau of American Ethnology Bulletin 180, 1961.

Trennert, Robert A., Jr. *Alternative to Extinction: Federal Indian Policy and the Beginnings of the Reservation System*. Philadelphia: Temple Univ. Press, 1975.

Underhill, Ruth. *Red Man's Religion: Beliefs and Practices of the Indians North of Mexico*. Chicago: Univ. of Chicago Press, 1965.

Van Orman, Richard A. *A Room for the Night: Hotels of the Old West*. Bloomington: Indiana Univ. Press, 1966.

Wagenknecht, Edward. *The Movies in the Age of Innocence*. Norman: Univ. of Oklahoma Press, 1962.

Wardell, Morris L. *A Political History of the Cherokee Nation, 1838–1903*. Norman: Univ. of Oklahoma Press, 1938.

Washburn, Wilcomb E., ed. *The Indian and the White Man*. Garden City, N.Y.: Anchor Books, 1964.

———. "The Society of American Indians." *Indian Historian* 3 (Winter 1970): 21–23.

Whitehead, Neil L., and R. Brian Ferguson. "Deceptive Stereotypes about 'Tribal Warfare.'" In *Talking about People: Readings in Contemporary Anthropology*, edited by William A. Haviland and Robert J. Gordon. Mountain View, Calif.: Mayfield, 1996.

———, eds. *War in the Tribal Zone: Expanding States and Indigenous Warfare*. Santa Fe, N.Mex.: School of American Research Press, 2000.

Wiebe, Robert H. *The Search for Order*. New York: Hill and Wang, 1967.

Willard, William. "Zitkala Sa: A Woman Who Would Be Heard." *Wicazo Sa Review* 1 (Spring 1985): 11–16.

Williams, Samuel Cole, ed. *Adair's History of the American Indians*. New York: Promontory Press, 1930.

Willson, Lawrence. "Thoreau: Student of Anthropology." *American Anthropologist* 61 (April 1959): 100–109.

Wilson, Raymond. *Ohiyesa: Charles Eastman, Santee Sioux*. Urbana: Univ. of Illinois Press, 1983.

Wright, Peter M. "The Pursuit of Dull Knife from Fort Reno in 1878–1879." *Chronicles of Oklahoma* 46 (Summer 1968): 141–154.

INDEX